RACISM AND INEQUALITY

Edited by
Harrell R. Rodgers, Jr.
UNIVERSITY OF HOUSTON

RACISM
AND
INEQUALITY
The Policy Alternatives

W. H. FREEMAN AND COMPANY
SAN FRANCISCO

229543

PHOTOGRAPHS

    Cover: Optic Nerve/Jeroboam, Inc.

Chapter 1: Optic Nerve/Jeroboam, Inc.

Chapter 2: Peeter Vilms/Jeroboam, Inc.

Chapter 3: Andy Mercado/Jeroboam, Inc.

Chapter 4: Photo by William Rosenthal

Chapter 5: Optic Nerve/Jeroboam, Inc.

Library of Congress Cataloging in Publication Data

Main entry under title:

Racism and inequality.

    Includes bibliographical references and index.
    1. Negroes—Social conditions—1964–
2. Negroes—Housing. 3. Negroes—Economic conditions.   4. School integration—United States.   5. United States—Race question.
I. Rodgers, Harrell R.
E185.86.R25   301.45'1042'0973   75-15640
ISBN 0-7167-0796-9
ISBN 0-7167-0795-0 pbk.

Copyright © 1975 by W. H. Freeman and Company

Printed in the United States of America   9 8 7 6 5 4 3 2 1

To Lynne,
with love

CONTENTS

PREFACE

I teach policy analysis courses, which frequently center on civil rights issues, at an urban university. My students, many of whom are blacks from the inner city, stimulated my interest in putting together this book. They frequently have expressed concern that they do not want to spend the semester discussing racial problems: problems they say they know because they live with them every day. What they want to know is why the problems persist and how they can be resolved.

This book attempts to meet this demand. The focus of the text is exclusively racism and racial inequality, and a level of sophistication suitable for introductory students has been adopted. Each of the chapters was specifically written for this volume. The authors are specialists on the topics they write about and most have written book-length treatments on their subjects.

A number of persons deserve my thanks. Professor Joel D. Aberbach and Everett F. Cataldo read the entire manuscript and made many helpful suggestions. Linn S. Woodward and Brenda King did an excellent job of typing the final draft of the text. My research assistant, Gordon Folkman, diligently performed a number of tasks associated with the volume. I would particularly like to thank my fellow contributors to this volume for working hard to develop a consistent theme and for meeting numerous deadlines.

To Lynne, for her love and companionship, my heartfelt thanks.

May 1975   HARRELL R. RODGERS, JR.

THE AUTHORS

Charles S. Bullock, III (Ph.D., Washington University) recently accepted a position as Professor of Political Science at the University of Houston. He is coauthor of *Law and Social Change: Civil Rights Laws and Their Consequences* (1971), and *Racial Equality in America: In Search of An Unfulfilled Goal* (1975); coeditor of *Black Political Attitudes: Implications for Political Support* (1972) and *The New Politics: Polarization or Utopia* (1970). In addition he is author of numerous publications in social science journals.

Robert E. Forman (Ph.D., University of Minnesota) is Professor of Sociology at The University of Toledo. He is author of *Black Ghettos, White Ghettos, and Slums* (1971), and coauthor of *The University and its Foreign Alumni* (1964). He has published articles on neighborhood interactions, delinquency rates, and collective behavior.

Neal A. Milner (Ph.D., University of Wisconsin) is Associate Professor of Political Science at the University of Hawaii and Visiting Associate Professor of Political Science and Urban Affairs at Northwestern University. He is author of *The Court and Local Law Enforcement: The Political Impact of Miranda* (1971), and coauthor of *Politics, Education, and Morality: The Sex Education Controversy* (1975). He is also the author of several papers on police reform.

Harrell R. Rodgers, Jr. (Ph.D., University of Iowa) recently accepted a position as Professor of Political Science at the University of Houston. He is author of *Community Conflict, Public Opinion and the Law* (1969); coauthor of *Law and Social Change: Civil Rights Laws and Their Consequences* (1971), and *Racial Equality in America: In Search of an Unfulfilled Goal* (1975); coeditor of *Black Political Attitudes: Implications for Political Support* (1972) and *The New Politics: Polarization or Utopia* (1970). In addition he is author of numerous articles in social science and legal journals.

H. V. Savitch (Ph.D., New York University) is Associate Professor of Political Science at the State University of New York at Purchase. Professor Savitch has published articles in the area of racial and ethnic politics and urban decentralization. His most recent publication is *Decentralization at The Grass Roots* (1974) which compares efforts at innovation in New York City and London. He is currently doing work on the comparative study of leadership among big city mayors.

RACISM AND INEQUALITY

Introduction

The chapters that make up this book are designed to describe why certain problems of racial discrimination and inequality persist in our society and to suggest ways of resolving them. The authors have not intended to provide treatments that exhaust all thinking on these problems but rather to provide thorough treatments that provide sophisticated insight into particular subjects. We have purposefully not included discussions of political alterations that might be considered ivory-tower radicalism, even though some seldom-discussed proposals such as voter stipends and random selection of some congressional representatives might have real merit. Instead we suggest changes that are highly probable and would be judged so by most people. Our goal is to convince the reader that social problems should and can be solved. This goal need not be clouded by charges of unrestrained idealism.

Because we suggest that racial discrimination and inequality can be overcome does not mean that we think the task an easy one. Many racial problems are intertwined with broader social and political ills in our society that must be cured or controlled if racial inequality is to be dealt with. In addition, many racial problems, including school desegregation in some urban areas, the drastic increase of black representation in certain jobs in the near future, the motivation of the most suppressed poor to political action, and saving the housing market in some of our cities, are almost intractable problems. But they can be resolved. In many instances, if existing laws were enforced, the problems could be alleviated (for example, some areas of school desegregation and employment). In others, large sums of money and considerable personnel would be required. More importantly, however, resolving some of these problems would require a shifting of political priorities in our society and some major political reforms. These changes would not come easily.

But whether a task is easy or hard does not seem important to us. The important consideration is whether the dilemma deserves resolution. If so, the effort is worthwhile. If, for example, we want to cleanse our society of racism, poverty, and urban decay, we cannot think exclusively in terms of dollars and cents. Solving these problems will undoubtedly cost less than they presently extract in terms of human misery, crime, and even economic loss. Nor can our approach to these problems be blind to political and class biases that spawn, nourish, and perpetuate these evils. If political changes are required, then these changes should be pursued.

One step in making significant gains in solving the problems discussed in this book necessitates the average citizen obtaining more political muscle. Savitch is concerned with the problem of political impotence of some groups in our society, particularly the powerlessness of blacks. His essay discusses the biases in our political system that favor some groups over others: most critically the powerful and wealthy over the poor. Savitch also analyzes the process by which powerless groups adapt themselves to the system in such a way as to aggravate their weaknesses. Last, he draws some lessons from contemporary efforts to produce political changes and suggests how citizens can gain the power to overcome racial and social ills. Savitch's prescriptions for political gains are interesting and deserve close evaluation.

Forman is concerned with providing adequate housing for the poor. He discusses the variety of conditions that create the housing crisis for low-income groups and recommends methods for ascending them. Forman believes that any rational solution to the problem requires preservation of the existing housing supply, and points out that in many European countries old housing still provides good homes and viable neighborhoods for the poor. As methods of preserving existing housing Forman discusses the merits of such proposed solutions as urban homesteading, rent subsidies, federal loans at low interest rates, and public housing. If public housing is to be used, Forman discusses how its design and the degree of tenant participation influences the success of a project.

Forman's prognosis is that we can house the poor if we try and if we develop a different perspective about the whole problem.

Bullock explores the problem of improving the economic conditions of blacks. After briefly examining the factors that generate black poverty and unemployment, Bullock discusses recent governmental responses. The legal authority and the operations of the Equal Employment

Opportunity Commission, the Office of Federal Contract Compliance, the Justice Department, and the Civil Service Commission are described. The shortcomings of these agencies are analyzed and improvements suggested.

Bullock points out that simply removing discriminatory barriers to employment will not benefit many citizens who are presently unprepared for anything but low-skill jobs. Because of a history of discrimination, blacks are disproportionately found in this category and Bullock discusses why manpower training programs are particularly important to them. He also discusses existing categoric programs and suggests the changes that are required to make them more effective.

Since policies geared to the needs of the labor force will have little impact on millions of citizens who cannot work because of age, infirmities, or dependent children, Bullock discusses the inadequacies of the welfare system and suggests alternatives. Through changes in a number of areas, Bullock sees ways of substantially removing the economic disadvantages of all the poor, including blacks.

Rodgers examines discrimination in education and advances the dual thesis that school desegregation can be achieved in all American communities and that successful school desegregation will ultimately have positive consequences for American society. In an effort to establish the validity of this thesis, Rodgers (1) reviews the progress of school desegregation to identify the areas in which this conflict must expand in the future if full school desegregation is to be achieved, (2) identifies the factors that have limited progress to suggest the obstacles that must be overcome if progress is to continue; (3) assesses the current standards of the Supreme Court on school desegregation and speculates on the implications of these standards for achieving further desegregation in both Southern and Northern school districts, (4) evaluates the benefits of interracial school systems and the merits of some recent attacks on school desegregation, and (5) suggests some methods of facilitating school desegregation.

Milner is concerned with making the police less racist and more responsive to citizens. Rather than discuss obvious but piecemeal approaches (for example, hiring more minorities), Milner discusses two models of police reform that would produce more systematic change. The police personnel model stresses improving the skills and professionalism of the police. The police function model stresses the clash between the role of the police in maintaining order and individual due process. Drawing upon suggestions for change implicit in these models, Milner offers an alternative model which stresses the need for police restraint, for political participation by outsiders in police policy making, for better apprenticeship programs for the police, and for methods of making the police more amenable to change. Through this approach Milner believes that important innovations can be achieved.

H. V. Savitch
STATE UNIVERSITY OF NEW YORK, PURCHASE

1

The Politics of Deprivation and Response

The political predicament of black Americans, like many critical issues, is by now a much overworked topic that has fallen prey to numerous versions of history. Conservatives, liberals, Marxists, revisionists, and counterrevisionists have jumped into the thicket and come up with contradictory but plausible accounts of the relation between power and race in America.

One school of liberal thought has viewed America as a democratic and benign society which has allowed its ethnic minorities to make it by dint of hard work and perseverance.[1]* If blacks were not capturing mayoralities and legislative seats as quickly as Italian or Irish Americans, their time was soon at hand. Political deprivation, like other inequities, was seen as a temporary aberration of the national psyche. With the proper dosages of due process and voting rights, the seizure would soon pass and so too would the political affliction felt by racial minorities. Another, more radical school, which emerged in the sixties, takes a dim view of American politics. This group holds to Cassandra-like interpretations of an elite conspiracy against the poor which has used the color line as the great divide of the working classes. Recent commentaries of this kind stress themes of American racism and a "subject peoples" argument that interprets black powerlessness as a manifestation of colonial servitude, similar to the imperialist experience of Africa and Asia.[2]

---

*Superscript numbers refer to notes listed at the end of this book.

Both of these very different interpretations of politics are, for the most part, convincing and quite valid when read apart from one another. When the arguments are joined, however, a question arises: how can such contrary explanations be plausible? The answer may be that each of these interpretations are pressing different sides of a story that has a common core. Traditionalists and liberals have concentrated on the "disadvantages" and liabilities under which black Americans labored for so many centuries. Racial prejudice, poll taxes, school segregation, and other bars to decent housing and employment have been foremost in the minds of liberals when analyzing the problems of race. Given this point of view, their conclusions point in the direction of eliminating these bars to opportunity so that blacks can make it on their own, in what is presumed to be a free and mobile society.

In the more radical literature which followed in the 1960s, the writers scoffed at the liberal's naiveté and pointed out that American politics was dominated by elites who were set on keeping their power and status. Racial discrimination and what came to be called "institutional racism," they argued, was all bound up with a political and economic structure which imposed intolerable conditions on blacks and would continue to do so.[3] Formalistic and legal methods to make opportunities available were seen as a sham which benefited only a tiny black bourgeoisie and kept the masses down. The only solution was to deal directly with the structure of power and the racism inherent in that structure.

As happens with complex problems, there is often more than one way to tell a truth, and a number of such truths can be found in the literature on race and politics. But truths can sometimes be reconciled, and such a synthesis might be made by proposing that a clue to understanding power in America lies in understanding the biases of the political system and how the proclivities of that system come to affect the fortunes of groups. Another clue toward that understanding lies in examing how aggregations of individuals—socioeconomic classes, ethnic minorities, interest groups, and so on—have adapted to that ambiguous entity called "the system."

The thesis of this chapter is that black Americans, taken as a socio-economic and ethnic group, have interacted with and adapted to biases within the political system, all of which have shaped the content of black politics. This interaction determined the course of the black struggle during the 1950s and early 1960s, brought it to a new plateau with the "revolutionary politics" of the middle and late 1960s, and has cul-minated in a new kind of "accommodationist" style which will stay with us for some time. In the following section I will examine the nature of political biases and how these biases work to the advantage or disad-vantage of particular groups. Generalizations drawn there will be applied to racial politics in the next section, where I will interpret the direction of black political action during the last three decades. The final section will deal with strategies for gaining power and affecting public policy.

Biases and the Political System

Politics as a Loaded Game. "Politics," say some, "is the art of the possible." For some, we should add, things are more possible than for others. The most obvious case is that of a wealthy scion with a "good name" being able to outdo his opponents by mustering greater amounts of money, resources, and prestige. Surely the man of modest means cannot compete against such odds.

But the issue, on all sides, is complex. Studies reveal that political activism depends also on motivation of the actors as well as their available time and existent interests. Robert Dahl points out that, contrary to prevailing myths about contests for power, inequalities amongst the contestants are not lopsided. As Dahl puts it, although "inequalities in political resources remain, they tend to be noncumulative" and dispersed in differing proportions amongst the actors.[4]

What Dahl and other liberal pluralists like him are saying is: there is no democratic nirvana on earth, and politics in this country has its defects. But, to the extent that democracy can be realistically applied, American government pretty well approximates that condition.[5]

This is true, but such an analysis hardly skims the meaning of political opportunity or its roots and consequences. Addressing these vital questions entails an analysis of what kinds of groups and social classes gain or lose from the system. It matters little whether individuals as such compete successfully within the system. What matters is what that participation means for a particular stratum of society, and what an individual has to do and become in order to hold a position of authority. The fact that a former sharecropper, or sharecropper's son, now occupies a governor's seat does not mean that sharecroppers have climbed to political ascendency.

Similarly, it matters little whether *possibilities* for political opportunities exist for a group. What counts are the *probabilities* of a group gaining power, given the prevailing biases of the system. By biases, I mean the proclivities and partialities of the political process which facilitate the quest for power by certain strata and hinder that of others. The concept of bias means that the political system and its attendant rules are not neutral.[6] The simple act of using at-large representation rather than ward-based elections can determine the direction in which the political wind blows. More intricate biases such as bureaucratic recuitment, methods for setting a legislative agenda, and media coverage have a profound effect on the fate of group demands.

Finally, biases, or rules of the game, have an enormous effect on the strategies and policy objectives of the participating groups themselves— even those organizations which have "revolutionary" claims are "conservatized" in the process of trying to achieve even minimal gains. Nationally sponsored health care is one example of a movement which has been so battered by medical associations and insurance companies that its ultimate passage may be more revealing of its failure than of any accomplishments. Other ill-fated movements which have gone the route of symbolic gesture are "no-fault auto insurance," which contains extensive clauses for making claims by finding fault, and "school decentralization," which is based on essentially centralist principles.* In each of these cases, the nomenclature was retained but the substance so diluted that the original movements for change lost most of their force, and their proponents were disarmed or co-opted into the system. The lesson to be learned is to determine the cost of compliance to political biases. Before we do that however, we should ascertain various types of bias and how they function to load the game.

Systemic Biases. Systemic biases can be defined as the prerequisites necessary for access to the political system and effective performance within it. American politics, in particular, places a heavy emphasis on these prerequisites, since it is heavily group oriented. That is, the more pressure a group can muster, the better able it is to shift policies toward its objectives.† Essential prerequisites for such participation are organizational and communications skills which in turn require money, commitment of personnel, a trained staff, propaganda apparatus, and the like.

Obviously, those organizations which are affluent and possess resources in greater abundance than their competitors are playing in a game where the ground rules invariably work in their favor. The upshot is a persistent class bias within the system where middle- or upper-class constituencies outdo their poorer neighbors.

---

*These examples are taken from experiences in New York State and New York City, where both "no-fault insurance" and "school decentralization" have been enacted in title, but with minimal substance and little impact.

†Although most democratic systems respond to pressure politics in some way, some are more vulnerable than others. Parliamentary systems with strong disciplined parties, for example, provide stronger insulation against external pressure. Some political scientists have argued that in Northern and Western European countries with parliamentary governments and strong parties, interest groups exert influence from within the party rather than outside it—few would claim however that these systems are as "group oriented" and amenable to their pressures as is the case in the United States.

Moreover, once having established themselves, powerful groups begin to define what kinds of demands are "legitimate" and what kinds are not. Effective participation by groups in the pressure system is not dependent on willingness alone, but on whether their demands fall within the established sphere of acceptability.[7] Anything outside the pale set by dominant groups is easily dismissed. Consider for a moment the widespread outrage that mothers on welfare face when they begin to speak of "welfare rights" and demand subsidies. Such general indignation is not aroused when farmers demand subsidies for not planting crops or when industries receive them in the form of tariffs, government loans, and special contracts.

Those socioeconomic groups which occupy positions of power and to whose advantage the rules of the game work, I shall call in-groups. Conversely, those groups which are at the periphery of the political system (that is, whose legitimacy is questioned or which are under-represented in the political arena) I shall call out-groups. Often, the processes by which persons become members of a socioeconomic group provide a clue to the group's potential for power. For instance, religious and occupational groups, whose recruitment processes are regularized and considered "normal," are likely to find the pressure system conducive to their aims. On the other hand, groups whose processes are considered illegitimate, held in low esteem, or connected with personal misfortune are likely to find such a system prejudicial.[8] Examples of in-groups are labor unions, farmers, and homeowner associations— each of which is esteemed by society and whose membership is recruited through either formal structures or the aspiration of those joining. Examples of out-groups are prison inmates, welfare mothers, the poor, and the infirm—each of which has lowly status and whose membership is formed as a result of chance or misfortune.

The reasons why certain groups have so little power are complex and difficult to reduce to a single explanation without finding exceptions, but uniformities do exist. Persons who find themselves belonging to out-groups are generally demoralized and stigmatized by society as well. While money is almost always in short supply, so are other commodities necessary for vigorous organizational activity, such as self-esteem, confidence, leisure time, and other attributes of middle-class life. Studies on political participation have found these attributes necessary for successful political action.[9] Without them a subtle but no less effective disenfranchisement takes place.

Recruitment into out-groups also has a marginal quality about it and a sense of impermanence. Persons who find themselves in such a situation have traditionally been more anxious to get out of their situation, or to disassociate themselves from the out-group than to stay and fight for it. Even when persons have deliberately undertaken to work for the improvement of the group as a whole, transience has been a major problem.

Transience leads to several difficulties. First, leaders and other important workers are constantly drained away from their original constituencies. In ghetto communities, for example, the most able leaders are soon hired by governmental bureaucracies and private institutions to fill executive positions. Although this may be considered advancement by some, others see it as co-optation (or more cynically, selling out to the establishment) when former activists are lured away from their communities.

Second, transience has an even greater impact on organizational membership. To use the example of urban ghettos, very often families are relocated around the city by welfare or urban renewal agencies, and this contributes markedly to the difficulties of maintaining community councils and neighborhood associations.

Third, the high rate of movement in and out of ghetto neighborhoods often breaks up what communication networks have been started and weakens group cohesion which is crucial to successful political action.

Fourth, out-groups lack a sense of permanence and a membership which readily perceives its "stake in society." In contrast, the energizing of in-groups for action when their existing stake is threatened, is a relatively simple task, and many leaders of these groups face the problem of restraining their more exuberant followers. Compare this situation with the difficulties of organizing high school dropouts to picket businesses for better employment opportunities or of rousing indigent families to lobby for better health care.

Scrutiny of what is required of groups for effective participation reveals the gravity of the obstacles faced by the disadvantaged. Prerequisites go far beyond a modicum of ability to organize and communicate. Group cohesion, permanence, stability, and a stake in the ongoing distribution of values are all prerequisites for effective participation and coincidentally, attributes of the more affluent classes.

What appears to be an open system is, on the contrary, one which structures effective political action along socioeconomic lines. Those strata which already have vested interests or which see the potential for winning high stakes are likely to develop a strong sense of purpose and to profit by pressuring the system. Those groups which are dispirited and whose condition mitigate against a strong consciousness, will be left helpless and also left out.

In spite of these systemic biases, out-groups have, from time to time, attempted to organize and work within the pressure system. In these instances, other biases have more aggressively been used to keep out-groups powerless.

Modes of Operation. Modes of operation may be defined as types of organizations which play a part in the process of decision making. They may intervene at any of the various stages of the process such as when issues are raised by advocates; considered by legislative bodies; implemented by executive agencies; or, if need be, resolved by judicial action. These organizations may combine several functions and this makes them especially powerful. Thus, local zoning boards exercise a number of quasi-judicial and legislative prerogatives by deciding on possible locations for industry, the acreage requirements for their population, and the size and shape of housing in a particular area. The distinctive characteristic of a mode of operation is that as an organization endowed with legitimacy it can shape the course of public policies.

Modes of operation may be of a public nature such as regulatory agencies, especially constituted commissions, electoral districts for purposes of representation (congressional, state, or local seats) or local school boards. They may also be private or quasi-public in nature such as interest groups, civic bodies, professional panels, and the like. The connection between public and private modes of operation can often be quite close. Studies of the national regulatory agencies, for instance, have found that "special" or favored relationships often exist between public agencies and the organizations they regulate.[10]

Close attention to modes of operation and their roles performed in decision making is important in ascertaining how particular operations work to exclude out-groups. Such exclusion may take place through one or a combination of the following techniques.

1. *Discriminatory selection of members to fill positions on appointed boards.* This may vary from the appointment of presidential commissions down to local zoning or school boards. The bias may be explicit as when chief executives appoint close friends or supporters to such positions, or it may be inconspicuous and put under the guise of a "screening panel." In the latter case, the process works with greater effect because it provides an aura of neutralism and over the years becomes institutionalized. These panels are drawn, almost always, from organizations which are entirely composed of affluent classes—chambers of commerce, established interest groups or "civic organizations," and professional associations. Sometimes these organizations may be rotated to give the impression of heterogeneity. Whatever the variances in arrangement, the effect is constant—the disadvantaged are left out. In New York City, for example, which has a school population consisting largely of black and Puerto Rican children from poor neighborhoods, the Board of Education prior to 1969 was appointed through a screening process. For more than 10

years, elite organizations chose their representation, whereas no spokesman ever sat on behalf of the city's poor.[11]

2. *Use of the formula* divisa et impera *to further weaken out-groups.* The classic use to which this formula was put is the gerrymandered electoral district. This often put important modes of operation such as state legislatures or city councils out of the reach of racial minorities. In northern cities today black and Spanish-speaking areas are often parceled out to surrounding middle-class communities.[12] The upshot is that out-groups are unable to elect their own representatives because their natural majorities are scattered. More recently, adaptations of the legislative gerrymander have been applied to other modes of operation such as planning boards and school districts.

Divisa et impera may be applied in other ways as well. For instance, it can be used to emphasize divisions between members of out-groups and make appeals to one then another segment of the group. Often such appeals are accompanied by tangible rewards or preferential treatment for "responsible" participants. Witness, for example, conflicts between blacks and Puerto Ricans which are structured (consciously or unconsciously) into fights over scarce antipovery funds. Similarly, old political clubs, encompassing within their jurisdiction large hunks of ghetto neighborhoods, have used a limited number of nonwhites as underlings and succeeded in maintaining white control long after their constituents have moved out of the area.[13]

3. *Loaded voting and administrative procedures used to preclude or discourage out-groups from gaining power.* Literacy requirements and "grandfather clauses" were used successfully in the South for over a century to keep blacks away from voting booths. In the urban North, the methods are less blatant and more a matter of political advantage than overt racism. As a result these practices are considered "fair play" and remain especially effective against weaker groups. Insurgent slates of black and Puerto Rican candidates are denied a place on the ballot because of picayune errors on nominating petitions. Names and addresses of registered voters are made excessively difficult for challengers to obtain because election boards are controlled by incumbent politicians. Elaborate weighting of votes and voting procedures, hardly understood by ghetto residents, discourage voter turnout.

Administrative procedures which are supposed to ensure fairness can be easily abusive, especially when entrenched groups see themselves threatened. Longevity and "time in grade" are used to monopolize skilled trades. Standards of "merit" selectively interpreted and ethnocentric criteria are used to determine promotion and entry into important administrative positions. In many areas of the country—Boston, Philadelphia, Chicago, Pittsburgh, and Los Angeles—it is quite common for particular ethnic groups which have moved into the middle class to "inherit" certain trade unions and bureaucratic posts. Though there are now campaigns by federal authorities to open these ranks, progress has been slow, because of the difficulty in distinguishing between honest criteria for performance and mechanisms of prejudice.

4. *Obstacles and petty harassment placed in the way of out-groups attempting to engage in civic or political activity.* These barriers may run the gamut from the use of police forces to "clear the streets" in the face of public demonstrations to hindrances placed in the way of disadvantaged persons wanting to attend public meetings. Out-groups are more easily intimidated by the constabulary and public officials than is generally thought. In the ghetto, a courtroom is regarded as a place people are taken to for sentence when they break the law, not a place of adjudication. Most of these people are fearful of authority and reluctant to press for their rights, even when they believe themselves to be correct. This attitude is especially prevalent among people who are receiving public assistance. As a matter of course, they are placed in a dependent position and made very much aware of it. Any conduct which might jeopardize their benefits is avoided.

Furthermore, public authorities take a jaundiced view of political activity by out-groups and are more likely to respond to them with stern measures. During New York City's school strike of 1968, police kept an especially watchful eye on the ghettos, despite the fact that that it was the white communities which were violating the law by cooperating with the striking teachers in keeping the schools closed.[14] In the Ocean Hill-Brownville district, citizens were arrested for congregating in the streets, while similar acts went unimpaired in middle-class neighborhoods.

Compare the harsh reaction to antiwar radicals in Chicago in 1968 and Washington in 1971 to the mild treatment accorded labor unions in New York in 1971, when the latter shut down bridges and thoroughfares—or for that matter, to the gentlemanlike settlements reached with municipal unions in San Francisco in 1974, after they paralyzed the city and forced the disposal of raw sewerage into nearby waters.

Differences between groups may be vast, and they have a direct bearing on the power groups are able to wield. That power in turn is related to the benefits they enjoy. In such a system equity is rarely granted according to the morality of a case. More frequently it is peace which is sought; and those organizations which can wage the most destructive warfare obtain the best peace.

Ideological Biases. I use the term ideology to mean an interrelated set of beliefs, attitudes, and goals which are used to guide the action of socioeconomic groups and organizations. An ideology may become a dominant one when it is defined by in-groups and treated as a general creed of the political system. A dominant ideology also serves as a justification for existing power arrangements.[15]

Ideological biases work to sift out "undesirable" political competitors and evaluate demands which come from out-groups. These biases become crystallized, forming a governing part of the political system through precedent and habit. Each victory by a stronger group is imbedded in an elaborate rationale in which the victories are identified with the desires and aspirations of the larger population. Thus, the so-called fight against "creeping socialism" in the 1950s carried out by "patriotic" organizations was successfully manipulated as a form of "Americanism" itself. During the depression, the Communist party attempted to use this technique through the slogan, "Communism is just twentieth century Americanism," but failed dismally. The tactic has been used by radicals and conservatives, in-groups and out-groups alike, although as conventional coalitions succeed and out-groups grow weaker, the more a dominant ideology is likely to take root.

Ideological biases may function as defensive or offensive weapons for in-groups. In either case, invidious comparisons are drawn between out-groups or those things which they represent and the orthodoxy of a dominant ideology. As a defense, these biases can be used to ward off potential change by calling it inimical to fundamental and presumably sacrosanct principles; hence, the claim by the American Medical Association that government-supported health care will destroy the doctor–patient relationship.

Ideological biases may also be used defensively to shore up the legitimacy of in-groups by pointing up the importance of "duly constituted authority."[16] The insistence that all change must take place through that authority and appeals to work through established procedures when they are loaded against out-groups is another ideological ploy to deflect demands for change.

As an offensive, these biases are used to brand proposals by out-groups "unfeasible," "idealistic," or "irresponsible." In more truculent versions, these label out-groups "extremists," "militants," or "criminals." Anything which departs from conventions set by in-groups is smeared by an ideological brush, often with a devastating effect and without regard to the merits of the issue.

In-groups reach their most effective control when their power passes from pressure to ideological finesse.[17] This happens when decision makers, and particularly local bureaucratic decision makers, base their judgment on the ideology of the in-groups. When in-groups remain dominant over a period of time, their ideological biases are bound to seep through all the rungs of the bureaucracy. A kind of conditioned behavior emerges in which administration is carried out in anticipation of what in-groups are likely to accept. Persons in key positions at local bureaucracies act according to what can "realistically be done" in the context of in-groups power, rather than Weberian models of administrative impartiality.[18] Most often these bureaucrats are experienced hands and have close rapport with representatives of in-groups. Having dealt with these groups for many years, they come to see their point of view and give them preferential treatment. Sometimes this may amount to a sympathetic nod, a helpful hint, or the communication of confidential information. At other times, these favors go so far as direct intercession on their behalf.

The reasons for this are many and tangled in an array of factors. In addition to lengthy experience with in-groups and empathy with their goals, local bureaucrats are prone to take the quickest short-run course, which means responding to the greatest pressure. Expediency then appears to be an important ingredient in building special relationships. Besides this, bureaucrats at the local level are more likely to share class, ethnic, and racial characteristics with in-groups and their goals and philosophies as well. When faced with a problem of discretion, their judgments are likely to fall on the side of the middle class rather than those they consider to be irresponsible and troublesome.

Bureaucratic decision makers have been able to obscure this bias in a number of ways.[19] Among these are the distribution of symbolic or emotionally satisfying rewards (that is, policy statements, elaborate ceremonies, speeches) while awarding tangible benefits to dominant interests; the appearance of undertaking activity to deal with problems, while actually doing little to change existing conditions; and selective responses to "crisis situations" which evoke publicity, while avoiding remedial action to deal with root causes.[20] In examining bureaucracies and their commitments, therefore, it is necessary to distinguish between *stated* and *intended* goals. Stated goals are aims which are pronounced as official policy and are for public consumption. Intended goals are aims which are actually operative in the implementation or nonimplementation of policy.

The successful confusion of these two goals has camouflaged real political situations and thrown out-groups off balance. As explained earlier, out-groups have great difficulty bringing about sustained pressure because of the transient nature of their social structure. Prolonged delay and duplicity by bureaucracies is quite effective in smothering out-group demands, since given a long enough period of time, pressure will disappear. We refer to the disappearance of out-group pressure as political quiescence—a state of political inactivity marked by frustration and futility.[21]

In the next section I shall examine how black political action alternated between heightened activity and quiescence in the last three decades. Finally, I shall attempt to draw some lessons from this experience in terms of strategies and avenues to power.

Liberal and Radical Responses to the Political System

Political Deprivation and the Liberal Response. The deprivations suffered by black Americans for the greater part of this country's history is not a new story nor something which should surprise the reader. The responses to that oppressive history, however, deserves close attention.

After Reconstruction, white terrorism was rapidly superceded by its political and social counterparts. Such devices as the "poll tax," the "grandfather clause," "good character" requirements, and the discriminatory use of literacy tests were used as a wedge with which to separate blacks from their political rights. After that, the restoration of black servitude was conducted more openly. When the Mississippi constitution was revised in 1890, its intent was stated quite baldly as "the policy of crushing out the manhood of Negro citizens."[22] One state senator at Virginia's constitutional convention readily admitted that its purpose was "to discriminate to the very extremity of permissible action . . . with a view to the elimination of every Negro voter who can be gotten rid of, legally, without materially impairing the numerical strength of the white electorate."[23]

The South did not have to wait very long either. By the turn of the century blacks were disenfranchised in virtually every Southern state. In Louisiana, for instance, the number of Negro voters fell sharply from over 130,000 in 1896 to 1,342 by 1904. The nadir of black voting strength in the South occurred in 1940, when so many were entering the armed forces. In no state did registration even reach 20 percent of the eligible black vote. Alabama had the lowest with just a fraction of 1 percent of Negroes voting. In Georgia, 1.71 percent of the black electorate was registered; in Virginia, 5.49 percent; in Mississippi, 0.09 percent; while

Florida allowed 3.20 percent of eligible blacks to register. Tennessee led the Old Confederacy with 16 percent of eligible black citizens voting.[24]

Jim Crow also had a future in the North, although it was of a different kind. The great black trek northward occurred between 1910 and 1920, while a second wave began in the years after World War II. Spurred on by hard times on the farm, mobility during two wars, and a search for work, blacks crowded into the cities. The increase in the black urban population during these periods was astounding. Between 1910 and 1920, Detroit's black population rose by over 600 percent, Cleveland's by 300 percent, and Chicago's by over 150 percent.[25] Once a base population was established, the increases in northern cities went beyond percentage growths to sizable pluralities. In 24 metropolitan areas with half a million or more residents, the central cities lost over two million white residents, but more than made up for that in black migration.[26] By 1960, the number of blacks in Philadelphia stood at over one-half million and many such centers as Newark, Cleveland, Gary, Detroit, and Washington, D.C., had black majorities or were on the verge of having them.

Everywhere they went in the north, blacks were segregated into their own turf. New York had its Harlem; Chicago, its South Side; Los Angeles, its Watts; and Boston, its Sugar Hill. In the eyes of whites, often immigrants themselves, the black influx was seen as a plague and they abandoned borderline areas as quickly as their neighbors arrived. As one early account in 1925 relates,

> the whole movement . . . took on aspects of an invasion; they became panic stricken and began fleeing as from a plague. The presence of one colored family in a block, no matter how well bred and orderly, was sufficient to precipitate a flight. House after house and block after block was actually deserted.[27]

Prior to the great treks northward, blacks enjoyed full employment, working in the trades with a modest number in the business and the professional class. Although there were living areas in which blacks were excluded, racial ghettos were as yet unknown. In Chicago as late as 1910, there were no areas where blacks constituted more than 61 percent of the population. More than two thirds of the Negro population lived in sections less than 50 percent black and a third lived in areas less than 10 percent black.[28]

But as blacks poured into the cities, their relative position deteriorated; and with increased numbers, racism grew uglier. In housing, blacks found themselves not only being barred from new areas of the city but paying more rent than their white predecessors in old dilapidated ones.[29] In education, the number of segregated schools rapidly increased in many cities; and with the racial separation came the all too familiar inferior treatment.* The cycle was completed as blacks found employment closed to them, making them unable to compete because they could not obtain the needed skills. Blacks were trapped into ghetto life—unable to break free because they could not get adequate employment and unable to get employment because they could not obtain an adequate education. The cycle of deprivation was also accompanied by a cycle of dependence. Blacks appeared in disproportionate numbers on relief rolls, police blotters, and drug treatment lines. In St. Louis blacks represented 29 percent of the population in 1959, but accounted for over 50 percent of the crime. In Detroit, in the same year, blacks constituted 30 percent of the population but 80 percent of the welfare recipients.[30]

The deprivation suffered by blacks was not exclusively a matter of institutional restrictions alone. At times racism burst out in its more violent forms. Beginning with the draft riots in 1863, Irish immigrants in New York City roamed the streets attacking free blacks. What Arthur Waskow calls a "pogrom," and Gunnar Myrdal a "massacre," took place with the police sometimes standing silently by. During the early years of World War I, there were numerous racial riots, usually the result of white depredations against black migrants. Racial conflagrations in East St. Louis in 1917 brought about the deaths of 15 whites and 23 blacks. In the summer of 1919, seven major racial riots occurred.[31] The most serious of these was in Chicago, when a black youth swimming off the Twenty-seventh Street Beach made the mistake of crossing over an invisible line separating the races. When he tried to come ashore, whites stoned him; and soon after the biggest race war in Chicago's history erupted. The final toll left 15 whites and 23 blacks dead, while 178 whites and 342 blacks were injured.[32] The North, blacks were beginning to find had all the trappings of Southern persecution, even if it lacked a statutory base.

At first blush racial oppression appeared to be largely a matter of political and legal factors: political, because it was rooted in a system of formal and informal power which disenfranchised blacks and deprived them of their means to influence public policy with respect to housing, education, and the like; legal, because racism was largely con-

---

*The presumably liberal city of New York may be a good case in point. The percentage increases in segregated black and Puerto Rican schools from 1958 to 1963 are as follows: at the primary level, 12% to 22%; in junior high schools, 10 to 17%; and at the senior high level, 0% to 2%. In one five-year span, 78 public schools had become segregated. See, for example, The State Education Commissioner's Advisory Committee on Human Relations and Community Tensions, *Desegregating the Public Schools of New York City* (New York: The Institute of Urban Studies, Teacher's College, Columbia University, 1964, p. 7).

ceived of as a denial of constitutional rights, which needed to be asserted through the courts. Most Americans, it was thought, were law abiding and once those rights were given legal sanction, racial prejudice would eventually disappear.

It was logical, therefore, that the fight against racial injustice would take place in political and judicial arenas. Spearheading the drive during the 1950s and 1960s was the National Association for the Advancement of Colored People (NAACP) and its special arm, the legal and educational defense fund. The general approach was toward securing "equal opportunities" for blacks. The spotlight was focused on an integrated civil rights movement which successfully obtained "equal opportunities" in the armed forces (1948, the abolition of segregated units); in education (1954, *Brown* v. *Board of Education* where the Supreme Court ruled that separate facilities were inherently unequal); in voting rights (1957 and 1960 Civil Rights Act); in public accommodations and employment (1964 Civil Rights Act); and in housing (1968, Open Housing Act).

The list by no means exhausts the accomplishments attained. Picketing, boycotts, and sit-ins were also carried out by grass roots participants as well as the national movement for integration. Usually such activism was a follow-up to securing the actual benefits of recent legislation or testing old discriminatory practices. But again, the intent was to gain for blacks those opportunities which other Americans enjoyed—nothing more nor less. In a word, what blacks were demanding during these years was simply the chance to play the game.

For a good part of the civil rights movement, and its sympathizers, this opportunity was sufficient. Many of these people were middle class and liberals, and their social status determined their ideological outlook. For possessing the wherewithal to compete, the game could be seen as a reasonably fair one with tangible rewards for those who could play it well. The rewards themselves were substantial, especially if one counts them within the contemporary period of black struggle, say the last 10 or 20 years.

The number of blacks being elected to legislative and other governmental posts can be encouraging to those with less than radical viewpoints. Throughout the 1940s and 1950s just two blacks sat in the House of Representatives—one a political maverick from Harlem, Adam Clayton Powell, and the other a party stalwart from Chicago's South Side, William Dawson. By 1966, there were six blacks in Congress, including one senator; four years later, the Ninety-first Congress had 10 blacks, and in 1973, the total on Capitol Hill rose to 16. Relative to the nation's black population of nearly 23 million or 11 percent of the total, 16 congressional representatives is a paltry sum.[33] But measured over a decade of struggle there was movement, no matter how cynical one might get in interpreting that movement.

Overall results, particularly at the local level, are also encouraging. As Table 1 indicates, there were over two thousand blacks holding public office in 1973, showing an increase over a five-year period of 121 percent.

Table 1 represents more than a simple compilation of numbers and percentages. What these figures mean is that black representatives now sit in the legislative chambers of most of the states in the union; that they have a place in county government and in many instances have been able to affect the kind of housing available to blacks and the police protection they receive or fail to receive; and that judges, constables, and boards of education are now subject to black influence. There are now 82 black mayors and 43 vice mayors overseeing, in some way, the delivery of municipal services to their constituents.[34]

What is interesting about the rise of black municipal executives in the past few years is that they have climbed to power with an increasingly large number of white votes. Mayor Richard Hatcher of Gary, Indiana, enlarged his share of white votes from 15 percent to 22 percent during his second election. This is no mean task in a city where racial tensions have run high and where Hatcher has attempted to build his power by strongly favoring black appointments at City Hall. Tom Bradley drew 47 percent of the white vote in Los Angeles in 1969, while that city's black population stood at only 18 percent. Bradley lost that year to the incumbent, Sam Yorty, who played on the racial issue, but came back in 1973 to trounce Mayor Yorty. Black mayors are incumbents today in such cities as Detroit, Atlanta, and Raleigh and have been building alliances across racial boundaries. Individual longevity may not be long, but the pattern appears to be set.

Indeed, taken from the perspective of one decade ago, these gains are quite dramatic. Voting rights legislation and politicization of blacks have, in the parlance of the previous section, dealt a blow to the overt biases of the political system. These overt biases, for the most part, consist of modes of operation or decision making instrumentalities—that is, legislative chambers, the courts, boards of education, councils of local governance, and executive agencies such as mayors and commissioners.

To the liberal whose main concern is the equalization of opportunity, the job of racial justice is on its way to being accomplished, though it is far from complete. Congress after all still has far too few black faces in it; black representation is not up to parity with the black population, and there are states where such representation is sorely lacking. But expectation is that progress will continue, and that as blacks come into

TABLE 1
BLACK ELECTED OFFICIALS IN THE U.S., 1969–1973

Year	Total	Differences from Previous Year	Percentage Increase	
			Previous Year	1969
1969	1,185	0	0	0
1970	1,469	284	19	19
1971	1,860	391	26	56
1972	2,264	404	22	91
1973	2,621	357	15	121

SOURCE: *The National Roster of Black Elected Officials*, Vol. 3 (Washington, D.C.: Joint Center for Political Studies, May, 1973), p. vii.

policy-making capacities within these modes of operation, substantive changes will occur. Thus by equalizing the rules in arenas where decisions are made, housing, education, and employment will improve for blacks, giving them a path out of the ghetto.

Political Deprivation and the Radical Response. Taken from one perspective black political progress during the last decade was formidable and could be ascertained with hard evidence. But statistics can mean many different things to different people, and what sticks out in the minds of critics is that 16 black congressmen represent less than 3 percent of that body's voting strength in a nation where blacks constitute 11 percent of the population. In state and local legislatures the record is far from satisfying. In 1973, six states in the union had no black representation in their legislatures, and in many legislatures where blacks were present, their numbers could be counted on the fingers of one hand.[35]

Table 2 shows 44 states plus the District of Columbia and their number of elected black officials. Omitted from the Table are Hawaii, Idaho, Montana, North Dakota, South Dakota, and Utah, which had no black representation as of early 1973.

A simple compilation of numbers does not take us very far however, unless we can interpret their consequences. To begin with, in the majority of cases the number of black officials in each state is so small that their power is virtually nonexistent, except for the moral suasion they can bring to bear. Table 3 indicates just how diluted this representation is when a number of states are grouped according to seats held by blacks.

Under these circumstances any concerted exercise of power is difficult, if not impossible. Thus while some can talk about impressive gains for blacks and cite over two thousand offices won within various modes of operation, that evidence can yield another picture when placed under different lenses.

TABLE 2

BLACK ELECTED OFFICIALS IN THE UNITED STATES AS OF APRIL 1973

State	Total	Federal		State			County		Municipal				Law Enforcement				Education		
		Senator	Representatives	State Executives	Senators	Representatives	Commissioners, Supervisors, Councilmen	Other County Officials	Mayors	Vice Mayors, Mayors Pro Tem	Councilmen, Aldermen, Commissioners	Other Local Officials	Judges, Justices, Magistrates	Chiefs of Police, Constables, Marshals, Sheriffs	Justices of the Peace	Other Law Enforcement Officials	State and College Boards	Local School Boards	Other Education Officials
Alabama	149					2	9	11	8	1	46		1	55				16	
Alaska	5			1		2												2	
Arizona	4					2					1							1	
Arkansas	141				1	3		1	8	1	47	11			19			50	
California	130		3		1	6			4	3	33	5	14	1			4	56	
Colorado	8				1	3					3		1						
Connecticut	48				1	5					20	6		4				12	
Delaware	12				1	2					8							1	
District of Columbia	8		1															7	
Florida	58					3			3	5	42	1	1					3	
Georgia	104		1		2	14	8	1	7	3	39	1	1					27	
Illinois	137		1		5	14	2		1		49	7	13	4		1	1	38	1
Indiana	57				1	6	1	1			23	6	3		5			11	
Iowa	8					1					2		1					4	
Kansas	22				1	4	1		2		6		1					7	

State	Total
Louisiana	130
Maine	3
Maryland	55
Massachusetts	20
Michigan	179
Minnesota	7
Mississippi	152
Missouri	85
Nebraska	3
Nevada	6
New Hampshire	1
New Jersey	134
New Mexico	4
New York	164
North Carolina	112
Ohio	111
Oklahoma	67
Oregon	6
Pennsylvania	65
Rhode Island	7
South Carolina	99
Tennessee	71
Texas	101
Vermont	2
Virginia	62
Washington	13
West Virginia	5
Wisconsin	9
Wyoming	2
TOTALS	2621

Column totals (TOTALS row): 2621 | 1 | 15 | 2 | 42 | 196 | 167 | 44 | 82 | 43 | 840 | 88 | 154 | 115 | 61 | 4 | 21 | 744 | 2

SOURCE: *The National Roster of Black Elected Officials*, Vol. 3 (Washington, D.C.: Joint Center for Political Studies, May, 1973), p. xvi.

TABLE 3
DISTRIBUTION OF THE NUMBER OF
BLACK ELECTED OFFICIALS PER STATE

Black Elected Officials per State	Number of States
0–29	21
30–59	5
60–89	5
90–119	5
120–149	6
150–179	3

SOURCE: *The National Roster of Black Elected Officials*, Vol. 3 (Washington, D.C.: Joint Center for Political Studies, May, 1973), p. vii.

Furthermore, talking about blacks elected to public office helps us very little unless we ascertain what these elected posts mean. In many instances blacks serving as commissioners, justices of the peace, and councilmen have little discretionary authority; such gains are merely ways of distributing patronage or allowing token appointments to office. As we discussed in a previous section there are numerous methods used to prevent out-groups from gaining power: gerrymandering, disallowing electoral petitions, screening panels, challenges to a group's legitimacy. When a group's claims persist over a number of years and become less resistable, however, a common response by in-groups is to concede some points but not those significant enough to make a difference. Thus, in North Carolina, state officials permitted larger numbers of blacks to vote during the 1960s in order to prevent federal registrars from coming into that state. The white elite calculated quite accurately that blacks could be elected to office in enough numbers to demonstrate a visible change but not enough to change the distribution of power and the content of policy.[36]

Such has been the case in a number of states and cities throughout the country. When blacks suddenly find themselves in the capacity of constituting significant pluralities, biases of various sorts are introduced which, intentionally or otherwise, curtail their power. Within modes of operation, for example, blacks have found ward-based voting replaced by at-large voting systems in many cities. The result has been that pockets of black strength within smaller communities have been overcome by a larger white voting majority which covers the entire municipality. In Jacksonville, Florida, just as black numbers began to make a possible difference in that city's power, adjoining white suburbs were annexed. There is, of course, a growing movement in American cities for annexation of suburbs and for many legitimate reasons, but a consequence of this is to dilute black political strength.

In instances where disenfranchisement is part of an intentional plan, newer biases have replaced traditional ones which were found illegal. Thus, the selective use of run-off elections was introduced when several whites found themselves running against a single black candidate. The use of "full slate" laws has also been selectively applied to prevent blacks from concentrating their voting power. Under this law, if there are multiple positions to be filled on the ballot, the voter must cast his ballot for the total number of offices to be filled, thereby preventing a lone black candidate from accumulating more votes than his white running mates.[37]

All this assumes, of course, an active black electorate which is highly motivated to vote. As we pointed out in the previous section, this is not usually the case. In addition to the ever-pressing needs of daily survival and a host of encumbrances mentioned earlier, out-groups such as poor blacks are not accustomed to expect anything from political participation. Thus, traditional means of political expression long enjoyed by whites and reinforced by tangible benefits have little credence in many black communities. When this fact is combined with the character of politics in the inner city, it is not difficult to see how vulnerable black neighborhoods really are. Politicians frequently parcel out black neighborhoods to surrounding white areas, where the politicians are guaranteed reelection. This pattern is particularly true in New York City, long the bastion of liberal values, except when it comes to the survival of incumbent legislators. As blacks and Puerto Ricans inhabit older white areas, electoral district-lines shift into the shape of contorted amebas in order to save old seats. Minorities have always been underrepresented in that city's state and congressional delegations, and only recently were they given the chance to elect representatives from their own districts to the City Council. City Councilmen however chose to increase their membership and dilute the minority vote rather than reapportion old friends out of office.

At first sight, it is curious that the most dramatic gains made by blacks and the largest number of elected offices held, should be in the South rather than in more liberal sections of the country. Yet as Table 4 indicates, nearly half the black elected-officials achieved their status in that region of the country thought to be the most racially oppressive.

Part of the answer as to why blacks should make the sharpest gains in the South rather than in the North belies the notion that all one need do to enjoy democracy is to legally ensure fundamental rights. While these rights were guaranteed in Northern cities for a good many decades, they counted for little in ghetto areas, where systematic biases have

TABLE 4
DISTRIBUTION OF BLACK ELECTED OFFICIALS
BY GEOGRAPHIC REGION AS OF 1973

Region	Number	Percentage
North	579	22
South	1,179	45
Midwest	685	26
West	178	7
TOTAL	2,621	100

SOURCE: *The National Roster of Black Elected Officials*, Vol. 3 (Washington, D.C.: Joint Center for Political Studies, May, 1973), p. viii.

operated to disenfranchise the population. Paradoxically, the history of legal segregation in the South enabled blacks to hold power once opportunities arose. For one thing, blacks were often a majority within segregated political jurisdictions such as towns, counties, and parishes. When the vote came, they already had a political framework within which to exercise that franchise and this prevented their absorption into white-dominated modes of operation. Secondly, having enjoyed a long history in most Southern communities, blacks were able to organize more effectively than their often rootless counterparts in the North. Much as the segregated black church enabled its members to control it, so, too, did segregated black political jurisdictions come under the power of its inhabitants, once legal barriers were removed. In the North, by contrast, the absence of such barriers was inconsequential so long as blacks remained transient and disesteemed wards of society.

A final objection to the argument that blacks have made political progress is that even if blacks do obtain the needed national policies, they will be undone by local bureaucracies working in alliance with in-groups. Thus, although the Supreme Court and the Justice Department proclaim an end to school segregation, local boards of education continue to segregate students; while Congress passes open housing acts, zoning boards make it impossible for blacks to obtain decent homes; and while Washington issues edicts for affirmative action, many unions remain closed. Power and policy, it should be noted, does not take place through proclamation but through actual implementation by willing officials. So long as these officials share the ideologies and beliefs of established in-groups, change will be resisted.

Politics entails an understanding of how different groups perceive the realities and the choices with which they are faced. Liberals perceived the black plight as essentially one of the denial of rights, and they labored hard to achieve those rights through relatively conventional means. Every legislative seat or executive post won by blacks was seen as a step toward implementing policies which would ultimately achieve racial justice. Although liberal activists sometimes showed impatience, they followed a set path by relying on conventional tactics and expected that a better society could somehow be pieced together. As noted earlier, these efforts were not without their rewards, and for a stratum of blacks they were quite encouraging.

The more radical perception of the problem and its attendant response was altogether different. For radicals, black political gains were not a matter of patiently or impatiently working for the awaited moment, but a denial that such a moment was conceivable, given the nature of the political system and the society. Incremental gains were not seen as steps forward but usually as situations in which black leaders were co-opted into a class and racially dominated power structure. Any gains that were made were seen as minimal compromises in order to defuse the black political movement.

Given this perception, radicals adopted a strategy more suitable to their expectations. The strategy may have not been consciously derived and neatly coordinated, but there was an intuitive response in the air during the early 1960s which became full blown several years later in mass protests and movements for black power and community control.

Each of these tactics is a complicated affair and will be treated more fully in the last section, but a few comments are in order here. The popularity of community control and black power represents a quasi and perhaps temporary withdrawal from the American political process. The words quasi and temporary should be emphasized in this description, because both community control and black power can be seen as ways of coping with biases within the system rather than a total withdrawal from it. In this sense the term "radical" is used in its most relative (and mild) sense, since the greater part of "militants" associated with these movements did not seek to transform society so much as to cope with it, as they perceived it to be. Coping with the system placed less emphasis on winning seats within existing modes of operation and more on developing a foundation of power which was distinguishable from the greater society. To this end, black power was used as an ideology for building support, and community control was to be the framework on which to locate that support. Similarly, the threat and practice of mass protest was a means of obtaining for blacks that which they were unable to achieve through conventional political expression.

In the final section, which follows, we shall explore each of these tactics along with conventional political practices. This will be done with

an eye toward ascertaining the utility of each tactic as a way of gaining
power and changing public policy.

Alternatives to Power and Its Synthesis

Thus far we have discussed two responses to political deprivation in
America, which were broadly termed as "liberal" or "radical" in nature.
The liberal variant primarily stresses conventional forms of political
expression such as running for elective office, challenging discriminatory
laws, influencing public opinion, and securing benefits through public
policy. While protest action of different sorts are by no means strange
to liberals, such action was usually subordinate to more conventional
methods and limited to peaceful demonstrations. On the other hand, the
radical method of expression relied quite heavily on mass protest or
what I shall refer to as direct action. Besides direct action, I have also
said that two other tactics are part of the radical style—community
control and black power.

The peak of the black movement for community control occurred in
New York City in 1968, when black communities demanded a voice in
the school system. The movement however has also spread to other
cities—Detroit, Washington, Dayton, Philadelphia, and Milwaukee, to
name of few—and has taken on different objectives.[38] In some cities
education is the primary target for reorganization; in other places "little
city halls" and other forms of decentralized control (such as those re-
lating to the police and housing) are in demand.

The concept of community control involves an effort to circumvent
the authority of a larger government and devolve its power to the neighborhood level. In this way, biases of the political system which work
against out-groups can be reduced or perhaps eliminated. Thus, to use
the example of education, neighborhoods within a city might exercise
direct control in hiring teachers and establishing curriculum priorities,
and in school construction. This would in effect curtail the advantages
enjoyed by in-groups (in this case unions, the educational bureaucracy,
and so on) and provide community residents with direct input into decisions affecting their children. The concept need not be limited to one
function alone and might include a variety of services which are essential
to community life.

The idea of black power is more ambiguous, perhaps, because it has
not had any tangible embodiment and remains largely an ideological
abstraction. In fact some political scientists have identified black power
as an ideology which calls for "black unity" and a "fair share" of social
and economic rewards for Negroes. Stokely Carmichael and Charles
Hamilton, in an exposition on the subject, define black power as

> . . . a call for black people in this country to unite, to recognize their herit-
> age, to build a sense of community. It is a call for black people to define
> their own goals, to lead their own organizations, and to support those
> organizations. It is a call to reject the racist institutions and values of this
> society.[39]

Black power, then, is more than a slogan, but is something of an
ideological movement or counter movement, which posits a set of principles—"unity," "heritage," and "community"—and makes a plea for
some future order—namely, support and leadership for black organizations. To be sure, along with these features come the slogans and
symbols (in this case, tricolor flag, clenched-fist salute, common salu-
tations, and the like) which are often connected with ideologies. But
these are devices used to promote cohesion and the larger aspirations of
the movement.

In short, both the notions of community control and black power
represent an inward turning of assertion in order to strengthen a powerless group. This inward turning is part of building out-group strength.
Thus, by asserting ethnic pride and "togetherness," and by directing
goals inward, toward the community, an out-group develops its own confidence and base of power. Where community control addresses itself to
constructing alternative modes of operation and transferring decisions
to local governing entities, black power attempts to face up to the problem of systemic biases by developing cohesion and a consciousness of
purpose.

Put another way, the use of community control and black power may
be described as the development of countervailing power for out-
groups so that they too can enjoy the requisites necessary for effective
political participation. As Carmichael and Hamilton readily admit,

> The concept of black power rests on a fundamental premise. Before a
> group can enter the open society, it must first close its ranks. By this we
> mean that group solidarity is necessary before a group can operate from a
> bargaining position of strength in a pluralistic society . . . .[40]

Mass protest, or direct action, has functioned similarly for black
radicals. Direct action may be defined as an unconventional mode of
political activity which is characterized by (1) mass participation, (2)
confrontation of protesting groups with authorities, or attacks upon
institutions, and (3) the use of whatever sanctions are available to
out-groups to achieve their demands. This characterization of direct
action obviously covers a multitude of acts and though I do not intend
to be exhaustive, the instances range from peaceful marches and picketing to sit-down strikes and building take-overs, from public disturbances
to the application of violence on a mass scale (riots or insurrections,
destruction of property, looting, and so on).

Again, in order to understand the occurrence of direct action through-out the 1960s, and particularly urban "rioting" between 1964 and 1968, one must understand the political perception of out-groups. If my position that out-groups are unable to muster the conventional pre-requisites needed (organization, intensive lobbying, communication, and so on) for effective political participation is correct, then direct action may very well be seen as an expression of available resources which out-groups do possess. Those resources which are available in the ghetto are an abundance of people and their willingness to act en masse in particular circumstances. Thus, direct action could be seen as the appli-cation of sanctions in the form of demonstrations, which could tarnish the image of an institution; or sit-down strikes, which could disrupt business; or violence, which could result in the destruction of property and the endangerment of lives.

It is not difficult to see how the sit-down strikes and picketing of the early 1960s had such a political motivation. But a great many of the riots which occurred in this nation's cities after 1964 had a similar political basis. Indeed the reports which were published in the wake of the rioting indicated that in most instances there were events which "triggered" the disturbances (alleged police brutality or police shootings of Negro youths). Many of the targets of destruction were white-owned shops thought to be exploiting the community, and the rioters themselves had a heightened sense of political injury. In the words of the National Advisory Commission on Civil Disorders,

> Characteristically, the typical rioter was not a hoodlum, habitual criminal, or riffraff; nor was he a recent migrant, a member of an uneducated under-class, or a person lacking broad social and political concerns. Instead he was a teenager or young adult, a lifelong resident of the city in which he rioted, a high-school drop-out—but somewhat better educated than his Negro neighbor—and almost invariably underemployed or employed in a menial job. He was proud of his race, extremely hostile to both whites and middle-class Negroes and, though informed about politics, highly distrustful of the political system and of political leaders.[41]

Thus, like community control and black power, direct action can be seen as a way of coping with the rigidities of the political system as out-groups perceive them. From the point of view of the actors, each of these tactics is a rational and adaptive response: rational, because they appear to be the most "logical" means for breaking through a system which is skewed against them; adaptive, because they appear to be the sole means through which political expression is possible and the only alternative to despair.

Synthesizing Alternatives. Looking at the liberal and radical re-sponses to political deprivation leads me to the conclusion that both

are pressing for racial justice with differing perceptions of what is politically feasible in American politics, which says little about what they
have in common. If a clue to a synthesis can be found it is that both
responses are means of survival within the political system rather than
outright rejections of it. This is not unusual for liberals, but it is ex-
traordinary for supposed "radicals" to be characterized by words like
"survival" and "adaptive." Radicals by nature emphasize rejection and
transformation of a system, not adaption to it. Yet, after all the rhetoric
has faded what comes through from more militant black groups is an
effort at functioning within the larger political framework by narrowing
goals (for example, the rejection of integration in favor of a more
separatist "black power") and building alternative mechanisms for
political participation (as exemplified in the shift from national poli-
ticking to community reconstruction).

The liberal and radical approaches are however by no means mutually
exclusive. There was, in fact, a period during the 1960s when the styles
complemented one another and, in my opinion, brought the black movement to a political peak. While sit-down strikes were occurring at segregated restaurants in the South and hospitals were being occupied in
Northern ghettos, black legislators were at the bargaining table attempting to secure redress through legislation and negotiation. The liberal
counsel was always one of "compromise" and "moderation," but it was
made more effective because blacks were acting in the streets. Martin
Luther King's appeal to nonviolence was made all the more powerful
because H. Rap Brown was ready to (and did) take the law into his own
hands. Black leaders for a time possessed amazing political leverage.
The not-so-veiled threat "You must accept our just complaints and you
must deal with us; otherwise, we will not be able to control our people"[42]
worked well for black liberals so long as another liberal was in the
White House.

What was wrong with these two approaches was that they were often
uncoordinated and sometimes disparate. Black leaders from either wing
would disavow or ridicule one another, undermining the leverage of the
other. Furthermore, a huge segment of the black community was leader-
less and their reactions spontaneous. This is particularly true in the area
of direct action where collective protests burst out into the streets as
the summers grew hotter, and raged into uncontrolled destruction.

This need not be the case in the future among blacks and whites;
liberals and radicals may be able to combine their talents to manipulate
the system to their own advantage. For if American politics contains
biases against the poor, it also has a few which can be turned around.
The system can be a double-edged sword, particularly when it comes to
ideology, and to a lesser extent when access to modes of operation are
involved. For example, ideological myths concerning the notion of

"equality" and the value of "progressive change" can be turned against status quo groups. This was at the heart of the black civil-rights movement of the 1950s and can be effective in the 1970s if used as an organizing tool in gaining access to modes of operation. Broadly speaking this would take the form of organizing tightly knit coalitions operating in spheres of public policy which most affect blacks. Full employment, job retraining, community-governed health care, and the channeling of energies toward environmental conservation and mass transit are just a few of the issues that afford opportunities to fulfill historical promises. These are essentially "nonracial" issues which cut across the concerns of all strata within the country. As such they are capable of energizing groups and providing them with a focus for pressuring various parts of the system.

Within the black community itself various factions may be able to work together in a two-pronged approach with each prong undertaking what it does best and easiest. No rigid demarcation is being suggested here, but what is urged is that liberal and radical blacks obtain optimal value for their efforts by reinforcing each other's claims. Thus, it is quite conceivable for black moderates in the halls of state legislatures to push for greater community control, and for radicals to reciprocate by supporting moderate measures which may assist blacks only indirectly (for example, aid for urban transportation).

One necessary beginning toward such cooperation is for all blacks to distinguish for the immediate future that which is politically possible from that which is socially desirable. One certain lesson from the experiences of 1968 and 1972 is that nothing happens in America without winning that "vast middle." Blacks must begin to think pragmatically about white America without getting caught up in a bitter reaction against its racism. An operative principle might be to allow middle America to identify and sympathize with black aspirations so far as that is possible, and this is where black liberals can be instrumental. From this, more specific tactics can be developed which might read as follows:

A. Work to identify out-group demands with the demands of the American center.
   1. Decentralization of city government is something which appeals to all communities, black or white. All urban communities should be empowered to make decisions affecting police, sanitation, or education. There is no reason why "community control" has to be a black issue, when whites are equally disgruntled about the quality of city services.
   2. Similarly, measures on comprehensive health care and full employment are issues which cut across racial and even class lines, and should be used to forge alliances.

B. Work to establish the legitimacy of "out-group" demands through resolutions, legislative bills, and national proclamation.
   1. Despite the seeming revolutionary positions of radicals on welfare rights, their positions can be quite tenable if the history of workmen's rights, women's suffrage, and free public education provides us with any guide.
   2. Furthermore, public statements and repetition of the unthinkable enable unorthodox claims to pierce ideological buffer zones.
C. Work to involve the "vast middle" in out-group causes.
   1. Potential allies might be the intellectuals, who often serve as transmission belts between radicals and the center.
   2. Other allies might be the mass media where reporters can "legitimize" ideas through articles and commentary. This can be a double-edged sword, but it is worth the risk, since most out-group ideas are not within the sphere of respectability anyway.
D. Work to establish coalitions with groups whose interests, no matter how minor, may be congruent with black demands.
   1. White working-class communities are as disgruntled with and alienated from the political system as many blacks. Common agreement on government taxation and spending may not be possible, but a demand that citizens get the most for their dollar in parks, recreation, and other services is entirely feasible.
   2. Establishing working coalitions with other groups can be important because of the very process of cooperative relationships such coalitions engender. Issues of a less controversial nature can be the basis for more elaborate alliances.
E. Where possible, avoid the trap of allowing elites to frame issues as one of class–race conflict. Black demands which touch all of society are unfortunately often couched as threats to white middle and lower-middle groups, thereby reducing the chances for social change.
   1. Measures toward racial equality in schools and employment, known as "affirmative action," have unnecessarily posed the issue as a squeeze for space between disadvantaged minorities and advantaged whites. This reasoning is specious and should be revealed as such. Black workers need not battle white trade unionists while the White House curbs government spending on sewerage treatment plants; black applicants need not have to compete for spaces in medical schools, while too few doctors are available for the nation and the need continues to grow.
   2. Elites in the courts and public agencies have been allowed to arbitrate such decisions, allowing token numbers of blacks entrance while institutions and jobs remain closed to greater numbers and whites labor under the mistaken impression that blacks have become a "privileged" group.

F. Black radicals should avoid excesses of verbiage and action which
    accomplish little and allow less preferable white candidates to win
    office. It does make a difference which candidates win office, because
    along with a change of personality comes a change in institutional
    structure and priority.
    1. The Nixon–Humphrey contest of 1968 will effect profound
       changes in judicial decisions for years to come, which will affect
       the future of blacks and whites.
    2. National programs have a way of continuing and developing a
       momentum of their own if given enough time to thrive and gen-
       erate constituent support. The premature death of the "War On
       Poverty" and its replacement with less generous revenue-sharing
       proposals is an instance where blacks have lost important potential
       advantages.
G. Varieties of direct action should be "rationalized" for public con-
    sumption so that public policies which assist out-groups are rein-
    forced and those which hinder them are protested.
    1. During the 1960s public protests were allowed to rage out of
       control long after they had made their point and after their
       effectiveness had ceased. The upshot of such excesses was a
       counterreaction, leaving white liberals embarrassed and helpless.
    2. Reinforcement of public policies designed to help the poor should
       come in the form of peaceful reconstruction and the formation of
       coalitions and alliances with other groups to work for additional
       positive programs.

This list of alternative tactics can, no doubt, be expanded and is intended as a guide not a political compendium. Its biases are admittedly
obvious for it stresses tactful accommodation not violent and abrupt
revolution. If, as was said earlier, politics is the "art of the possible,"
there are few choices left short of national catastrophe.

Nor need these recommendations be interpreted as a cynical and
Machiavellian ploy to gain power simply for the sake of it. Power can
be used for many purposes, and among those purposes lies the possibility of fulfilling social reconstruction. This is of course easier said than
done, for it requires unity and a sense of purpose to win power, neither
of which is in abundant supply among black activists.

As a segment of the black population moves into the middle class,
the separation between black liberals and black radicals may widen into
a chasm. Color alone does not determine a group's behavior nor even
its identification, although it is a significant bond. Social class and economic opportunities also set the agenda for the political commitments
a group is willing to make. Consequently, difficulties besetting blacks

may well stem from an internal separation of blacks into "haves" and "have nots." This would indeed be ironic, for it was radical and liberal action that made a larger black middle class possible. Such an occurrence would be a political misfortune, but such are the ways of a political system which is geared to incrementalism and a middle-class ethos.

Robert E. Forman

THE UNIVERSITY OF TOLEDO

2

Housing and Racial Segregation

The essentials of life are usually stated as food, clothing, and shelter. This chapter is about one of these most basic needs, shelter or housing. In contrast to many creatures in nature, man has severe physical limitations which make the adequacy of his shelter practically a matter of life itself. In a complex urban-industrial society such as the United States, both climate and health needs make housing of vital importance. And, of course, beyond the basic creature-protection function, housing as a result of its location and characteristics is related to a person's social world in matters of social status, chances for earning a living, interactions with other members of his family, and his or her self-concept, to mention just a few obvious aspects. Clearly, housing is very important to physical and social well-being both from the standpoint of the individual and of the society.

The problem of housing will be considered in two parts. First is the question of the physical housing supply. This includes the total national stock of housing and the meeting of housing needs in specific areas and for different groups within the society. We need to keep in mind that the provision of housing is a complex operation which includes land, physical materials, workers, building codes and regulations, financial institutions, economic conditions, population movements, taxation policies, transportation and land use, styles of life, socioeconomic levels, and beliefs and attitudes concerning housing. Although each of these presents a possibility for something "going wrong" and making housing problems worse, each offers an opportunity for improving housing conditions.

The second part concerns the racial aspects of housing. We know that our cities are sharply segregated into black ghettos and almost completely white areas, so much so that if a completely even distribution of blacks were to be made over the whole of a typical American city, approximately 90 percent of the blacks would have to relocate.[1] If the segregation is voluntary on the part of the blacks, that is their right. To the extent it is imposed on them and handicaps them and frustrates their desires, possibilities for alleviation must be considered.

Providing Sufficient Housing

The Housing Supply

If one has enough money, housing is not likely to present serious difficulties regarding either type of accommodation or its location; major housing problems are confined to an overwhelming degree to those with lower incomes. This is not a new situation either in this country or in other urban-industrial nations. "The housing problem," then, is how to provide adequate housing for people with lower incomes.

In the United States, more so than in most other urban-industrial countries, real estate interests have promoted the theory of the "filtering-down" (or "filtration") process for meeting the needs of low-income families. In this process, new housing would be built for higher-income families who would occupy the homes until they no longer wanted or needed them at which time the homes would be sold. Age and neighborhood changes would make the houses less desirable and hence lower in cost so that they could be bought by lower-income families. Successive changes over a period of time would permit homes to filter down to low-income families. Although the constant churning of population required by the process would help increase the earnings of real estate brokers, it is less clear that neighborhoods would benefit from the resulting mobility of families. If one accepts, however, the proposition that low-income families can hardly expect to live in expensive new homes, the filtering-down process might seem to offer the mechanism for providing adequate housing for families of limited means.

We must ask how well the filtering-down process works in practice, and this leads us to inquire about the adequacy of the total housing supply within the country. First, let us begin with a brief conceptual definition of housing adequacy: a housing unit may be considered adequate if it does not *add* to the problems of those who live within it. All people encounter problems and difficulties with which they must deal. As a minimum, housing should be a neutral factor so that it does not increase a person's burden. Housing which, through poor heating, ventilation, or sanitation, causes illness and its attendant problems for its residents obviously creates additional difficulties, as does a housing unit which is so crowded that it exacerbates difficulties by creating interpersonal frictions which generate tension and keep a person from gaining a reasonable perspective on things. There is nothing in this concept of adequacy which requires that housing be new, luxurious, or stylish. The definition is a minimum one.

Existing data permit an operational definition approximating the conceptual one. In a study of urban housing for the period 1950–1990, the Douglas commission used the concept "housing needs," which encompassed housing units in dilapidated buildings, units without their own complete plumbing facilities (hot running water, toilet, and bath or shower), and units considered "crowded" because of containing more than one person per room. The commission also included as a housing need an additional number required only during the 1950–1960 decade to produce a reasonable number of vacancies.[2]

The housing needs concept corresponds roughly to that of housing inadequacy mentioned above. Data in the Douglas commission report indicate a decline in housing needs by about one half during the 1950 to 1970 period. Despite the improvement, 1970 census data show that there were still 10.4 million housing units that were either substandard or overcrowded or both, slightly more than half of this figure being overcrowded units, with the remainder being physically substandard. While the commission expects a continuing reduction in the number of substandard units, they predict an almost constant number of approximately 3.9 million crowded units through 1990. Although the 1970 census showed fewer substandard units than was expected by the commission, it revealed a total of 5.6 million crowded units.[3]

Commission data and estimates for 1950–1970 point to a rate of new housing construction faster than that of new household formation so that for every two new households formed, three new housing units were built. This is contrary to the experience of 1890–1940 when rates of construction and new household formation were approximately equal. Despite losses of some existing housing since 1950 there has been a substantial gain in both the number and the percentage of sound housing units. The housing supply today is not only larger in proportion to the population but also includes a substantially smaller number of inadequate units than it did in 1950, both for the central cities and the country as a whole. If the filtration process is to work successfully, certainly the conditions of the quarter-century following World War II were favorable for it.

The commission nevertheless concluded that the progress in housing was "unevenly distributed," with the greatest gains being made in the higher income brackets. Those in a "lower economic status," including many blacks and other minority group members, "have lagged badly" so that "the gap in the housing status of the poverty group—roughly one-fifth of all households—and the more affluent four-fifths has been widening."[4] Filtering-down does not appear to be an effective means for meeting the housing needs of those at the lowest socioeconomic levels. The commission stated: "If the market process is to be improved upon, methods must be devised for dealing directly with the needs of housing deficit families."[5] This means that building homes for the wealthy is not the way to meet the housing needs of the poor.

Racial and Economic Factors

We must focus attention on socioeconomic differences among those who make up the market for housing. One may think of this market as including people in three broad categories. At the top are those whose incomes are sufficient to enable them to obtain completely satisfactory housing, including new homes, without undue financial hardship. This category probably includes about the top two-fifths of the population in terms of income. In the middle is a moderate-income group of about the same size whose earnings range from slightly above average to considerably below. These people can provide at least minimally adequate housing for themselves providing they are not confronted with too many handicaps such as income reduction and higher housing costs resulting from price increases and high financing charges. Finally, there are those at the bottom of the economic ladder, estimated by the Douglas commission as about one-fifth of the total population, who under no ordinary circumstances can pay enough to obtain adequate housing in the conventional market. It is this bottom group that filtering-down will not help.

We must not make the mistake of thinking of these economic groups as being only racial groups with blacks at the bottom. There are more poor whites than poor blacks, and an increasing number of blacks are finding their way into middle- and higher-income positions. A considerable improvement in the socioeconomic position of blacks has been shown by Scammon and Wattenberg using data mainly from the 1970 census.[6] These data show that blacks, particularly the younger married urban families outside the South have obtained incomes nearly equal to those of whites, and that blacks made substantial gains in getting better jobs and more education during the preceding decade. The combination of legal action, legislation, and protests did produce substantial gains for blacks so that many were able to move into middle-class income levels. One statistic, however, gives cause for serious concern—almost one-third of all black families are female-headed.[7] Such families, without a male present to provide income and control of the children, tend to have the most severe financial and behavioral problems that result in their living in the poorest, most inadequate housing. We must be aware of these differences among the blacks if we are to deal with their housing problems effectively.

Socioeconomic differences among blacks are not new, of course, and have been recognized in the literature for decades. Recent data, however, have thrown more light on the housing and locational aspects of intra-black differences which are our concern here. Analysis by Williams of a special census conducted in Cleveland in 1965 clearly revealed a pattern of developing polarization *within* the black ghetto so that while an increasing number of blacks earned normal incomes and were able to live in decent neighborhoods with standard housing, a "crisis ghetto" had developed in which things got worse between 1960 and 1965.[8] Whereas incomes had gone up within the black community as a whole, they went down in the crisis ghetto. As Williams stated, "In relative terms the Crisis Ghetto was further away from the rest of the city than in 1960 in terms of major economic indices."[9] The crisis ghetto also showed a decrease in the number of male-headed families and an increase in female-headed families along with an increase in the number of families in poverty even though population within the crisis ghetto fell during the 1960–1965 period. Williams concluded that "those with economic strength *can* flee the Crisis Ghetto. . . . But it is also clear that entrapment in the Crisis Ghetto springs directly from poverty. The price over the wall is primarily money, not skin color."[10]

The Scammon and Wattenberg data indicate that many urban blacks have been moving into better and higher-paying jobs and thus have been acquiring the means to escape from the crisis ghetto in their cities. Those remaining tend to be the ones with the most disorganized families and the lowest incomes, all of which makes for an unstable neighborhood high in the whole range of social pathologies —a neighborhood which by its very nature encourages those who are able to do so to flee, thus accentuating the division between blacks. The division is economic, not racial, a view which has also been advanced by Banfield.[11]

The crisis ghetto concept was used in the National Urban League's recent study, *The National Survey of Housing Abandonment*.[12] The study resulted from concern with a phenomenon which has been increasing rapidly in the past few years: abandonment of housing by the owner, frequently an absentee landlord, who simply has utility services to the building cut off and renounces all claim to it. Within twenty-four hours of abandonment vandals may so damage the building that it is lost forever as part of the housing supply. We will need to consider abandonment more fully later, but here will note its contribution to the making of a crisis ghetto in that a vacant vandalized building can harbor socially dangerous people as well as contribute a hazard of its

own through the threat of fire. This tends to drive out of the neighborhood the more stable, responsible families who can afford to move
elsewhere thus leaving in the crisis ghetto only the poorest, most disorganized families.

When we contemplate the considerable range of socioeconomic
differences within the typical black community, it becomes apparent
that our search for solutions to problems of housing cannot be thought
of simply as one of providing adequate shelter for "the black." Housing
problems and what needs to be done to deal with them vary according
to life circumstances and socioeconomic characteristics of individual
families, whether black, white, or other. For each of the three broad
income categories mentioned earlier the housing problems and approaches to meeting them are different. To the extent that a black in
the top income group has a problem it is almost certain to be one of
racial segregation hampering his ability to live in the kind of house and
neighborhood he wants and is able to afford. Those in the middle category will encounter more problems of racial segregation, and in addition
need an adequate supply of moderate-cost housing. Those in the lowest
group cannot provide for their own housing needs and also have severe
problems of life adjustment. It is to the meeting of the needs of the latter
two groups that we will now turn.

Moderate-Income Housing

Those in the moderate-income group are basically capable of paying
their own way in the housing market providing only that there is an
adequate supply of housing and that costs are reasonable. Let us look at
issues affecting that supply. Given the cost of conventionally constructed
new homes in most parts of the country plus their financing costs, we
may conclude that those with average incomes and less are largely
shut out of the conventional new home market. Although they can
obtain adequate housing, it will be mainly in older homes and apartments, and increasingly in mobile homes. Reliance on older homes for
people in this group necessarily means reliance on filtering-down and
this implies that their housing supply is affected by the health of the
new-home market even if they are not able to buy new homes themselves. What it comes down to is that anything which helps to keep
down housing costs benefits the moderate-income family.

Interest Costs and Government Assistance

The cost of buying a home is not just the cost of the home itself but
the total amount of money the family has to pay including, for the great
majority of people, the cost of interest on the mortgage. In the late
1960s interest rates increased dramatically and have remained high
since then. This has a profound effect on the amount of income a family
must have even in order to qualify for a mortgage.

Let us consider a family applying for a $20,000 mortgage at an interest rate of 8 percent. The interest cost alone during the first year of the mortgage will be almost $1,600 or over $130 per month. Additional amounts for payment toward the principal, taxes, and maintenance can easily bring the amount required for housing expenses to over $200 per month. Following the common guideline that housing expense should not be more than one-fourth of the total take-home income (so that there is an adequate amount for food, clothing, medical expense, and so forth), a family would need a gross income in the vicinity of $12,000 per year to qualify for the mortgage and buy the home. But the average conventional new home costs more than $30,000, which would require proportionately higher payments and income.

Now let us assume an interest rate of 4 percent on the $20,000 mortgage. The amount required for interest is reduced by half—approximately $67 per month. Because of the one-to-four ratio of housing to total income the monthly income required for the mortgage would be reduced by about $265 per month or $3,200 per year. With everything else being equal the family would only need a $9,000 per-year income for the house rather than $12,000. In other words, given only some help on the interest payments, millions of families could purchase housing they otherwise could not afford.

Section 235 of the 1968 Housing Act actually went much further than this in providing for mortgage subsidies for lower-income families that would require them to pay as little as 1 percent interest on home mortgages with no down payment required and up to 40 years to pay. Under the program the majority of houses were to be new ones, which undoubtedly is one reason why it has had the support of real estate interests. In the first two years of the program, over 100,000 homes were started or occupied under the program. Section 235 has made it possible for families with incomes as low as $4,000 per year to purchase homes.

Unfortunately, as has happened with other federal programs, abuses quickly developed which marred the reputation of Section 235. Sales of overpriced deteriorated homes to buyers unable to meet the terms of repayment resulted in many foreclosures at considerable financial and reputational loss to buyers, but at no hardship to lending institutions who were covered by the Federal Housing Administration (FHA). Outright fraud amounting to possibly two hundred million dollars and involving lending institutions, real estate men, and federal officials was found in the New York City area alone.[13]

At the time of this writing the future of Section 235 is unclear. The fact that there were criminal abuses does not mean that such a program need inevitably have them. It should not be beyond the capabilities of this country to operate a vital housing program honestly. Regardless of what happens with Section 235 specifically, I wish to support the principle of aiding lower-income families to pay for their own housing which many families can do if they receive some assistance with interest costs. A mortgage interest subsidy program enables many families who would otherwise be doomed to slumlike conditions to live in safe, adequate housing. Such a program also could play a crucial rehabilitative role in the cities of our society. We simply cannot let the older parts of our cities decay into oblivion. By enabling families to buy and rehabilitate older homes we help preserve our cities; failure to do so is a foolish economy which sacrifices dollars later in order to save pennies now. Any rational housing program must include the preservation and improvement of the existing housing supply.

The matter of housing assistance brings up an issue which should be discussed, namely, the rationale or justification for subsidizing part of the housing cost of some families when other families are providing for their housing on their own. Why should some people, simply because they have a lower income, get a housing subsidy from the government? Put this way, the question overlooks the fact that a substantial part of the population of the United States benefits from housing assistance from the government, and the higher-income families do so more than the lower-income ones. The chief means for this is the income tax deduction for interest and property tax expenses.

Using our example of the $1600 mortgage interest, a family with a taxable income in the $12,000 to $16,000 range would be able to reduce their federal income tax payments by $400—amounting to the equivalent of a housing subsidy of $33.33 per month for this above-average income family. They could also deduct money paid for property taxes, which would give them a total housing subsidy of over $40 or $50 per month from the federal government. A family with a $50,000 a year taxable income would receive as a housing subsidy one-half of its mortgage and tax payments, an amount which could easily run to several hundred dollars per month.

Let us consider an even more extreme case. While Richard Nixon was President he received an income totaling over one million dollars during the period from January 1969 through May 1973. On his federal income tax returns for that period he deducted $257,376 as interest payments on properties he was buying, as well as the $81,255 property taxes he paid on them, these two deductions amounting to almost one-third of his income for the period. The tax on this money at the 70 percent rate stipulated for his income would have been over $237,000. By not having to pay it he was in effect given a housing subsidy from the government averaging almost $4,500 per month in addition to the residence provided for him at the White House. Worthy of note also is that during this same period Nixon's net worth increased by $681,381.[14]

Although questions were raised about the legality of some of Nixon's financial manipulations, there seems to be no doubt but that his housing deductions were legal. They did not depend upon his being President; deducting interest and property taxes from income is a game anyone can play. The higher the person's income is, and the more he spends on property, the greater will be his housing subsidy from the government. At the other extreme, a low-income family taxed at a small rate would receive little dollar benefit from the income tax provisions. A mortgage subsidy, on the other hand, would be of real value and might well be a smaller dollar amount than the middle-income family would receive from its income tax deductions. It seems hard to argue that what the low-income family would receive would be any more of a "government giveaway" than the benefits extended to those financially more fortunate.

The inequities of the federal income tax provisions regarding housing have led some to propose that they be eliminated. On a purely rational basis one could probably make a good case for this, arguing that our present policy provides a larger housing subsidy for rich families than for poor families.[15] This tax "loophole," however, benefits millions of families, and politically it would be practically impossible to remove. It is not my intent here to argue for its removal in any event. Rather, I would maintain that the existence of federal housing benefits for higher-income families justifies federal assistance in housing for lower-income families, who because of the fact that their incomes are small, receive little or no benefit from income tax provisions, but could receive real benefit from a mortgage subsidy.

Land and Exclusionary Zoning

Providing adequate housing for moderate-income people is largely a matter of making an adequate supply available at a reasonable price. This includes both the construction of new moderate-cost homes and the maintenance or rehabilitation of existing homes. Allowing that some families in the moderate-income group will benefit from the filtering-down process, their housing supply will also be influenced by the adequacy of new housing construction for income levels above theirs. Whatever helps to keep housing costs down will benefit the lower-income family.

A basic component in the housing picture is land itself, and problems related to land are becoming increasingly important. At the end of World War II land around most cities was plentiful, and easily obtained, and millions of acres were gobbled up during the 1950s and 1960s in our tremendous burst of suburban development.[16] Larger sized lots, the construction of one-story, rambling residential and institutional buildings, and a leapfrogging pattern of development leaving vacant spaces scattered about all resulted in a land-wasteful low-density pattern of development that could not be efficiently served by public transportation and required many families to have two and even three cars, which they poured out onto the ever-expanding but always over-crowded expressways.

For better or worse, that era is over. The ecology movement, fed by the air pollution created by the exhaust products of over 100 million vehicles might have been sufficient to end it by itself. The energy crunch and the passing of low-cost gasoline will supply whatever additional impetus is needed. This trend seems clear and irreversible. We need to do some serious thinking about the direction in which our cities are going, and one of those directions will most certainly be toward greater density and more efficient land use.[17]

There are direct implications for housing in these trends. Although housing costs have increased steadily for the last 30 years, the cost of land for housing sites increased twice as fast as that for the building itself.[18] Casual expansion of low-density urban development has used up much of the conveniently located land readily available for urban development. When one is interested in providing reasonably priced housing for moderate-income families, the availability and cost of land become very important.

It is not that there is no land left, but that a good part of the scarcity of land has been created by actions of suburban governmental bodies. One does not have to be a graduate in accounting to conclude that a moderate-income family living in a home on which it pays $500 per year in taxes and sending three children to school, upon each of whom is expended $800 per year for education, is not going to be a great financial asset to the local community. In an effort to protect themselves from this situation many suburban communities have enacted zoning laws which in effect permit only expensive homes on large lots. The resulting higher property taxes per unit would be much more favorable to the community. In a survey of the greater New York City area it was found that "Today, almost all vacant land suitable for large-scale home building is zoned precisely to discourage large-scale home building. On the average, each house has to have at least half an acre of land; on most of the remaining vacant land—two-thirds of the vacant land in New Jersey—each home must have an acre or more."[19]

In the Toledo suburb of Oregon, Ohio, a change to larger-lot zoning was made only after the first steps had been taken in a development of new lower-cost homes. Eighty-seven families who had bought lots and had contracts for building the homes were thus stopped in their tracks. Although city officials said that the change had been planned for over two years, the change was made suddenly in an emergency meeting of the city council. The zoning change not only increased the required lot size, but raised the minimum home size by more than 50 percent as well as required the developer to provide two and a half acres of park space for every 250 homes. While making a provision for parks may be desirable, requiring that the developer, rather than the community as a whole, provide the land increases the cost of the new homes. The changes effectively bar any federally assisted lower- or moderate-income housing in Oregon and ensure that only above-average-cost homes will be built in the suburb.[20] Restrictions such as these, in evidence all over the country, led the mayor of Milwaukee to call large-lot zoning that excludes minority and low-income families "the greatest metropolitan evil in the United States" and to note that "the green walls of suburbia are built higher and higher."[21]

It is not that there is no more land available for moderate-cost housing, but that much suburban land has been locked away for occupancy by higher-income families on large lots. If some of this could be freed for multiple dwellings, town houses, or small-lot detached homes, there would be sites for housing moderate-income families either directly or through the filtering-down process.

One factor which will tend to make for more efficient land utilization, in my opinion, is the pressure generated by transportation-ecological forces. Also, there seems to be a move away from the local property tax as a means of providing the basic support for local education. Great inequalities in ability to support public school systems have resulted from heavy reliance on local property taxes because of large differences in taxable property per pupil. Reducing reliance on local property taxes, however, also reduces one of the major reasons for suburban large-lot zoning.

Legal Challenges to Exclusionary Zoning

Beyond these considerations, however, there are legal questions involved. Large-lot zoning practices have an effect not just upon the individual community itself, but upon the whole metropolitan area. The people denied housing in a community because of large-lot zoning necessarily must concentrate at greater densities elsewhere, thus imposing an undue burden on those parts of the metropolitan area. The United States Supreme Court held in 1926 that zoning was a valid exercise of local power. However, the court recognized "the possibility of cases where the general public interest would so far outweigh the interest of the municipality that the municipality would not be allowed to stand in the way."[22]

Exclusionary zoning has generated renewed interest in the legal issues involved, leading to an increased number of challenges of zoning ordinances, the basic argument being that while large-lot zoning may shelter the individual community it increases problems elsewhere which are contrary to "the general public interest." In 1965 the Pennsylvania Supreme Court struck down a minimum four-acre lot size requirement in Easttown Township on the basis that it did not serve the general welfare,[23] the case becoming a precedent for subsequent Pennsylvania decisions. A 1971 New Jersey Superior Court decision similarly overturned a Madison Township zoning requirement for one- and two-acre lots, saying that a municipality has an obligation to help meet the housing needs of the region.[24]

The above cases involved challenges in state courts to exclusion resulting from zoning regulations. In another approach to restricting growth the San Francisco far-suburb community of Petaluma, California, passed an ordinance in 1972 limiting the number of building permits which could be issued for the construction of new homes to 500 per year, an amount only a little more than half the number that had been built there the preceding year. The ordinance was overturned on constitutional grounds in a 1974 United States District Court decision which ruled that it interfered with the rights of citizens to travel and to "abide and settle" in a community. Judge Lloyd Burke ruled, "No city may regulate its population growth numerically so that residents of other cities cannot enter and establish residency there."[25]

The Petaluma decision signals another means by which exclusionary legislation may be attacked, in that it places emphasis upon the rights of the individuals who are being kept out of the community rather than just upon a broad concept of the welfare of the region as a whole. In a recent article, attorney Frederick C. Mezey distinguishes between the "old zoning," whose legal basis was established in the 1920s and which emphasized protection of economic values of the individual community, and the "new zoning," which began in the 1960s and challenges land-wasteful practices which increase housing costs and discriminate against low-income and minority groups. Mezey states, "Suits by members of the excluded groups ... are now causing the courts to shift the emphasis from the protection of the regulating municipality to the protection of the excluded groups. The focus on *people* rather than fiscal needs is the chief characteristic of the new zoning. This humanistic cast can bestow benefits because the new zoning will be scaled and related to the *entire* community of people and their needs."[26] He notes that the legal support for the old zoning was developed before "Supreme Court cases which evolved the principle that the poor are entitled to equal protection of the laws."[27] Under this newer philosophy, then, the rights of the person who is being kept out of the community are taken into account and there has been a trend toward giving him legal "standing" to question the laws or regulations which exclude him.

One indication of the effect that land and building zoning has upon the ability to purchase a new home comes from data in a report concerning the greater New York City area. As of 1973 it was estimated that only one family in five in the area had an income high enough to allow it to purchase a new home, but that if local governments would permit town houses and garden apartments for families with children, and modest detached houses on small lots, then almost half the families in the area could afford new homes.[28] Restrictive economic zoning is thus shown to have a decided effect upon the housing market, reducing by more than half the number of families able to enter the new-home market.

Exclusionary zoning has also been used to keep public housing projects and privately sponsored low- and moderate-income developments from locating in some areas. There have been a number of successful legal challenges in federal courts based on the argument that such zoning is in violation of the Equal Protection Clause of the Fourteenth Amendment to the Constitution. In reviewing three significant 1970 cases concerned with this issue a report of the National Committee Against Discrimination in Housing concludes, "The Lawton-SASSO-Lackawanna rulings constituted an impressive first round of 14th Amendment challenges to exclusionary zoning. They set forth strong principles of law indicating that the federal courts were prepared to protect minorities and the poor from zoning and planning decisions which would deprive them of their rights."[29]

A subsequent adverse decision was made in the case of *James* v. *Valtierra* where refusal of a California community to permit a public housing project resulted from a local referendum required for such projects by the California state constitution. Overruling a California district court, the United States Supreme Court held that the local referendum provision in California was valid and democratic.[30] Subsequent lower-level court decisions have tended to follow the earlier pattern, indicating that the equal protection argument may apply except in a state having a constitutional provision requiring a local referendum on the issue.

Low-Income Housing

Although one may define low-income families strictly by number of dollars received, it is a functional rather than a purely categorical income in which we are interested. Some retired people, for example, may show a very modest income on paper and yet live quite comfortably in a home that was paid for when they were younger and working. Students also may live at the poverty level, but with the expectation that it will not be permanent and with resources and expectations that the average poverty-level family does not have. Our main concern here is with younger and middle-aged families, including broken ones, who live all or most of their lives at or below the poverty level and who simply cannot afford adequate housing through the normal operation of the housing market. They are the perennial inhabitants of the slums whose only hope is government-assisted low-income housing. Many of these families are black, Puerto Rican, Amerindian, and Chicano.

The existence of slums well back into the nineteenth century leads one to question whether the private housing market has *ever* been able to provide *adequate* (as defined earlier) housing for the poor. Accounts of housing for the mid-nineteenth century Irish immigrants and those from Europe around the turn of the century chorus unanimously that their housing was dangerous, unsanitary, and overcrowded, and a menace to health.[31] We need to ask how much better things are for the poor today.

Three-quarters of a century after Jacob Riis and other housing reformers began their "battle with the slums" in this country, a student of the problem concluded, "Slums are one of America's major social and economic problems in the 1960s. This in spite of the fact that we live in an 'affluent society'; in spite of the fact that we have had housing and slum clearance programs for many years. . . . The slums are still with us."[32] I have argued elsewhere that part of the problem of the slum is that it tends to be viewed as only a temporary phenomenon which will soon be corrected through an urban renewal or a "slum clearance" or a "rehousing" program. Clearly, the slum is not that easy to eliminate, while the belief that it will soon be eliminated leads to a casual attitude towards it, to the detriment of generations of slum inhabitants.

It should be noted that it is neither the age of buildings nor the poverty of their inhabitants that in themselves make slums. Students of housing have commented on the virtual absence of slums in cities in such urban-industrialized nations as West Germany, the Netherlands, and the Scandinavian countries, despite their having both very old buildings and low-income families.[33] The problem of slums is a complex one.

Existing Private Housing

If buildings can be old and yet not slums this means that the solution to the slum problem is not necessarily to tear down all slum buildings in a massive program of "slum clearance." Europe has too many buildings a century or more old that are well maintained and occupied by people of considerable social status to permit the view that age in itself is an important factor. On the contrary, some quite new public housing projects have themselves become "federal slums."[34] Although some old buildings were slums practically from the day they were built and fully deserve demolition, mass destruction of all old housing is simply inconceivable. We must look for ways in which existing housing can be maintained and rehabilitated.

The system our society has evolved for dealing with old inner city property is like a study in insanity. Fast tax write-offs for depreciation the first few years of ownership motivate the owner of a property to keep it for only a few years and then resell it, thus discouraging him from having a long-range interest in the property. If he does try to borrow money for improvements he is likely to find that the part of the city his property is in has been "red-lined," that is, defined by the lending agency as a risky place in which to invest money, and that he cannot get a reasonable loan. The property, then, continues to deteriorate. Providing obviously substandard housing, the building is nevertheless rented out for whatever the owner can get until a major crisis arises— failure of the heating or plumbing system, or health department orders for major changes—at which time the owner may simply walk away, abandoning the building so that its occupants are deprived of their housing completely.

In the study of housing abandonment cited earlier which was made by the National Urban League it was found that abandonment was most likely to take place in the crisis ghettos of American cities, in which conditions had gotten worse during the 1960s. Abandonment reached as high as 20 percent of all buildings in some neighborhoods studied. The report stated, "The abandonment process has reached the stage where it poses a clear threat to the survival of certain central cities as viable environments for human habitation."[35]

The survey found that Detroit and Atlanta had comparatively little abandonment which seemed to be due to the fact that "local financial institutions still have an interest in the central city" and that decisions on lending money on property were based on individual financial responsibility and not on automatic ruling out of certain areas through red-lining.[36] Detroit also benefited from having a relatively low unemployment rate and high per capita income for a central city, as well as a less rigid segregation pattern than most cities. The survey found whole blocks of boarded-up structures in New York, Chicago, and St. Louis, and widespread vacancies in Cleveland. Abandonment went hand-in-hand with lack of mortgage funds: "The flow of conventional mortgage funds to most areas within the City of St. Louis has been shut off," but not to the all-white far South Side.[37]

Not only does abandonment reduce the total available housing supply, but abandoned buildings become like a cancer in the area; as a fire hazard and a center for vandals they threaten the neighborhood around them and frequently lead to the abandoning of sound, adequate housing which happens to be located near them. The process of abandonment ordinarily begins several years before the final step of walking away is made by the owner. Abandonment eventually results after the owner has begun disinvesting in the property—not putting enough money back into it to maintain it adequately—and an early indicator of disinvestment is failure to pay property taxes. Tax delinquency may go on for years before the city takes action, each year making it less likely that the owner will be able to pay off the taxes, although the fact he initially decided not to pay taxes indicates he gave up on the building at that point. The building really died then.

Shore estimated in 1973 that some 300,000 housing units in New York City alone were "creaking toward abandonment" to join the 100,000 units in the metropolitan area which have already been abandoned. This represents housing for more than a million people and its demise represents a serious tax loss to the budgets of struggling cities. He points out that many of the abandoned buildings remain sound structures and adds, "Though from the owner's point of view they were not worth keeping, from society's point of view, they could be rehabilitated into satisfactory housing for less than any other decent housing could cost."[38]

Proposals for dealing with abandonment involve a combination of legal means for promptly acquiring control of buildings undergoing disinvestment by their owners, financial support outside normal market channels to maintain and rehabilitate buildings which have been subject to disinvestment, action by the city itself to make sure that it does not disinvest in a declining neighborhood through curtailment of municipal services, and programs by neighborhood groups to assist local residents in dealing with housing and family problems.

As an example of the last-mentioned activity, there is the case described by Shore of the Upper Park Avenue Community Association (UPACA) in East Harlem, New York City. The association is engaged in a program of providing rehousing in new and rehabilitated units for 8,000 persons who have been living in substandard housing in the area and had a schedule that called for almost 6,000 people to be rehoused by the end of 1974. UPACA is headed by two housewives, but the organization requires that applicants for the program "take a 10-week course, prepared by Cornell University, at which problems of living together in an apartment and in a city are discussed."[39] Although some applicants have had to be rejected to protect other tenants, the program generally has been quite successful. Writers concerned with the immigrants of the past frequently emphasized that the immigrants needed training in how to adapt to the ways of the city.

The National Urban League study of abandonment emphasizes that action taken to prevent abandonment must be based in each case on the stage of the abandonment process being dealt with. Strict enforcement of building codes would be helpful before a neighborhood has started to decline, for example, but too-strict enforcement could invite abandonment at later stages of neighborhood decline. Although genuine hazards could not be overlooked in enforcing building codes in declining neighborhoods, some violations that might be more of a technical nature could be permitted to continue. If the code required, for example, that ·

electrical outlets be no further than 12 feet apart, it would not be wise to force an expensive rewiring job because existing outlets were 15 feet apart. Also, to try to compel major structural changes because a room was 10 percent smaller than permitted would be inadvisable.

The Urban League emphasizes that racial factors are of great importance in initiating neighborhood decline. "The crisis ghetto phenomenon is the product of a process which commenced with racial transition. The appearance of blacks had a profound psychological effect on property owners in transition areas."[40] The league believes that racial change led to decreased maintenance of property, reduced city services, fears of capital loss by owners, and flight from the neighborhood by the residents who could afford to leave and by business and professional people who served them, intrusion into the neighborhood of undesirable business and land uses, and an increase in illegal activities. In most cities, legitimate sources for mortgage money dried up and the exploiters took over. Racial segregation and the concept of a neighborhood as "changing" or "going black" were obviously causal factors at work. More geographically widespread housing opportunities for blacks, particularly low-income families, would not lead to the concentration of poor disorganized families that could send a neighborhood into decline.

The Urban League report concludes that further research into abandonment is needed and that their proposed solutions need further investigation and development. No doubt considerable governmental assistance will be needed to halt and reverse the disinvestment process, but however much the amount, it will certainly be less than allowing sound, albeit old, buildings to deteriorate to the point of becoming unlivable. As a society, we simply cannot write off our major cities.

A new approach which offers hope for both saving abandoned buildings and upgrading them and their neighborhoods is urban homesteading, analogous in its operation to the rural homesteading of the nineteenth century. Pioneer experiments in urban homesteading began in 1973 with local legislation enacted by Philadelphia, Baltimore, and Wilmington, Delaware. Other cities are sure to follow their lead. Details of the programs vary from one city to another, but the basic similarities are that abandoned homes acquired by the city are turned over to low-income families who agree to rehabilitate them and live in them for periods of three to five years. In Philadelphia the abandoned homes are sold to the highest bidder, it being possible for a successful bid to be as little as one dollar. Wilmington provides for a lottery system to decide which applicants will receive the homes. Wilmington also provides that money spent in improving these homes can be credited toward a reduction in the local property taxes. If the local governments would provide close consultation with and assistance to homesteading families, their chance of success would undoubtedly be much greater. Although some families may underestimate the costs and effort of rehabilitating a deteriorated dwelling and may not be successful, urban homesteading deserves watching as an innovative attempt to deal with abandonment constructively.[41]

Public Housing

The term public housing is used to refer to housing which has been built or paid for with governmental funds and is managed by a local housing authority. Families living in public housing projects pay rent, but not at a rate high enough to pay for all costs of the project. For a number of reasons, an important one being that they were relatively small in size, the public housing projects of the 1930s were quite successful from the standpoint of both their residents and the cities in which they were located.

By the mid-1950s housing projects were being built on a much larger scale in many cities. High central-city land costs plus considerations of eliminating as little existing housing as possible led to massive high-rise projects concentrating thousands of families in a small area. Because public housing is for low-income families, those whose incomes increased beyond the ceiling limits were forced to move out, leaving only the least successful and the most disorganized families in the projects. A high proportion of families without fathers present plus socioeconomic and life-style characteristics of the residents meant minimal supervision of juveniles and soaring rates of delinquency. The impersonal, anonymous atmosphere led to alienation from the project itself and high rates of vandalism and destruction. Clearly, many modern, high-rise projects are unsuccessful.

The most spectacular failure is the Pruitt-Igoe project in St. Louis, which never managed to obtain full occupancy and whose buildings and residents have been subject to extremely high rates of crime and vandalism. A federal official visiting the project found "complete and total" alienation on the part of Pruitt-Igoe residents.[42] As one step in an attempt to salvage the 1955 project, three of its buildings were dynamited to destruction in 1972. The cost of rehabilitation for the remaining buildings is likely to be greater than the $36 million the project cost initially. Although not as dramatic as Pruitt-Igoe, the Rosen Apartments project in Philadelphia and the Columbus Homes project in Newark have also been cited as failures.[43]

Defensible Space

A recent study by Oscar Newman, an architect and city planner, may be of considerable importance in pointing the way toward salvaging existing housing projects and designing more successful ones in the future.[44] Newman's work is based primarily on extensive data available for the 169 public projects housing more than 528,000 people in New York City. His book specifically acknowledges a debt to the ideas of Elizabeth Wood and Jane Jacobs, and one can see relationships between Newman's ideas and those who have emphasized the importance of territory for both humans and animals.

Newman points out that the high-rise apartment, first advocated back in the 1920s by Le Corbusier, managed to be a relatively successful form of housing because it was, up to the public housing projects of the 1950s, basically a facility for middle-class people, a substantial number of whom did not have children. The middle-class emphasis on respect for property rights and individual autonomy, possibly augmented by a guard at the door to screen visitors, did not produce serious problems of crime or a feeling of alienation from the apartment building itself. Newman doubts, however, that the high-rise concept can be used successfully in its present form with low-income families, most of whom have children, without producing major problems of crime, destructiveness, and alienation.

Beyond differences in socioeconomic level and family situation, Newman sees similarities in human response to territory and spatial features that seem to transcend cultural differences, indicated by examples from cultures as different as Neolithic Turkey, African Sudan, Pompeii, and eighteenth century Holland. Newman's specific conclusions, though, come from comparisons of data from different housing projects in New York City. Built over a number of years, of different sizes, with different types of buildings having different entrance, stairway, and hall arrangements, the various projects offered an excellent opportunity to learn of social consequences of project design.

Newman cites the case of the Van Dyke and Brownsville housing projects in New York City. The two projects are in the same neighborhood, being across the street from each other, and are practically identical in number of persons per acre and in the social characteristics of their residents. Yet the high-rise Van Dyke project had four times as many robberies and 66 percent more total crime incidents as Brownsville and a 72 percent greater maintenance outlay than the older Brownsville low-rise project. Similarly, the high-rise buildings in the Rosen Apartments project in Philadelphia suffered an incidence of vandalism, robbery, and loitering drug addicts more than seven times as much as the low-rise buildings in the same project.[45]

The sheer number of relatively new high-rise public housing projects means that they cannot all be demolished as were the few buildings in Pruitt-Igoe; for better or worse low-income families (many of them black) can look forward to living in them until well into the twenty-first century. Given this expectation, we must ask if anything can be done to make them more livable and humanized. Fortunately, in a number of cases it should be possible to put into effect even in existing projects many of the principles deduced by Newman that he designates collectively as *defensible space.*

I will not attempt here to summarize systematically the principles of defensible space but only to give a general idea of his approach. Two basic principles seem to be involved: one is the distinction between public and private space, the other is a matter of encouraging safety through facilitating natural public surveillance of public areas. To be more specific, a person living in an apartment will regard the unit as "his," and will feel he has the right to determine its use and who can enter, and so on. The apartment unit itself as a minimum is his private defensible space. How he feels about the corridor it opens onto or about the stairs and the lobby in the building will be influenced by the design and usage patterns of the building. Where a corridor serves no more than five apartments it will come to be viewed by the residents as an extension of their apartments and will be used and watched by them. Children may play in it and parents will keep track of them, and this, plus the physical setting, will deter intruders. A corridor serving more than five families will come to be defined as public space and may be roamed freely by an outsider without being contested by the residents.

Similar principles work for building stairways and entrances. Likewise, project grounds may come to be defined either as "belonging to" building residents or as public space which can be frequented without challenge by drug addicts, juvenile gangs, and so on. Simple landscaping arrangements of such things as walks, hedges and shrubbery, steps, and low walls may be all that it takes to publicly signify that the residents in that building or part of the project view it as part of their territory and subject to their control. It then becomes safe for children to play in with their parents watching them in the background.

Natural public surveillance is also important in ensuring safety. Corridors, elevators, stairways, and lobbies are dangerous places in many housing projects. A robbery or rape victim may be accosted in a lobby or corridor and forced into an elevator or stairway for the attack. If these places serve more than a few families they will be defined as public and not the responsibility of the tenants (with the police not likely to be near when needed). Design factors in such instances can provide for maximum visibility to the public so as to deter attacks. A rapist will think twice before attempting his attack in a well-lighted stairway with ample windows providing ready visibility from the street and sidewalk. Similarly, a building lobby and its elevators easily visible from the street will be safer than one in which an attacker is not detectable until the victim is already inside and it is too late.

Newman offers examples of existing projects which were modified to decrease crime and increase resident safety. He concedes that electronic devices might have to be used in some cases; for example, a television camera in the elevator with the picture shown on a screen in the lobby. It is important to emphasize that defensible space concepts are not just to cut down on vandalism to save repair money for the housing authority. As a society we have built high-rise monstrosities for those whose family size and age of children, as well as their socioeconomic and cultural background, are completely inappropriate for their occupancy. The concepts discussed here offer the opportunity to make life in them somewhat safer and more sociable than it would be otherwise. Although Newman emphasized crime reduction, it would seem that a safe and congenial living environment would confer social benefits that go considerably beyond just the lessening of crime.

Tenant Participation

Given that existing public housing projects will continue to be used for the foreseeable future, in addition to possible design alterations that may make them safer and more socially cohesive, we must ask whether administrative changes can be made that will reduce alienation of the residents and make for improved community relationships. In a way it may be surprising that St. Louis, which led the nation in public housing horrors with its Pruitt-Igoe project, is now taking the lead in developing new management approaches for its public housing. The key factor is tenant participation in management decisions.[46]

Not only in Pruitt-Igoe but in the city's eight other projects, rent delinquency was common despite extensive legal action by the authority to force rent payments. Other difficulties included crime and vandalism and inadequate maintenance, the latter attributable heavily to insufficient funds because of rent delinquency. A widespread rent strike by the tenants in 1969 brought on a crisis which resulted in a new rent schedule based on tenant income, but the most important factor was probably the replacement of the director and the appointment by the mayor of two tenants to the authority's Board of Commissioners. Also, a city-wide Tenant Affairs Board and local boards for each project all elected by tenants, have been given considerable authority to mediate tenant–management differences and to influence management decisions.

Regarding the changes, Hirshen and Brown concluded that "the essential validity and workability of tenant involvement has been demonstrated," with crime and vandalism reported as being lower and rent delinquency "almost nonexistent."[47] Applications exceed the number of existing units, a situation with which St. Louis had not been confronted for years. The authority has employed many tenants for jobs within its projects in maintenance, security, and social services. Reduced overhead costs leave more money for maintenance and improvements.

Philadelphia is also notable for its inclusion of tenants in its public housing management. Tenant participation not only makes for more wholesome relationships between tenants and management, but is frequently instructive for tenants. A tenant who does not pay his rent on time knows that his case will be handled by the Resident Advisory Board (RAB) rather than just an impersonal management. However, the RAB makes it plain in its Public Housing Tenants Rights Handbook that, for example, buying a new television set is not considered a good excuse for not having the rent money when it is due.[48] Both the St. Louis and Philadelphia experiments indicate that tenants are capable of taking more responsibility in the operation of projects, and that when they do, feelings of alienation decrease as they acquire more control over the management of their lives.

Non-project Housing

Despite the possibility of ameliorating some problems of housing projects, we need to question seriously the very notion of a housing project. In the United States the current concept of a government housing project was developed in the 1930s as part of the New Deal efforts to fight the depression through providing jobs for construction workers, the resulting housing being an additional side benefit. They were of a modest scale, were located so that they replaced slums with obviously superior housing thus also benefiting the surrounding neighborhood, and were actually associated with improved living conditions for their residents.[49]

The increase in size of projects in the larger cities after World War II, along with their racial and socioeconomic isolation, has led to their offering a quality of life giving rise to some of the types of problems discussed just above. Harrison Salisbury described the giant housing projects in these terms: "They spawn teen-age gangs. They incubate crime. They are fiendishly contrived institutions for the debasing of family and community life to the lowest common mean. . . . Some projects seem more like Golgothas designed to twist, torture and destroy the hapless people condemned to their dismal precincts than new homes for unfortunates."[50] Also, public opposition has developed to housing projects so that practically any location proposed for a new project is almost sure to start opposition from the neighborhood in the form of protests to the local government, picketing, petitions and legal suits, mass demonstrations, and even violence.

The housing project generates another serious problem. Because it is low-income housing there is a ceiling on the amount a family may earn and still remain in the project. The smaller size, generally older, projects especially can offer a low-income family safe congenial housing definitely superior to that available to it on the housing market. Given these circumstances, a promotion or pay raise becomes a threat to the family by possibly raising its income beyond the limits for the project. The situation creates an adversary relationship between the tenant and the project management which is always looking to see whether the family should be evicted from the project because of its own success. From the standpoint of the project community itself, the income ceiling functions adversely by constantly forcing out the more successful stable members. Studies of slum neighborhoods have repeatedly shown that despite a relatively poor socioeconomic level overall, each neighborhood has some relatively successful frequently better-educated leaders who help hold a community together and offer a stabilizing influence. Many of these natural neighborhood leaders would not be permitted in a housing project because of income ceilings, so that the large project deprives its residents of the opportunity to live in a normally cohesive natural type of neighborhood. Those living in a small-scale project are less likely to be so isolated from the community-at-large that they are deprived of a more normal type of neighborhood organization.

The housing project seems to have enough drawbacks and difficulties so that we may seriously question whether it has run its course and can best be supplanted by other means of assisting with the housing for low-income families. Evidence on the disadvantages of concentrating large numbers of low-income people together has led to the greater emphasis on small-scale or "vest-pocket" sites scattered throughout the community. But we must ask whether housing assistance for low-income families necessarily must be in the form of new buildings made specifically and only for poor families. When we consider how adequate housing may be provided for these families rather than how housing projects should be designed, a number of alternatives suggest themselves.

Rent subsidy is one possibility. If an apartment in a housing project would have to be rented out at $150 dollars per month in order to fully pay for all the costs of its construction and maintenance, and we rent it out to a family for $75 per month, we are subsidizing the housing expenses of that family at the rate of $75 per month or $900 per year. We might, instead, simply give the family the $75 housing subsidy directly and let it obtain its housing through normal channels in the community.

A massive program of rent subsidy instituted suddenly, though, would defeat its own purpose by producing a large increase in demand without a corresponding increase in supply; the result would be mainly just an increase in rents charged. But if introduced gradually and coupled with insistence that subsidized units conform to building and health codes, a rent subsidy program could encourage maintenance and improvement of existing housing and indirectly stimulate the construction of new housing. Another major advantage would be that the family could live in a normal community setting rather than in an institutional project likely to carry with it a social stigma.

Perhaps even more important is that success would not be penalized by eviction as is the case now with projects. A family which increased its income would simply receive a reduced amount of subsidy and could continue living in the same unit. Initiative could be greatly weakened by a system that reduced subsidy by a dollar for each dollar of income increase. Rather, an arrangement, say, in which the subsidy would be reduced by one dollar for every four dollars of income increase would be much more equitable. The same principle could be used to provide an increase in subsidy in the event of family-income reduction.

The Leased Housing Program initiated in the 1960s by the federal government points the way. Under this program administered by the federal Department of Housing and Urban Development (HUD), local housing authorities may lease privately owned dwelling units for rental to low-income families. Families pay rent according to their income, and the federal government reimburses the local housing authority for the difference between the actual costs and the amount paid by the families. A building may be acquired for the program without arousing all the community antagonism attendant upon the construction of a housing project, and the families benefit from living in a more normal community situation and without the fear they will have to move out if their income increases. The program has been quite popular with some 70,000 dwellings receiving support under the program in 1969, only four years after its adoption, a number which was 10 percent of the total amount of publicly supported low-income housing.[51]

Another approach to breaking the traditional public housing project concept is being made in Minneapolis. Not far from the central business district in a poor, deteriorated area a private developer, Cedar-Riverside Associates, is building a "new-town in town" which started attracting considerable attention even before the first tenants began moving in. By time the first buildings in the development were only half-occupied, it had been visited by delegations from 70 cities in 30 states and 20 foreign countries. Using expert planning and exhibiting a high degree of social consciousness, the total development has a timetable of from 15 to 20 years. The location nearby of the University of Minnesota, two substantial hospitals, and Augsburg College ensure that many residents of the development will be associated with these institutions. Yet, the development plan includes provision for low- and moderate-income families.[52]

The Stage I project, which is to be typical of the entire development, includes 117 units of public housing with rents as low as $41 per month and 552 units of federally assisted (Section 236) housing for moderate-income families in the total of 1299 units, which also includes 222 units of "semi-luxury housing" with rentals ranging up to $550 per month. With the exception of some low-rise town houses, the individual apartment units, which vary considerably in size and floor plan, are in high-rise buildings with the low- and moderate-income subsidized units integrated in the project as a whole so that they are undistinguishable architecturally from the others.

The 117 low-income housing units are rented by the Minneapolis Housing Authority which assigns tenants to the development. Some of these tenants are very likely to be black. There is no question but that the management of the development is committed to a policy of no racial discrimination, one-seventh of the residents being black or Spanish-speaking minorities. The surrounding neighborhood is largely white, having been a locus earlier for Scandinavian immigrants of modest circumstances. Thus, the development has the possibility of true stable racial integration of families having a wide range of incomes. At the time of this writing the earliest families in Cedar-Riverside had been in the development only a few months, but the management reported that the combination of racial and socioeconomic mixing of tenants appeared to be working out successfully. We certainly need alternatives to the large present-day housing project. The approach taken at Cedar-Riverside seems to offer real possibilities.

Racial Residential Segregation

One of the most striking and profound facts of modern American cities is the separation of their residents according to race. A thorough study of the extent of racial segregation, using 1960 census data, on more than 200 cities made by Karl and Alma Taeuber showed that more than half of these cities had segregation indexes of more than 85.[53] The segregation index tells the percentage of nonwhites in a city who would have to relocate in order for each block to have the same proportion of blacks and whites as the city as a whole. The substantial number of index numbers in the 90's and high 80's points to a near complete separation of races. A more recent study of segregation changes between 1960 and 1970 using census data from 19 metropolitan areas concludes "that in general there was an increase in the spatial concentration of blacks and all nonwhites over the decade."[54] Segregation was more complete in 1970 than in 1960. If automobiles were to progress like this they would not need reverse gears.

The existence of segregation in itself would not be a problem if it were voluntary. Many people desire to live near other people who are like themselves, whatever characteristics they may wish to emphasize in defining likeness. We certainly cannot assume either that all blacks would want to live in predominantly white neighborhoods or that a goal of zero on the Taeubers' segregation index should be the ideal for the typical American city for the foreseeable future. Rather, the difficulty arises from involuntary segregation—from a system in which a minority family that wants to live in a certain neighborhood for whatever reason and can afford financially the costs, finds that it is denied residence simply because of race.

The Development of Segregation

Racial separation seems so complete and so well established in our cities today that it seems it must be inevitable, and yet a look backward reveals that this was not the case. European immigrants remained segregated from the white natives of the city going as far back as the mass of Irish who fled to this country from the potato famine of the 1840s. Later immigrants settled in the slums and immigrant ghettos of Northern American cities in Little Polands, Little Sicilys, and so on, frequently clustering together so that those from the same village back in the Old Country clustered togethered on the same street in Chicago or Cleveland. Native whites isolated themselves from these minorities through the equivalent of moving to the suburbs in the same manner as has taken place in recent years with regard to the blacks.[55]

Up until the decade of World War I there were not many blacks living in the Northern cities. During the half-century between 1860 and 1910 some 90 percent of all blacks in the United States lived in the South, the figure changing by only three percentage points during the whole period. Most of what blacks there were in the Northern cities lived mixed in with immigrants and were frequently viewed as better tenants than their white neighbors. World War I shut off the labor supply from Europe and Northern industry recruited heavily in the South to meet its increased labor demands, thus giving birth to the "Great Migration" which saw large and regular increases in the number and proportions of blacks in the cities. That the increase in numbers did not in itself automatically lead to complete segregation is indicated by the extremely revealing statistic that even by 1920 the most well-established and blackest part of Chicago's "black Belt" was almost half white in its occupancy.[56]

The present arrangement of almost complete separation of the races would undoubtedly never have developed by itself. Rather, it is clear that it was systematically and deliberately promoted, with the major responsibility being attributable to real estate brokers. In 1924 the National Association of Real Estate Boards adopted as part of their Code of Ethics a provision which had the effect of restricting a realtor from selling a home in a white neighborhood to a person of another race. Thus, it became "unethical" for a realtor to take part in a transaction which would produce a mixed neighborhood.[57] Aided by mortgage lending agencies, the segregated pattern as we know it today was quickly evolved in the 1920s.

A half a century of following that pattern has now gone by and our society is in a whole new era. It is inconceivable that we should continue to follow the old ways. The actions of people in the real estate field seem to have been more important in bringing about our present system of segregation than a clamor for it from the population at large. I have argued elsewhere that racial segregation contributes to prejudiced attitudes and racial strife over housing and may be more of a cause than an effect of prejudice.

Yet, despite the origins of the present pattern and the tangle of cause–effect relationships between prejudice and discrimination, the current system has developed its own self-perpetuating dynamics. With the availability of housing for blacks having been seriously limited and the avenues of ghetto expansion severely restricted, it was only natural that an area into which blacks *could* move would soon become largely black. The *expectation* of this has tended to affect the reactions of whites. It has been observed that neighborhoods have a threshold or "tipping point" and that if black occupancy stays below this level—generally about one-third—the area can continue as an interracial one, but that if the proportion of blacks becomes greater than this then whites are likely to leave rather quickly. Given the animosities between the races it is not surprising to hear of cases where remaining white families in largely black neighborhoods have been harassed to encourage them to leave.

We must ask, though, whether rapid white exodus after the tipping point has been reached is due to an aversion of whites to living in a neighborhood which is divided, say, fifty-fifty or whether the fact of increased black occupancy is viewed by whites as predicting the future course of the neighborhood, that is, that it will soon become all black. A number of reports indicate that although many whites do not mind having some black neighbors, they do not want to live in a neighborhood which is mostly black. In moving from an area which they define as "going black," whites may create the very condition which they expect, the situation being a good example of the "self-fulfilling prophesy." An excellent remedy for this is the knowledge by whites that blacks are free to move anywhere in the city so that they will not be forced to concentrate in one area.

Reducing Residential Segregation

Segregation and the Law

Two landmark events in 1968 seem clearly to have made illegal any form of racial residential discrimination. One of these was the passage

of Title VIII of the 1968 Civil Rights Act (the fair housing act) which
outlawed racial discrimination in the sale or rental of all housing except
owner-occupied housing sold without services of a real estate broker
and owner-occupied apartment buildings that contain no more than four
dwelling units. The second event eliminated even these exceptions. It
was a ruling by the United States Supreme Court upholding an 1866
law reading, "All citizens of the United States shall have the same right,
in every State and Territory, as is enjoyed by white citizens thereof to
inherit, purchase, lease, sell, hold and convey real and personal property."
This ruling in the case of *Jones* v. *Mayer* "rendered all housing, with no
exception, open without regard to race, at least as a matter of legal
right."[58]

With complete racial equality in housing guaranteed to every United
States Citizen, the real question now is the implementation of these
legal rights. Although *Jones* v. *Mayer* is complete in its coverage it does
not provide enforcement, it being necessary for the wronged party to
take private legal action on the basis of this law. Suits by individuals
are also possible under the fair housing act, and in a major decision the
Supreme Court ruled in 1972 that whites could also be considered
"persons aggrieved" by racial discrimination.[59] Two tenants of an apartment development in San Francisco filed suit under the act claiming
that they had suffered social, business, and professional injury as a result of living in a "white ghetto." The opinion of the Court noted that
the fair housing act relies heavily upon action taken by individuals and
that whites can be adversely affected by discrimination as well as blacks.
The opinion encourages individual enforcement actions and means that
action taken to oppose discrimination in a housing development can be
taken by whites who are already in it as well as by blacks who are being
kept out. The implications of this seem to be considerable.

In addition to private lawsuits the 1968 fair housing act also provides
for HUD to take enforcement action, although this is limited to informal methods of conference, conciliation, and persuasion. HUD can
refer the cases to the Department of Justice for legal action but cannot
force follow-up. The political realities do not incline one to believe that
enforcement by HUD or the Attorney General will be thorough and
vigorous. The penalties for noncompliance tend to fall on the property
owner-taxpayer-party contributor who is certain to exert pressure on
both Congress and the Administration to tone down attempts at "forced
integration." Also, effective enforcement costs money and is not apt
to be extensive in a period of austerity budgets for government services.
Nevertheless, HUD has been responsible for some significant gains.

Either as a result of individual lawsuit or of HUD action or a combination of the two, there is the powerful threat of financial loss to the

individual or organization practicing racial discrimination resulting from having to pay damages as well as correcting the abuse. A buyer or renter who has been denied a dwelling unit because of racial discrimination may sue the seller or landlord for damages suffered as a result of being denied the unit. Damages could include lost income resulting from inability to take or keep a job because of the housing discrimination, additional housing expense incurred because of being denied the unit in question, but also damages for pain, humiliation, or mental suffering because of the rejection. A court might also impose additional damages as a punishment for having violated the law. Damage awards or settlements up to several thousand dollars have been reported.

It can be argued that the private suit for damages requires that the wronged party undertake the legal action himself with its attendant risk of paying the cost of the legal fees (if the decision went in the plaintiff's favor he would ordinarily be able to recover the legal costs), and that a majority of those discriminated against would have neither the temperament nor the social class orientation to initiate legal action. There is also the definite possibility that despite the law and the evidence some courts would rule against the plaintiff. I will not try to deny these objections. Rather I would maintain that even *some* victories by only *some* people would have a powerful effect in breaking down the *system* of racial discrimination that has developed.

The pattern of racial residential segregation which began to take its modern form in the 1920s is based on *total* separation of the races into their different sections in the city. This pattern allows for only three types of areas: black areas (into which no "right-thinking" white would consider moving), white areas (in which no "ethical" realtor would sell a home to a black), and areas which are "changing" or "turning" (white areas adjacent to existing black areas which have been broken by "blockbusters" and in which the only whites are those who have not yet moved away so that the area eventually can become all black). In this context, talk of neighborhoods in terms of property values, "desirability," and "deterioration" are all oriented toward their likelihood of becoming black.

In other words, segregation has become an all-or-nothing phenomenon, similar in its totality to virginity. According to the traditional views a neighborhood which has become slightly integrated is tainted just as much as the girl who said she was only a little bit pregnant. It is the *completeness* of the segregation which has been important. This is why I think that even some successful actions by only some individuals will have a profound effect upon the segregation pattern. As blacks start to show they have the ability to buy a house here and rent an apartment there in white areas, they break down the concept of a neighborhood as being either all black or all white. Without completeness, segregation loses much of its meaning, and systematic opposition to any residential integration becomes unrewarding.

Another effect of successful damage suits needs to be mentioned. Even if a particular applicant for an apartment has neither the inclination nor the resources to initiate a suit for damages, the landlord will not know that. Having heard of some other landlord who not only had to stop discriminating but also had to pay substantial damages, he is likely to think twice before sending away the person before him. His second thought may be not to turn down the applicant. Thus, the *possibility* of legal action may be enough to make many people stop discriminating without ever actually being confronted with the ultimate means for dealing with it. Again, the elimination of some discrimination removes its all-or-nothing character and reduces the "value" to whites of continuing discrimination.

It is probably true that a small landlord—say an owner of one building containing six apartments—could have an easier time resisting the law than a large rental operation. Turnover would be low, it would be more difficult to prove that a particular refusal was actually due to race, and the inclination of the occasional applicant might be simply to let the matter pass and seek elsewhere. Opposite conditions would tend to prevail with large-scale operations. Consistent refusal to rent to blacks or restriction of them to certain areas would be evidence of a "pattern of discrimination," which is prohibited by the 1968 fair housing act. A large rental organization would soon confront someone who would seek to break the discrimination pattern, and a local or national civil rights organization might well be interested in assisting the person.

One rental firm in New York City controlling the rentals of 20,000 apartment units in various buildings in the city followed the practice of assigning blacks to certain of its buildings and whites to others. As a result of legal action protesting this pattern of discrimination it agreed in 1971 in the United States District Court in Brooklyn to relocate and to provide a month's free rent—a considerable financial consideration— for as many as 50 black families it had denied access to certain of its buildings that it had previously reserved for whites only. Also part of the agreement was a stipulation that it would accept blacks in any of its units and ensure fairness by stamping applications with a time clock and dealing with them on a strictly first-come, first-served basis.

The largest apartment management firm in the Cleveland area signed a similar agreement with the Department of Justice and the Urban League. A large real estate agency in Washington, D.C., likewise settled a lawsuit by agreeing to end discriminatory practices and paying $3,000 in damages as well.[60] With large blocs of housing units removed from the discrimination pattern in different cities around the country the occasional resistance of the small-time operator becomes irrelevant and the old pattern of total discrimination becomes increasingly unable to maintain itself.

Goals and Attitudes

When we look at integration in housing we need to take account of some very basic white fears and attitudes. The traditional total segregation residential pattern, plus the consequences of social and economic discrimination against blacks in our society, has led to black ghetto areas having a higher incidence of various types of social pathology than most white areas. That there are wide differences within the black ghetto is apt to be overlooked by the average white, who when he thinks of the black ghetto is apt to think of crime, drugs, and delinquency as well as deterioration in property values. Given that blacks have generally been denied access to new housing in the suburbs (except for the occasional all-black suburb), the only means for providing additional housing for blacks was by expansion of the black ghetto, block by block, into white areas.

The very resistance of whites to black expansion generated the back-pressure in the ghetto that made expansion more difficult to resist. With exploiting blockbusters sowing fears and driving down prices (usually only long enough to panic whites into selling), the prospect for a white having a black neighbor has not been one which he was likely to take casually. However, what we have been talking about here is not expansion of the black ghetto as such, which is simply a continuation of the traditional pattern of segregation, but rather a moving out of some of the residents of the black ghetto and settling in integrated neighborhoods, not as the first invaders in a wave of ghetto expansion but as individuals who are simply moving into the neighborhood.

Studies have repeatedly shown that whites do not mind having some black neighbors but that their biggest fears and resistance result from the desire not to be isolated in a largely black neighborhood. In other words, it is not having black *neighbors* that the white resists, it is the likelihood of living in a black *neighborhood*. With the residential segregation barriers lowered, the back-pressure for housing would be correspondingly reduced. Most black ghetto residents would probably prefer to remain in a black area just as immigrants earlier congregated near each other in their ghettos. If most whites would not want to live in a predominantly black neighborhood, it is understandable that many blacks would likewise not want to live in a mostly white neighborhood. We are talking here about making it possible for those blacks who wish to do so to live outside the ghetto, not about mere ghetto expansion. Looked at in this way, the arrival of a black neighbor in a white area is not the first signal of an approaching invasion but is simply a new neighbor. It is a statistical fact that there are not enough blacks in any metropolitan area for all of them to move everywhere at once; removing racial barriers cannot possibly result in all white neighborhoods suddenly becoming all black.

Whites must not be guilty of taking it upon themselves to decide for blacks where and how they should live. They certainly have done this every time they have practiced racial residential discrimination. Whites would be doing this just as much, however, if they decided that complete integration should take place and that the black ghetto should be broken up with all blacks being scattered about in predominantly white neighborhoods. Political, social, and psychological advantages can come from people living together in a community with people with whom they can identify and feel congenial. This has been noted repeatedly by black writers from at least as far back as DuBois in the late nineteenth century up to the 1970s, one recent example coming from the poet Lucille Clifton, who characterizes the ghetto as a place of love and freedom.[61] Black leaders have also argued, and probably correctly, that breaking up the black ghetto would greatly weaken their effectiveness in trying to wrest greater equality for blacks.

We should keep in mind that the term ghetto refers only to separation of a racial or ethnic group in a particular area of a city. A free society has to allow for the possibility of voluntary segregation of a group. A ghetto need not be a slum with all that implies by way of inadequate housing, personal demoralization, poverty, and social pathology. This caution is inserted here to remind us that our goal is not to break up the black ghetto and bring about a condition of zero segregation; it is to eliminate *involuntary* segregation so that those who do wish to live outside the ghetto may do so.

Opposing the Blockbuster

Given the tendency to view neighborhoods as either black, white, or in process of changing, a white neighborhood which is adjacent to a black one and which is perceived as being in the path of black expansion is certain to attract the attention of "blockbusters," real estate operators who specialize in using high-pressure scare tactics to panic whites into selling out so that their property can be resold profitably to blacks. Blockbusting, defined as the attempt to induce a person to sell property through claims that people of another race, religion, or ethnic status are likely to move into the neighborhood, is prohibited by the 1968 fair housing act. The use by blockbusters of subtle statements and innuendos, however, can make it difficult to prove legally that the appeal to sell was really based on a threat of racial invasion.

Although the act does not specifically prohibit mere solicitation of property owners to sell, the cumulative effect of a dozen or more real estate firms soliciting heavily in an area can induce mass sales even if no claims of racial invasion are made. In other words, regardless of the kinds of appeals used with property owners, the fact of mass solicitation can have a substantial effect just in itself in leading a neighborhood to become all black.

In this context a 1973 United States District Court decision in Detroit can be of considerable significance. A neighborhood group of property owners organized as the Emerson Community Homeowner's Association initiated a class action suit against 15 real estate firms claiming that heavy solicitation in their neighborhood by these firms tended to panic whites into selling and thus was a form of blockbusting. In a precedent-setting opinion, Judge Damon Keith upheld them, ruling that heavy real estate solicitation in itself is in violation of the 1968 fair housing act because of the fear and panic which such solicitation generates.[62]

In an attempt to deal with this problem in another way a number of cities have enacted antisolicitation ordinances. Details vary from city to city, but in general they provide a means for restricting solicitation by real estate firms. Blockbusting statements are frequently prohibited, and the use of "For Sale" and "Sold" signs may also be restricted. The impression of instability in an area generated by a rash of real estate signs in front of buildings can alone obviously have a considerable effect on residents.[63]

A 1972 Baltimore County ordinance prohibits real estate canvassing anywhere within the county. A real estate firm is permitted to seek business through general advertising and of course can serve any customer who contacts the firm to arrange for selling his property. The ordinance also provides that if 10 residents in an area (its boundaries being defined by the residents) request it, a hearing must be held which can result in banning real estate signs from display within the area for a period of up to two years, with extensions of the ban being possible. Blockbusting claims—that property should be sold because another race is moving into the neighborhood—are also prohibited. Fines up to $1,000 for violation of the ordinance by real estate firms are possible.

A Philadelphia ordinance prohibits solicitations by real estate firms who have been notified by a property owner that he does not want to be solicited. Although a few individuals might take the time and effort to notify all the real estate firms who might solicit them, the only effective way of implementing the notification provision is for community groups to canvass property owners in likely neighborhoods and get signatures on a petition which can be used to notify the various real estate companies not to solicit. Dayton provides that the Human Relations Council can declare a neighborhood a "sensitive area" either after receiving a substantial number of complaints from residents of the area within five days alleging improper activities by real estate people or if 25 percent of the homes of any block of the neighborhood have "For

Sale" signs on them. Real estate solicitation and the use of "For Sale" signs may then be banned in the sensitive areas. By the time, however, that many complaints result and one-fourth of the homes are already up for sale, the stability of the neighborhood has already seriously been threatened, and the ban is very likely to come too late to be effective.

It can be seen from these examples that the approaches to restricting real estate soliciting are varied both in methods used and in effectiveness. It is important that action can be taken before an area has already been decimated by solicitation. Although relying for enforcement on a city council or a local community relations board does not require action by individual citizens, the motivation of resources of official bodies may not be equal to the task. Ordinances requiring petition actions by citizens place the burden on the affected homeowners, but do provide a means for action be to be taken. What would be best for a particular community could depend upon local circumstances. It certainly seems important that a ban on solicitation be implemented promptly and before the neighborhood is torn apart by real estate activity, and that a ban be of long enough duration to really protect the area. A 60- or 90-day restriction, as provided by some ordinances, is clearly too short, particularly if the procedures used to obtain it require considerable effort.

Regardless of the specific form a local antisolicitation ordinance might take, just having it on the books will not be sufficient for it to have an effect. Active use must be made of its provisions. Detroit has had a Fair Neighborhood Practices Ordinance since 1962 which provides for restriction on the use of real estate signs and of soliciting upon notification of real estate firms by property owners. Yet, this did not prevent extensive soliciting and blockbusting activities in northwest Detroit, which led residents of the area to take legal action under the 1968 fair housing act as described earlier. A local antisolicitation law is not a substitute for citizen vigilance but rather a means for making it effective.

Finally, we should be clear about the purpose of antisoliciting legislation. We have pointed out elsewhere that although the blockbuster makes considerable personal profit through causing great hardship for white homeowners by manipulating them into selling at panic prices, and greatly increases racial antagonisms by his scare tactics, at least he is one of the few people in the real estate business who is actually increasing the supply of housing for blacks. Given a situation where little new housing was built for blacks and where conventional realtors viewed it as "unethical" to sell to a black a home in a white neighborhood, the development of the occupation of blockbuster became inevitable as the only means to provide new sources of housing for blacks.

Antisolicitation legislation, then—whether local, state, or federal—can only be workable if alternative sources of housing for blacks are available. The social purpose of antisolicitation laws must be to permit an area to become and remain genuinely interracial without it being forced into becoming solidly black. It is the intense soliciting in an interracial area which can eventually drive out all whites and leave it completely segregated. Preventing solicitation in areas which might be turned completely, requires that at least an equivalent amount of housing must be made available for blacks in other parts of the city. The obvious way to do this is simply to have all housing open racially (which, incidentally, is in accord with federal law). We are back again to questioning the traditional view that a neighborhood must be either all white or all black or in process of change from one to the other.

Private Desegregation Efforts

Most attempts to bring about stable interracial neighborhoods and apartment dwellings have either resulted from governmental actions involving legal or financial pressures or from religious and philanthropic organizations. Desegregation has come to be associated in the popular mind with falling property values and deteriorating living conditions. In this situation it may come as a surprise to learn that at least some real estate people have approached the task of bringing about stable interracial housing as a money-making commercial enterprise.

Perhaps the best example of profit through interracial housing is Mr. Morris Milgram, who since 1952 has directed a number of businesses—with names such as Planned Communities, Mutual Real Estate Investment Trust (M-REIT), and Partners in Housing—which all have had as their goal the provision of housing on an interracial basis for families of various economic levels on sites ranging from Massachusetts to Illinois and Texas. Altogether Mr. Milgram claims to have established 4,500 dwelling units on an interracial basis, so that whether the units were suburban homes or city apartments, the goal was to maintain a racial mix of residents so that the neighborhood or building became neither all black nor all white.[64]

A recent organization of Mr. Milgram, Partners in Housing, is designed to attract higher-income investors who can profit economically at the same time that they supply capital to facilitate interracial housing. A prominent feature is that the investor can share in the heavy depreciation permitted by the federal income tax laws in the early years of a housing development and use the paper loss to offset income obtained from other sources, thus reducing his income tax.[65] Although one may question the propriety of our present tax laws which permit an accelerated depreciation of rental property, given that this is possible, Partners in Housing takes advantage of it to attract people who wish to make their investments serve social purposes. So much attention has been directed to the economic exploitation of increasing segregation that it seems worthy of mention that profits apparently can also be made (although perhaps more modestly) in nonsegregated housing.

When we move beyond the issue of making it possible for the individual to buy a home or rent an apartment wherever he wishes, which has been our concern so far, and enter the area of larger-scale developments which are avowedly interracial, the problems become more difficult. I will consider some of these here.

Public Housing

Public housing was discussed earlier simply as housing for low-income families without regard to race. Here we will concentrate on the racial factor. Although many public housing projects were officially operated as segregated institutions in earlier years, any official acceptance of or legal justification for segregation was eliminated during the 1960s with President Kennedy's Executive Order 11063 of 1962 and passage of the 1964 Civil Rights Act. It is hardly surprising, however, to find that most public housing projects show a high degree of racial separation resulting both from the location of a specific project—a project in the middle of a black neighborhood is certain to be occupied almost entirely by blacks —and/or from management policies of the local housing authority that in some way seem to result in the blacks winding up in project A and the whites in project B, even if A and B are across the street from each other.

In a major lawsuit initially filed in 1965 against the Chicago Housing Authority, it was clearly shown that an extreme degree of racial segregation existed—out of 54 projects in the city, 50 were more than 99 percent black, whereas the remaining 4 were practically all white.[66] The evidence showed that projects were systematically located within the city so that their racial identity would be clearly established at once. Each city councilman in effect had a veto over any project proposed for his ward, and the council would not override it.

When a decision was finally rendered in 1969, Judge Richard B. Austin ordered that henceforth three projects had to be built in a white area of the city for every one built in a black neighborhood, and that future projects had to have density limits so that they would be smaller in size and could be scattered more about the city. The decision was upheld upon appeal and let stand by the Supreme Court. City council refusal to approve sites in white areas led Judge Austin in 1972 to order housing authority officials to bypass the Chicago City Council and to acquire property in white areas without council approval if necessary. Thus, the case was still active seven years after being initiated and undoubtedly will continue to be so for some time into the future. The expense and duration of such a case requires the support of a well-established organization; in this instance it was the American Civil Liberties Union. However, most cities would not have as large or complex a situation as Chicago, and the legal precedent has now been established so that future actions should not require as much effort as the original case. Legal pressure is very apt to be needed in most cases, as a housing authority, like almost any bureaucracy, is not likely to change its *modus operandi* without external compulsion. It is possible that with some local housing authorities, negotiations to end discrimination could be successful without court action simply because the legal remedy existed and could be used if the housing authority were recalcitrant.

The greater emphasis on small-scale, scattered-site projects possibly in connection with the use of existing buildings could help to reduce opposition to public housing and to make race less of a factor in public housing in the future.

Summary

The example of Europe shows us that poor people living in old buildings do not necessarily have to have degrading housing that threatens their health and life itself. Neither is an attitude of hopeless despair inevitable. We have seen that although massive high-rise projects may be workable for middle-class people, they do not meet the needs of low-income families. The design of new public housing projects, and alterations to existing ones, need to take into account the lessons learned from the experience of the past, particularly the defensible space concepts. Given the many disadvantages of housing projects, we should be seeking for alternatives to the project.

Providing adequate housing for moderate- and low-income families will require both preserving and improving the quality of existing housing and facilitating the construction of reasonably priced new housing, either to be occupied by these families directly or for occupancy by others so that the filtration process can operate. Any programs that help to minimize building abandonment or to salvage abandoned buildings will obviously contribute to meeting housing needs. The continuing growth of land costs as a factor in housing emphasizes the importance of exclusionary zoning in restricting housing opportunities for these families and underscores the importance of legal decisions which have tended to limit the extent of such zoning.

Honoring the rights of blacks to live where they wish includes the possibility that some blacks may prefer to segregate themselves voluntarily in neighborhoods that are predominantly black. This, of course, is their right. The major problem, however, has been involuntary segregation, which has denied housing opportunities to blacks who desired to live elsewhere. The combination of the 1968 fair housing act and the *Jones* v. *Mayer* case has clearly established the legal right of blacks to live in whatever housing they wish to and can afford. Continuing action to implement these rights will be needed for some time in the future.

Charles S. Bullock, III
UNIVERSITY OF HOUSTON

3

Expanding Black Economic Rights

D uring the 1950s and much of the 1960s, equality in the political, educational, and social spheres received most of the attention of civil rights activists. The emphasis was on getting blacks registered to vote and desegregating schools and other public facilities. Although these objectives have not been fully achieved, the energies of civil rights activists are increasingly directed toward economic goals.

The shift in emphasis to economic objectives is partially attributable to the discovery that achievements in other areas, while often heightening self-respect, did little to improve the quality of life for many black Americans.

> During the decade of the 70s, the civil rights movement must move to be an economic movement. We must put economic flesh and bone on Dr. [Martin Luther] King's dream—otherwise its going to be just a dream.[1]

To elaborate, although school desegregation may improve the educational program provided blacks,[2] realization of the benefits will be thwarted in a labor market subdivided by walls of prejudice which deny blacks good jobs, regardless of qualifications. So also, the value of the vote and the right to use public accommodations may be diminished in the eyes of people who, because of past or present discrimination, are unable to earn a decent living.

There are two distinct target populations for programs intended to advance black economic rights, the employable and the unemployable. The first category consists of two groups. First, there are those who are currently working but, because of discrimination, earn less than whites having equal qualifications. Second, there are people who through education, training, or other remedial programs could be prepared for participation in the job market. The unemployable are those who because of age (too old or too young), health, mental capacity, or family responsibilities (heads of female-headed households in which there are small children) are unlikely to be efficient participants in the labor force. These distinctions are important since programs geared to eliminating inequities confronting the employable will do little for the unemployable. If the unemployable are ignored, large segments of the black population will continue to exist without the basic rights of an American citizen.

In this chapter I shall first consider the status of employables and later turn to the unemployables. The same format will be followed in each section. First, the programs which are intended to regulate behavior in a policy area, for example, equal employment, will be described. This will involve explanations of the goals established and the techniques by which the objectives are to be achieved. Second, the progress made pursuant to the programs will be discussed. Where performance has been inadequate, explanations for the deficiencies will be suggested which may enhance the likelihood that policy objectives can be achieved.

Employables

Equal economic opportunities are contingent upon three major conditions being met simultaneously: (1) Employment opportunities must be accessible to all regardless of race; (2) competitors in the job market must have available opportunities for necessary education, training, and health care; and (3) there must be an adequate demand for labor. Until recently there has been little government recognition of an obligation to meet any of these three prerequisites.

What has been done to improve the conditions of blacks in the labor force? I will first describe and then evaluate the operation of equal employment opportunity programs to determine the success of programs directed at removing racial barriers to employment. Manpower programs will next be dealt with in an effort to appraise progress in preparing blacks for fuller participation in the labor force. Finally, attention will be focused on the extent to which the Employment Act of 1946, with its commitment to maximum employment, is being honored.

Equal Employment Opportunities

An essential first step toward equality of economic opportunity is elimination of racial discrimination. In the absence of fair employment practices, well-educated blacks may be limited to poor-paying jobs for which they are overqualified. The imprint of discrimination is clear in 1969 data showing that the average black having one to three years of college earned $6,909, less than the average white who had completed elementary school ($7,064).

Federal support for equal employment opportunities extends back to a Roosevelt executive order (E.O. 8802). This initial commitment to equal employment opportunities was narrowly applied and short-lived, with its impact limited to the defense industry. Enforcement muscles were flaccid and once the forces of democracy had defeated the Axis powers the largely ineffectual enforcement agency, the Fair Employment Practice Committee, quietly expired from lack of congressional appropriations.[3]

For almost two decades, federal commitment to minority employment rights was limited to executive orders which provided, at most, symbolic benefits. Calls, like President Truman's, for "fair employment throughout the Federal establishment without discrimination because of race, color, religion, or national origin . . ."[4] went unheeded on Capitol Hill and in the bureaucracy. Not until the first half of the 1960s was action taken to protect minority workers.

Efforts directed at private employers will now be discussed, followed by a look at efforts in the public sphere. In dealing with private employers, the activities of the Office of Federal Contact Compliance, the Equal Employment Opportunity Commission, the Justice Department, and state fair employment practices commissions will be described and evaluated. The primary focus in public employment will be the United States Civil Service Commission.

Federal Contractors

President Kennedy's 1963 Executive Order No. 11114 forbade racial discrimination in all federally financed construction projects. In late 1965, E.O. 11246 extended the prohibition to all of a federal contractors' projects, including work sites not under federal contract. Contractors were obligated to obtain pledges of nondiscrimination from subcontractors and unions with whom they dealt. Contractors who continued to discriminate would be subject to loss of contracts and debarment from future contracts. The Office of Federal Contract Compliance (OFCC) was created to oversee the compliance activities of 26 federal agencies, each charged with implementing the requirements among its contractors.[5]

The potential importance of requiring federal contractors to establish equal employment opportunities is clear. At least 100,000 and perhaps as many as 225,000 contractor facilities supply the federal government with everything from buttons to missiles and office buildings.[6] In 1969 federal contractors employed 20 million workers, approximately one-fourth of the national labor force. The OFCC estimates that the cost to minority members of discrimination by federal contractors amounts to some $24 billion annually.[7]

Federal contractors are obligated not only to avoid discrimination but also to actively recruit minority workers. The OFCC guidelines of 1968 set forth the obligation in the following terms:

> A necessary prerequisite to the development of a satisfactory affirmative action program is the identification and analysis of problem areas inherent in minority employment and an evaluation of opportunities for utilization of minority group personnel. The contractor's program shall provide in detail for specific steps to guarantee equal employment opportunities keyed to the problems and needs of members of minority groups, including when there are deficiencies, the development of specific goals and timetables for the prompt achievement of full and equal employment opportunities. . . .[8]

Thus the OFCC recognizes that agreements to no longer discriminate are inadequate to achieve meaningful minority participation in businesses which had previously discriminated. To facilitate minority penetration of what had been largely, if not exclusively, white job categories federal contractors must establish numerical objectives for minority employment to be achieved within a specified time-frame. By 1970 contractors were also required to collect data needed to evaluate the effectiveness of affirmative action programs. However, in 1973 the OFCC was criticized for lacking specific guidelines for evaluating contractor compliance and for not gathering data sufficient to permit evaluation.[9]

Although E.O. 11246 applies to all federal contractors, the most aggressive efforts have focused on construction contracts. Several techniques have been used to establish employment objectives for entire metropolitan areas rather than deal with individual projects. Employment goals have been set with an eye toward bringing minority participation in the better paying skill trades up to the size of the minority component of an area's population. In Philadelphia and a few other cities, the OFCC established annually increasing proportions for minority employment in the skilled trades.[10] A second technique, hometown plans, has goals and timetables negotiated by representatives of unions, contractors, and the minority community for the training and employment of workers. In some areas where hometown plans have failed, minority employment goals have been included among contract bid conditions. Although the Nixon Administration announced its intention to develop goals and timetables for 100 cities, only 54 had been developed by 1973. The OFCC has considered setting regional goals and timetables but has yet to act.

Although goals and timetables are necessary to expand minority job opportunities with federal contractors, they are by no means sufficient.

For the objectives to be reached, compliance officers must alertly monitor the minority hiring procedures of contractors and aggressively enforce the law against those found deficient. The second year goals of the
Philadelphia Plan were met only after the issuance of more than 100
show-cause orders threatening contract termination and one debarment
from future government contracts.[11] Hometowns plans, which are
largely voluntary, have been less effective than the Philadelphia Plan.
NAACP labor specialist Herbert Hill charges that "After some four
years of experience with the plans, not a single hometown plan has
produced any gains for the minority community."[12]

How extensive have monitoring activities been? Prior to 1969 compliance agencies reviewed, on the average, fewer than 10 percent of the
contracts for which they were responsible.[13] OFCC Order No. 1 required
that at least half of the contracts be annually reviewed. The impact of
this order was first seen in fiscal year (FY) 1971 when 31,000 contract
compliance reviews were conducted by the agencies reporting to the
OFCC.

In evaluating performance, compliance agencies consider the progress
made toward meeting goals and timetables for minority employment.
This usually involves appraisal of the contractor's recruitment, promotion, and training policies to insure that they are free of bias. If the
review of material provided by the contractor leaves unresolved doubts
whether the affirmative action plan is being honored, an on-site inspec-
tion may be conducted.

The OFCC selects a portion of the reviews done by the agencies for
desk auditing, which serves as a check upon the work of the reviewing
agencies. This monitoring device will turn up deficiencies in agency
reviews and will also provide the OFCC with feedback on the impact
of various procedures on minority employment. Discovery of lack of
progress not noted by the initial reviewer may lead to another on-site
visit, or even an OFCC takeover of the enforcement process when a
large, recalcitrant corporation with multiple problems is involved.

Agencies responsible for contract compliance now have review procedures which, on paper, appear thorough, but progress may remain
limited in the absence of a viable threat of punishment.[14] Although the
OFCC has potent weapons at its disposal, for example, contract termination and blacklisting, it has hesitated to use them. First notices of debarment (that is, notices calling upon the recipient to show cause why
he should not be denied federal contracts) are infrequently sent, and by
September 1971 only one contractor had actually been debarred.[15] It is
also rare for a contractor to be sued for noncompliance, or for a low
bidder to be denied a contract because of his employment practices.

Spotty and infrequent use of available sanctions belies a lingering
infatuation with voluntarism. Agencies responsible for protecting the

rights of minorities frequently fail to enforce affirmative action agreements, which has led to the charge that "Contractors will readily agree to comply with the affirmative action clauses in federal contracts because they are totally aware of the historic failure of the agencies to use their sanctioning powers against contractors."[16] Where concerted and consistent actions have been taken, as in Philadelphia, goals have been met and exceeded.

Although a number of explanations can be offered for the failure to achieve greater progress, a common denominator is lack of commitment. This charge can be laid against several units of government. In the early days, the OFCC's oversight capacity was restricted because of understaffing on account of tight-fisted appropriations from the Bureau of the Budget and from Congress. Consequently, individual compliance agencies diverted few personnel to policing contractors' employment policies. For example, in 1969 the Treasury Department, which is responsible for 12,000 banks, assigned three employees to monitor employment behavior.[17] Compliance agencies are now required to employ sufficient personnel to review at least half of their contractors annually.

There are accomplices, but the bulk of the guilt must be ascribed to the OFCC. It has often been dilatory in promulgating guidelines for agency behavior. No guidelines were issued for 30 months, and standards for data collection sufficient to measure minority employment progress, and guidance in evaluating affirmative action plans have been slow in coming and sometimes vague once formulated. The Commission on Civil Rights further charges that the OFCC has done a shoddy job of training compliance personnel.[18]

Although the OFCC has always been characterized by a lack of aggressiveness, it is now further impeded. In October 1971, the OFCC fell in status from being an agency within the Department of Labor to simply a unit of DOL's Employment Standards Administration (ESA). Even if the reorganization has not sapped all of the energy of the sometimes lethargic OFCC, the move symbolized the lack of support given OFCC efforts by the Nixon Administration. DOL, by making the OFCC's field personnel answerable to ESA assistant regional directors rather than to the OFCC director in Washington (in Peters' terminology the OFCC hierarchy is now a free-floating apex),[19] has relegated considerations of race to being but one of a variety of equally important terms of federal contracts. This may be quite damaging to fair employment since frequently when an agency is given an additional responsibility, the new duty is subordinated to preexisting programs. Therefore, we suspect that ESA will assign low priority to its equal employment responsibilities.

A clear illustration of how ESA supervision has accorded the OFCC the type of loving kindness popularly associated with stepmothers involves OFCC staffing. In 1971, the OFCC had filled only 76 percent of its authorized positions—superiors said reorganization had made full staffing unnecessary.[20] As of August 1972, only 64 percent of the OFCC's positions were staffed.[21] Given the delays which mar the OFCC's history in formulating guidelines, and given the infrequent use of sanctions, the shrinking OFCC staff indicates that the poor performances of the past are likely to continue, if not degenerate.

Private Employment Other than
Federal Contract Work

Private employment not done under federal contract is regulated by the 1964 Civil Rights Act, as updated in 1972. Title VII of the 1964 statute prohibited racial discrimination by employers or unions having at least 25 employees, and covered an estimated 75 percent of the national labor force.[22] To enforce it, the five-member Equal Employment Opportunity Commission (EEOC) was created.

The EEOC has chosen to restrict its activities, adopting a largely passive role. Most of its resources have been devoted to processing tens of thousands of complaints. Typically the commission has opted for a narrow gauge response to complaints, handling them on a one-by-one basis. Not until 1974 did it follow the OFCC's hesitant lead and begin to fashion voluntary nondiscrimination plans for entire industries. The EEOC has generally been reluctant to establish goals and timetables to increase minority employment.

Prior to 1972, the EEOC's powers were somewhat limited. When it determined that an employer was guilty of discrimination, its enforcement authority was restricted to "conference, conciliation, and persuasion." For respondents unmoved by persuasion, there were no remedial sanctions at the EEOC's discretion. Redress came either through a private suit by the complainant, or the EEOC could refer the case to the Attorney General for prosecution. This major deficiency in the EEOC's authority was corrected when it was empowered to bring suit if negotiations failed to produce a settlement. The 1972 statute also expanded the EEOC's authority to include employers and unions with at least 15 workers, and extended coverage to employees of state and local governments.

There are two basic EEOC approaches to discrimination. The first is passive, with the commission responding to complaints filed by people who feel they had suffered discrimination. In the second approach the commission takes a more active role and initiates efforts to eliminate discrimination. These two techniques will now be described and evaluated.

Complaint Processing. Upon its creation the EEOC was designated to receive and resolve charges alleging job discrimination based on race, ethnicity, sex, or religion. When it receives a complaint, the commission will refer it to a state Fair Employment Practices Commission (FEPC) if it originated in a state having an FEPC. If there is not an FEPC to assume jurisdiction, the commission will investigate to determine the merits of the complaint. If the investigation produces evidence to support the allegations in the complaint, efforts will be made to resolve the problem. Unsuccessful attempts at resolution may lead to the employer being sued.

The EEOC has been deluged with an ever-growing number of complaints. During its first seven years some 110,000 charges were filed, and by FY 1976 more than 85,000 complaints are expected annually. Although a number of complaints are dismissed or are handled at the state level, almost 80,000 were recommended for investigation between FY 1966 and 1972 (see Table 1).[23] By the end of FY 1972 slightly more than half of these had been investigated. The thousands of complaints which annually clog the EEOC's mailbox have demanded the full-time attention of 70 percent of the Commission's staff.[24]

Charges of racism account for almost 60 percent of the complaints and constitute two-thirds of the investigations. Complaints against employers are almost nine times more numerous than are accusations against labor unions. Employers are most commonly charged with discriminatory firing or hiring practices.

Since the EEOC has devoted so much attention to complaint processing, one might expect that it would become quite adept at this facet of its work. Despite the emphasis on complaint processing, very few complaints are resolved in favor of the worker. Although more than 41,000 investigations were completed during the EEOC's first seven years, conciliations were undertaken in only 9,188 cases (22 percent). Even partial success was achieved in only 27 percent of the conciliations attempted. This amounts to successful resolution of 6 percent of the investigations completed and a microscopic 2 percent of the complaints filed. This miserable batting average appears even worse—if that is possible—when compared with the opinion of an EEOC chairman that *80 percent* of the complaints are valid.[25]

The EEOC's record is further marred by the limited vision with which it has responded to complaints. Even within its defined role of handling complaints, the agency could have done more. A more aggressive stance would be to broaden individual complaints into class actions wherever possible, to look for misdeeds other than those cited in the complaint when investigating, to check for patterns of discrimination, and to give priority to complaints offering the maximum potential for interdicting systematic discrimination. Not until mid-1971 was maximum elimination of systematic discrimination embraced as a goal. Even that commitment became suspect when national impact cases were limited to no more than 10 percent of the commission's resources.[26]

TABLE 1
EEOC Annual Complaint Processing, FY 1966-1972

Fiscal Year	Work Load[a]	New Complaints Received	Investigations		Conciliations (Respondents)			Deferred to States	Referred to Justice
			Recommended	Completed	Attempts	Success[b] (#)	(%)		
1966	8,854	8,854	3,773	1,659	68	52	76	977	0
1967	12,927	9,688	5,084	3,549	174	88	51	1,158	35
1968	15,058	10,095	6,056	5,368	640	306	48	2,136	26
1969	17,272	12,148	9,152	7,543	1,451	376	49	2,980	51
1970	20,122	14,129	11,255	5,090	1,192	270	23	4,201	78
1971	33,214	22,920	16,309	7,321	2,441	815	33	8,516	36
1972	51,969	32,840	28,337	10,688	3,222[c]	594	18	14,256	13
1966-1972		110,674	79,966	41,218	9,188	2,501	27	34,224	239

[a]Includes complaints recalled from state agencies.
[b]Includes partial as well as complete successes.
[c]Includes pre- and post-decision efforts.
Sources: Issues of Equal Employment Opportunity Commission, *Annual Reports* (Washington, D.C.: Government Printing Office).

Another weakness is the inability to process complaints with dispatch. Since the EEOC's first year, when it was staffed to handle 2,000 complaints but received 8,854, it has been buried in paperwork. By the end of FY 1974, the backlog of unprocessed cases was a staggering 97,761, up from 53,416 two years earlier.[27] The backlog means that instead of processing complaints in 60 days, as was the goal, the average has elongated to two years.[28]

The backlog of complaints reveals much about the EEOC's institutional health. The commission is doing poorly precisely on the item which it has chosen to stress. Its performance is unlikely to inspire either staff or clients. The former may adopt a lackadaisical approach to their work when confronted by an ever-growing mountain of complaints. Lack of pride is apparent according to a congressional study which found that a quarter of the commission's work had to be redone because of deficiencies.[29] Organizational malaise is reflected in the high turnover of personnel. During its first half decade, four chairmen, five general counsels, and six executive directors passed through the EEOC's revolving door. Indicative of restlessness in the ranks was the filing of 220 charges of discrimination against the commission by its employees, a rate of complaints 28 times greater than was generally found in federal offices.[30]

Processing delays result in continued discrimination for those who file complaints. Moreover, complainants may lose faith in the EEOC as a corrective agent and perhaps in the government as a whole. If skepticism about the utility of lodging a complaint spreads, many who have felt discrimination will not even bother to file charges.

A number of problems remain, but some aspects of the EEOC operations have improved, including liaison with state FEPCs. Because of poor FEPC performance, the EEOC now defers complaints only to states having standards comparable to federal ones. Under these new criteria, the finding of possible cause by FEPCs rose to 81 percent, during the first half of FY 1972. This is a vast improvement over FY 1968–71 when states found possible cause in only 19 percent of the complaints they handled.[31] A high rate of successful resolutions by the states might reduce the EEOC's workload to proportions which it could handle.

A second aspect of the EEOC complaint process which has been changed is the disposition of cases not susceptible to voluntary resolution. The pre-1972 recourse of sending unresolved complaints to the Justice Department for prosecution proved unsatisfactory. In litigation, as in other aspects of its operation, the EEOC moved with frustrating slowness, referring slightly more than 200 of its unreconciled cases to Justice, even though negotiation had been unavailing in hundreds of instances. Justice did little to encourage the EEOC, taking few referrals to court. By FY 1971 the situation had deteriorated to the point where of 36 complaints forwarded to Justice, only 1 prompted a suit.[32] Some of Justice's seeming lack of enthusiasm to prosecute may be attributed to problems at the EEOC. The commission's long delays in processing complaints meant that the material forwarded to Justice was dated and some cases had become moot. Another problem was that the EEOC's investigations were generally inadequate to sustain a conviction, necessitating a time-consuming investigation by Justice.[33] Despite the early recognition of these problems, little was done to coordinate efforts of the two agencies.

It is to be hoped that this obstacle was corrected in 1972 when the EEOC was granted authority to file suits. Although at first slow to use the new tool, the EEOC initiated more than 160 cases in FY 1974.[34] Increased litigation, particularly when it leads to costly back-pay assessments against employers, should prompt more firms to settle out of court to avoid court costs and bad publicity. One study of EEOC enforcement efforts concludes that conciliation is much more likely when the costs of continued noncompliance are perceived to exceed the costs entailed in settlement.[35]

Despite the numerous shortcomings in EEOC complaint processing, this activity has produced some standards for private employment practices. The commission annually collects data on employment by race and sex from all firms with 100 or more employees. These data have been used to create rebuttable inferences of discrimination. The

EEOC has succeeded in compelling employers to recruit in ways likely to attract blacks, instead of continuing to rely on practices which produced a white work force. Other EEOC decisions have helped define standards for tests and other employment prerequisites and for the use of seniority systems. Among job prerequisites which have been generally disallowed in the face of EEOC challenges are requirements of a high school diploma, a good credit rating, and no arrests or convictions. What is needed is for these decisions to be applied systematically to all employers and unions and not just those against whom protests are lodged.

Affirmative Action.   Affirmative action techniques offer the potential for broader application of EEOC standards. Despite heavy emphasis on complaint processing, the EEOC has long been aware of the inadequacies of a passive response.

> Recognizing that complaints are an insufficient measure of the extent to which job discrimination exists, the Commission strove . . . to transcend the case-by-case compliance process and stimulate the kinds of broadscale affirmative action by the employment community which would combat the effects of past and present discrimination.[36]

Affirmative action has come in a number of guises. EEOC has investigated several industries and has launched industry-wide conciliation efforts for airlines, shipping, trucking, and construction, to name some. It has held hearings to determine the overall job status of minorities in some major urban areas. Such investigations may be undertaken in the absence of a complaint and have a much broader range than a single case of discrimination. The rationale for the 1968 New York City hearings illustrates the potential of such endeavors.

> Progress here can serve as a model across the country; decisions made and policies executed at the headquarters site of many major corporations may control and certainly can influence, behavior patterns in providing equal job opportunities throughout every plant and branch office.[37]

Another aspect of affirmative action is the filing of charges by commission members when they believe discrimination is being practiced. Commissioner charges have usually come as a result either of public hearings or of evidence turned up during investigation of a complaint. In addition to the possibility of using commissioner charges for challenging discrimination in an entire industry, the facts asserted in charges can be used by private parties to sue their employers.

A fourth technique has been the intervention of the EEOC in the policy making of independent regulatory commissions. For example, the EEOC has intervened in Interstate Commerce Commission rulemaking procedures in an attempt to eliminate discrimination in the transportation industry. The EEOC also appeared before the Federal Communications Commission to delay a rate increase requested by American Telephone and Telegraph until the communications giant agreed to correct discriminatory personnel policies. AT & T ultimately paid $15 million in back wages and granted raises totaling $23 million to women and minority men against whom it had discriminated.[38]

The EEOC has also worked with employers and unions to devise schemes for increasing black employment. Under the New Plant Program, the EEOC approaches employers while plants are under construction and offers to help recruit minority workers. Operation Outreach seeks minority youth for union apprenticeship programs. At the request of employers, the EEOC will participate in developing affirmative action programs. Seminars have been held to acquaint trade associations with their fair employment obligations and with EEOC services.

The potentially most significant example of affirmative action occurred in April 1974 when, for the first time, an industry-wide plan was negotiated. The United Steelworkers Union and the nine companies whose workers it represents agreed to replace dual seniority systems with plant-wide seniority.[39] Goals and timetables were set for minority recruitment and advancement. Also some $31 million in back wages will be paid to almost 50,000 victims of discrimination. While NAACP's Herbert Hill and some other civil rights spokesmen have criticized the wage settlement as too small,[40] the plan is a major achievement. If it serves as a prototype for other industries and if these plans are enforced, they will vastly expand equal employment opportunities.

The EEOC has several affirmative action strategies available but has not fully developed them because it assigns priority to complaint processing. The experiences of the federal government when trying to desegregate schools and to extend black voting rights in the South indicate that a passive federal role is less productive than is a more active approach.[41] It would therefore be advisable for the EEOC to reorder its priorities and give greater emphasis to affirmative action techniques. Negotiation of industry-wide settlements should reduce the number of new complaints as well as resolve problems raised in complaints already in hand. Switching personnel from complaint handling to affirmative action would, of course, mean that delays in resolving complaints would lengthen. Nonetheless an industry-wide approach would seem to be a more efficient utilization of personnel. Once uniform standards have been established, the EEOC can use the employment data which are collected annually to monitor progress and to guide the selection of targets for follow-up monitoring.

Litigation
When the EEOC or the OFCC is unable to resolve complaints, a court suit may be in order. Until 1972, when respondents rejected EEOC

conciliatory efforts, a private suit was typically a complainant's only recourse. Because of the expense of litigation, the absence of a body of case law, and a paucity of attorneys experienced in the subject matter, fewer than 10 percent of the unreconciled complaints in which the EEOC found for the plaintiff were taken to court.[42] Obviously the right to file suit after the EEOC has had a complaint 60 days is not a major bulwark of workers' rights to employment that is free of discrimination.

If a complainant pursues redress in the courts, the EEOC may file an *amicus curiae* brief. This form of participation was little used prior to FY 1968, but had occurred more than 500 times by the end of FY 1971.[43] Filing a brief can be an effective means of enforcement because, as the Commission on Civil Rights observes, "The Commission [EEOC] has had noteworthy success in its *amicus* activity in persuading the courts to adopt its position. . . ."[44]

As an incentive for employers not to litigate, courts have assessed attorney's fees on the defendant not only when the plaintiff wins, but sometimes even when he loses. The latter decision has been justified on the basis that a plaintiff's attorney functions as a "private attorney general."[45]

The other alternative prior to 1972 was for the EEOC or the OFCC to refer unresolved complaints to the Justice Department for litigation. However, during the early years, this option was unsatisfactory since Justice's Employment Section had the lowest priority among the Civil Rights Division units.[46] The activity of Justice as protector of minority employment rights has fluctuated, spurting from 10 cases in FY 1967 to 26 in FY 1968, only to fall back to 10 in FY 1970. FY 1972 saw the greatest new suit activity with 34 initiated.

Rather than proceed on every case referred to it, Justice's strategy was to prosecute referrals which promised area-wide or industry-wide impact or which had multiple defendants.[47] Operating along these lines, suits were filed against Household Finance Corporation (the nation's largest lender), Roadway (the nation's third largest trucker), United States Steel Corporation (the nation's largest steel producer), and construction unions in several cities. Winning these suits, it was hoped, would provide models for other industry members.

Justice-filed employment suits have given the legitimacy and influence of court precedent to policies pursued through administrative channels. Some of the more important decisions have ruled against union practices which disadvantage minorities, not because they specifically exclude minorities, but because they establish standards which are more likely to thwart minority participation. For example, all tests and educational requirements for hiring or advancement which disproportionately exclude blacks are illegal, unless they can be shown to be necessary to the business.[48] Justice suits have also succeeded in barring seniority in several contexts. For example, seniority is discriminatory when a union hiring hall, from which blacks were previously excluded, counts white seniority prior to when blacks were permitted to join.[49] Seniority systems are also forbidden when they dissuade blacks from moving into jobs previously denied them by forcing them to forgo seniority already earned in other jobs with the same employer.[50]

Other suits have helped define illegal recruitment practices. Requirements that union apprentices be recommended by members, or that they have worked under union contracts when such jobs were previously denied blacks are illegal.[51] Suits have also led to the establishment of quotas for future recruitment of blacks. In the *United States* v. *Ironworkers Local 86*,[52] the union was ordered to have at least 30 percent minority representation in future apprenticeship classes, and to waive maximum age limits so that 90 blacks who had been barred from construction unions because of race could become apprentices. Even a state agency, the Alabama State Highway Patrol, has been given recruitment quotas, being ordered to hire 50 percent blacks until they constitute a quarter of the force.[53]

Although the Justice Department has not acted against as many discriminators as one might wish, its actions are important. Its successes help legitimize bureaucratic efforts and provide precedents for private plaintiffs. Moreover, the victories, by establishing court-recognized standards of behavior, may prompt other employers and unions to voluntarily forgo discrimination. Rulings against discrimination may also inspire similarly situated workers in other companies to seek redress.

Civil Rights Gains in Nonfederal Employment

The wisdom of our forefathers holds that the proof of the pudding is in the eating. This aphorism is certainly appropriate to an evaluation of civil rights programs. If there has been progress, then blacks should be obtaining jobs previously denied them. Blacks should be appearing in white collar and skilled blue collar occupations in industries which had previously restricted them to menial tasks. Holding better jobs should also lead to higher wages.

In this part, longitudinal data on the participation of blacks in various industries and in certain broad occupational categories will be offered. It is impossible to demonstrate conclusively that any of the civil rights programs has produced changes. Nonetheless, if black participation and wages increase, then—given the history of black exclusion—we may assume that the programs have contributed. If no increases are discernible, we may conclude that the programs have had little impact. To get a reading on possible program impact, four sets of observations are presented.

Data showing changes in the distribution of nonwhites across occupations since 1950 are given in Table 2. Entries in the Table are ratios

TABLE 2
RATIO OF NONWHITE WORKERS TO EXPECTED DISTRIBUTION OF NONWHITE WORKERS IF EVENLY DISTRIBUTED ACROSS OCCUPATIONS, 1950–1974

Occupation	1950	1960	1965	1970	1974
White collar workers	.26	.37	.43	.60	.65
Professional and technical	.39	.42	.55	.64	.71
Managers, officials, and proprietors	.19	.24	.26	.34	.38
Clerical workers	.27	.49	.53	.76	.86
Sales workers	.17	.23	.28	.35	.38
Blue collar workers	1.00	1.10	1.10	1.20	1.17
Craftsmen and foremen	.38	.47	.53	.63	.68
Operatives	.95	1.12	1.14	1.34	1.38
Nonfarm laborers	2.61	2.55	2.43	2.18	1.79
Service workers	2.97	2.60	2.50	2.11	1.96
Private household	5.99	4.74	4.55	3.90	3.60
Other	1.98	1.91	1.93	1.77	1.75
Farm workers	1.54	1.54	1.37	.98	.70
Farmers and farm managers	1.20	.75	.57	.47	.35
Laborers and foremen	2.17	2.47	2.35	1.64	1.31
TOTAL	9.6%	10.5%	10.8%	10.7%	10.9%

SOURCE: Computed from data in Department of Labor, *Manpower Report of the President* (Washington, D.C.: Government Printing Office, 1973), p. 143; the 1950 Census; and *Earnings and Employment*, Vol. 20 (February, 1974), pp. 43–44.

which indicate the over- or underrepresentation of nonwhites in each occupation. A 1.00 indicates that nonwhites constitute the same proportion of a particular occupational category as of the total labor force, that is, 10.9 percent in 1974. Ratio's less than 1.00 mean that nonwhites are less often found in an occupation than in the overall labor force, whereas scores above 1.00 mean that nonwhites are overrepresented.

Since 1950 nonwhites have constituted approximately a tenth of the labor force. Their distribution in the labor force has changed, however, with nonwhites more often having white collar jobs while less often being found in the lower paying service and farm work categories. Nonwhites have been slightly overrepresented among blue collar workers since 1960. Changes visible in the blue collar strategy are that nonwhites now have a larger share of the better paying craftsmen jobs and are less often laborers. Although nonwhites remain underrepresented among the highest paid white collar workers, a 51 percent increase has been achieved between 1965 and 1974. The proportion of nonwhites in each white collar occupation grew by more than 25 percent after 1965.

These gains are notable, but there are indications that the rate of change is slowing even though further realignment is necessary before nonwhites have a proportionate share of the better paying jobs. For example, between 1965 and 1970 the proportion of nonwhites in white collar jobs grew by 3.4 percentage points annually; between 1970 and 1974 annual growth averaged 1 point. Although growth has continued at about the same rate in the professional class since 1970, it has slowed in the other white collar categories. The skid marks may well have been caused by the economic slow down.

That growth of nonwhite representation among professionals has not decelerated may be explained by the more rapid growth of college graduates among blacks than whites. Between 1960 and 1973, the proportion of blacks aged 25 to 34 who were college graduates increased 102 percent, compared with a 60 percent increase among whites.[54]

Despite gains registered in white collar occupations, nonwhites remain seriously underrepresented among managers and sales workers. Although empirical evidence is lacking, it is likely that discrimination frequently restricts nonwhite entry into these positions. Employers may decline to hire black managers or salespersons, fearing that to do so would reduce profits. Because of status anxieties, some whites may refuse to work under a black supervisor, and the morale and productivity of other whites may be impaired. Merchants may hesitate to employ black salespeople for fear that some of their customers will be offended and therefore shop elsewhere.[55] So long as some businesses have all-white managerial or sales staffs, competitors who have a largely white labor force or white customers may be reluctant to hire blacks in these two categories.

The gains registered should not blind us to other remaining inequities. Nonwhites were still underrepresented in all the better paying and more prestigious job categories (white collar occupations and craftsmen). They are disproportionately found in the less attractive jobs, especially private household work. The causes are twofold. Weaknesses in equal employment enforcement efforts have already been noted. The adequacy of enforcement cannot be fully determined until the second matter is known, that is, the supply of nonwhites currently qualified or trainable for occupations in which blacks are underrepresented. Discriminatory education policies and other consequences of racism have restricted the number of blacks who are prepared for many jobs, especially occupations with a high educational requirement. For example, blacks constitute only 2.9 percent of the college and university faculties (1972–73), 0.7 percent of the engineers (1971), and 1 percent of the attorneys. They constitute 5 percent of the medical students (1972) and 1 percent of the engineering students (1971).[56]

TABLE 3

RATIO OF NONWHITE WORKERS TO EXPECTED DISTRIBUTION
OF NONWHITE WORKERS IF EVENLY DISTRIBUTED ACROSS
OCCUPATIONS, CONTROLLING FOR RACE

Occupation	Blacks		Spanish-speaking (1973)	American Indians (1973)
	1966	1973		
White collar workers	.32	.51	.56	.75
Professional and technical	.29	.43	.44	.59
Managers and officials	.11	.25	.34	.75
Clerical workers	.43	.79	.76	.75
Sales workers	.29	.47	.61	.75
Blue collar workers	1.32	1.29	1.39	1.25
Craftsmen	.44	.60	.88	1.00
Operatives	1.32	1.43	1.32	1.00
Laborers	2.59	1.92	2.31	1.67
Service workers	2.82	2.29	1.51	1.00
TOTAL	8.2%	10.8%	4.1%	0.4%

SOURCE: Computed from data in Department of Labor, *Manpower Report of the President* (Washington, D.C.: Government Printing Office, 1974), pp. 383–384.
NOTE: Data based on firms having 100 or more employees.

The patterns of occupational change noted for nonwhites in the labor force also appear for blacks when firms with 100 or more employees are scrutinized. Using the same presentation format as in Table 2, Table 3 shows more than a 50 percent increase in the ratio of blacks in white collar jobs between 1966 and 1973. Undeniable gains have occurred, however, blacks remain woefully underrepresented in the high paying professional and managerial occupations. The distribution of blacks in 1973 in the set of firms in Table 3 also appears less favorable when data on the Spanish-speaking and Indian minorities are introduced. Generally both of these other minorities are more equitably represented in the better paying categories, that is, white collar occupations and craftsmen, and less often found among the poorest paid (service workers) than are blacks.

Analysis of the data in Tables 2 and 3 lends insight into the nature of blacks' occupational gains. Since blacks constitute more than 90 percent of the nonwhite labor force, data in Table 2 are greatly influenced by the distribution of blacks. Therefore the proportionally more frequent representation of Indians and Orientals in the better paying jobs cannot explain all the differences in the occupational ratios in Tables 2 and 3. Blacks are less well represented in better paying jobs in the larger firms reported in Table 3 than in the overall labor force. If we assume that larger firms generally pay higher wages and extend more fringe benefits, then the less frequent representation of blacks in the better paying jobs of larger firms than in the labor force means that a number of blacks in the "good jobs" categories are less well remunerated than whites similarly classified. Moreover a number of black professionals, managers, officials, and proprietors may well have largely black and poor clienteles, thus reducing their earnings.

Although the EEOC and the OFCC have responded to complaints leveled at discrimination in virtually all segments of the economy, some industries have received particularly intensive federal scrutiny. By 1970 the OFCC had been most active in dealing with the construction industry. The Justice Department had brought a number of suits against trucking firms and railways. The EEOC had held hearings on gas and electric utilities (1968) and the textile industry (1967).

If these enforcement activities have had an impact, then there should be an exceptional increase of black employees in these industries. Table 4 presents data on the proportion of blacks by industry and occupation for 1966 and 1971. Although 1971 may be too soon for the results of federal efforts to be fully manifest, the industries studied had been subjected to federal compliance efforts by that time. If more recent data were available, greater changes might be seen.

Of the total number employed in three of the industries, the percentage of blacks has increased, exceeding 50 percent in textiles and utilities. The gains are commendable, however, blacks still constitute a smaller proportion of the work force in all but two of the industries than of the total labor force (9.5 percent in 1971 in firms of the size for which data are reported in Table 4). Moreover the proportion of black workers in two industries—railroads and construction—actually declined slightly.

The changes in the proportion of blacks holding white collar jobs deserve praise for gains made, tempered by realization of the remaining maldistribution. In 1966 blacks held no more than 1.3 percent of the white collar jobs in any of the industries. Four years later this figure had been exceeded in all five industries, but the maximum (3.9 percent) was below the national figure (4.6 percent). Within the white collar category, black presence remained token in managerial, professional, and sales positions. Greatest real increases occurred among technicians and clerical workers, but even here blacks remained underrepresented and with two exceptions (clerical workers in utilities and technicians in trucking) substantially below total United States figures.

The situation of black blue collar workers remained much the same between 1966 and 1971. All the industries except textiles stayed in the same relative position vis-à-vis total United States figures. Blacks experienced a 94 percent gain in the share of blue collar textile jobs which

TABLE 4

BLACK PARTICIPATION IN FIRMS WITH 100 EMPLOYEES OR MORE
IN SELECTED INDUSTRIES, BY OCCUPATION, 1966
AND 1971 (IN PERCENT)

Occupation	Total U.S.		Construction		Utilities		Railroads		Textiles		Trucking	
	1966	1971	1966	1971	1966	1971	1966	1971	1966	1971	1966	1971
White Collar	2.5	4.6	.8	2.3	1.3	3.9	.8	2.5	1.0	2.3	.8	3.4
Professionals	1.3	2.6	.3	1.1	.4	1.3	.1	.8	.3	.9	.7	2.3
Technicians	4.1	6.1	1.3	3.7	.7	2.3	.3	1.0	1.2	3.6	2.7	10.9
Mgrs. & offs.	.9	2.0	.7	1.4	.2	.6	.2	.6	.3	1.1	.8	1.9
Clerical	3.5	6.8	1.2	3.7	2.5	7.3	1.0	3.2	1.6	3.6	1.1	4.2
Sales	2.4	3.9	.5	1.4	.6	1.6	.1	.6	.3	.4	.7	1.2
Blue Collar	10.7	12.7	16.4	15.3	4.7	7.8	8.8	8.5	8.5	16.5	7.7	10.8
Craftsmen	3.6	5.4	5.2	6.7	1.5	2.8	2.2	3.4	2.6	7.0	5.0	6.3
Operatives	10.8	13.8	13.9	14.3	5.7	11.1	5.1	6.3	7.1	16.8	5.7	8.8
Laborers	21.1	21.1	41.2	35.2	20.2	24.8	30.4	28.7	22.9	27.4	16.8	18.9
Service	23.0	24.7	27.7	23.0	31.7	35.0	49.3	42.5	30.2	32.6	22.1	26.0
TOTAL	8.2	9.5	12.7	11.8	3.8	6.3	7.9	7.5	7.9	14.6	6.3	8.9

SOURCE: Equal Employment Opportunity Commission, *Equal Employment Opportunity Report, 1966,* Vol. II (Washington, D.C.: Government Printing Office, 1968); and *Equal Employment Opportunity Report, 1971: Job Patterns for Minorities and Women in Private Industry,* Vol. I (Washington, D.C.: Government Printing Office, 1974).

they held. In trucking, railroads, and utilities, blacks held a smaller proportion of the blue collar jobs than the 12.7 percent of all blue collar jobs held nationally. A bright spot is that the percentage of black craftsmen in three industries is greater than that nationally, although in no instance did it approach the 9.5 percent which blacks constituted of the nation's total labor force.

Overall the greatest black employment gains occurred in the textile industry. During the four years black employment soared by 73 percent, including gains of more than 100 percent among white collar workers, craftsmen, and operatives. These gains are tarnished, however, if one accepts the evaluation of the Commission on Civil Rights that the increases stem from spreading white disinclination to work in the poor-paying textile industry.[57] Support for this surmise comes from December, 1973, statistics showing the textile and apparel industries to be two of the three lowest-paying manufacturing industries.[58]

The changes observed between 1966 and 1971 in these five industries are in the direction anticipated if government efforts to protect equal employment opportunities were having their desired effect. Despite those gains, the status of blacks in 1971 in the industries which received special federal attention remained generally less favorable than in the total labor force of firms of comparable size. In none of the five industries did the proportion of blacks equal the national proportion in any white collar occupation. In two industries there were fewer craftsmen. While there have been some notable improvements in the industries receiving special attention, they are not numerous. Indeed the more common pattern in the better paying jobs was for the disparity between the proportion of blacks in the United States labor force and their proportion in the five industries to actually increase during the five years.[59] It is therefore difficult to applaud federal enforcement in these industries.

A final measure of equal employment gains is income. Effective programs to curtail discrimination will not only eliminate racial obstacles to better paying jobs but will also assure that blacks and whites are paid equal salaries for equal work. Despite the gains chronicled in the three preceding Tables, the relative economic position of blacks remains little changed. Thus, although median black family income grew by $1,394 between 1967 and 1973, white income improved at a slightly faster rate.[60] Consequently median black family income as a percent of the white figure was less in 1973 than in 1967 (58 percent in 1973; 59 percent in 1967). Taking a longer look, black incomes, relatives to white incomes, were only six percentage points higher in 1973 than in 1959.

A second measure of income is the proportion of families with earnings below the low-income level. Between 1959 and 1973 the proportion of low-income black families declined from 48 to 28 percent. The drop for whites, however, was from 15 to 7 percent. Thus, again, compared with whites, blacks were worse off by 1973. In 1959, blacks were 3.2 times as likely as whites to be poor; by 1973 the ratio was 4.0. Although many black families are escaping poverty, whites are doing it at a much faster rate.

Progress to Date

The preceding discussion has presented a mélange of facts, some indicating progress in black employment, others noting weaknesses in enforcement or showing the gaps remaining between whites and blacks. The mixed findings point to a conclusion that while conditions are certainly improving, much remains to be done. The redistribution of blacks across occupational categories so that they more often wear white than blue collars is certainly encouraging. Our optimism is checked, however, upon realization of the persisting disparities. Particularly disheartening is evidence that the rate of black progress is declining. Among managerial and sales occupations, blacks still have less than 40 percent of the jobs which their proportion of the population suggests would be their fair share.

The underrepresentation of blacks is especially acute among larger employers (see Table 3), even though these have been subject to federal standards longer than smaller businesses have. In 1966 at least 39 of every 100 black employees in the firms reported on in Table 3 would have to change from a job in which blacks were overrepresented to one in which they were underrepresented to achieve an equal distribution of blacks across job categories. Data for 1973 indicate that, on the average, only one black worker per year negotiated the change, with 31 of every 100 blacks still needing to change jobs before maldistribution could be corrected. Put in this perspective, progress in eliminating the effects of discrimination in private employment has been very slow.

A second disquieting feature is the failure of the incomes of black families to catch up with those of white families. Since 1970 median black incomes actually have become smaller in proportion to white incomes, dropping from 61 to 58 percent of the white figure. Thus, while some blacks are gradually infiltrating white occupations, the overall economic position of the race is deteriorating. Black income gains produced by the war-heated economy of the late 1960s have been wiped out by the economic foundering of the 1970s.

Finally the gains reported in Tables 2 through 4 may overstate actual improvements because of the breadth of the occupational categories used. This would help account for the seeming anomaly of improving occupational distributions coincident with incomes declining relative to whites. Black professionals are more often dental technicians than dentists, more often practical nurses than registered nurses, more often elementary school teachers than university professors. Moreover, black clerical and salespeople more often work for smaller concerns which probably pay less well than do larger ones.

Declining black purchasing power, slow adjustments in occupational distributions, and the numerous defects in federal enforcement efforts lead to the conclusion that more could be done. While recognizing that upper limits for black economic achievement are set by the supply of qualified and qualifiable blacks and by the demand of employers for workers, racial discrimination continues to restrict blacks' job opportunities. More aggressive federal enforcement, especially greater attention to affirmative action and less reliance on complaints, should open up additional jobs to black Americans.

Federal Employment

In public employment, concern for the unlawfulness of discrimination is augmented by interest in policy implications of black underrepresensation. While the argument has not been resolved, some contend that the absence of blacks from policy-making positions will result in an agency being less likely to act to satisfy black needs.[61] Therefore, racist government employment practices may, in addition to contributing to the economic hardships of blacks, reduce both the input of black demands and the federal response to these demands.

It was only with President Johnson's Executive Order 11246 (1965) that the federal government can be said to have seriously shouldered its responsibility to hire and promote minority workers. Johnson's executive order named the Civil Service Commission (CSC) to institute an equal employment opportunity program, to establish regulations for federal units and to process charges of discrimination. While the CSC was to lead the equal employment effort, each constituent unit of the federal government was to rid its personnel program of discrimination.

In implementing E.O. 11246 the CSC spoke boldly of an affirmative action program. A March 1966 memo urged that

> An affirmative program must go beyond mere nondiscrimination. It must be devised to overcome obstacles that impede equality of opportunity for minority group persons and should be governed by a plan of action tailor-made to the problems and needs of the installation.[62]

Later that year, however, the CSC began hedging on its commitment, assuring agencies that numerical goals would not be used for evaluating equal employment programs.[63] This policy was not reversed for four and one-half years. In 1969 President Nixon (with E.O. 11478) reiterated the federal government's commitment to equal employment opportunities and called for efforts to help minority employees win promotions to administrative positions and to create special programs for the disadvantaged.

When the federal government embarked upon its fair employment program in 1965, black workers were overrepresented in the lower ranks and underrepresented in the higher ones. As of June 1965, blacks constituted 19.3 percent of the grades 1 through 4 of General Schedule jobs (these are the bulk of the federal government's white collar jobs), but a scant 1.3 percent of the grades 12 through 18.[64]

Federal equal employment efforts have been directed at recruiting additional minority workers, helping those already employed obtain promotions, and excising discrimination. Recruitment activities include publicizing that the federal government is eager to hire minorities, and more energetically, recruiting at predominantly black campuses. Training programs geared to preparing minority workers for promotions offer both on-the-job preparation and classroom training, including allowing lower level workers time off to pursue college degrees.[65] A minority worker who feels that he has been discriminated against can file a complaint. If the complaint is not resolved, it can be appealed to the CSC.

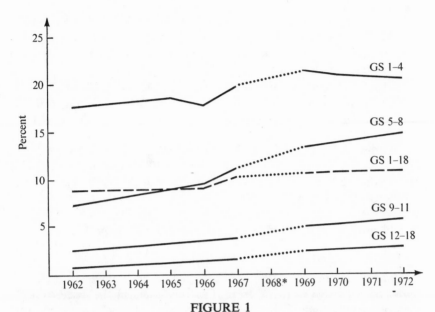

FIGURE 1

Proportion of Blacks in Federal Employment by GS Grade, 1962–1972.
SOURCES: U.S. Civil Service Commission, *Study of Minority Group Employment in the Federal Government* (Washington, D.C.: Government Printing Office, 1967); appropriate volumes of the U.S. Civil Service Commission, *Annual Report* (Washington, D.C.: Government Printing Office).   *Data not available.

The Equal Employment Opportunity Act of 1972 calls for greater CSC activity. The CSC is to conduct annual reviews of agency equal-employment opportunity plans and to make on-site inspections. Agency plans are to include training programs to prepare minority employees for positions of greater responsibility.

Evaluation.   Data with which to trace the success of federal equal-employment opportunity exertions go back to 1962. As shown in Figure 1, the proportion of blacks in each set of General Schedule grades increased during the decade ending with 1972. The overrepresentation of blacks at the lowest levels became more pronounced, standing at 21.7 percent in 1972. At the GS 5–8 grade, the proportion of blacks almost doubled (to 15.0 percent) as they moved from underrepresentation to overrepresentation. Blacks remained underrepresented at the upper levels, although more than doubling at GS 9–11 to 5.9 percent and quadrupling at GS 12–18 to 3.2 percent. Despite the gains, the Commission on Civil Rights estimates that it will take another 35 years of progress at the 1967–70 pace before the proportion of blacks at the

GS 12–18 grade equals the proportion of blacks in the United States in 1970.[66] The disparity between blacks and whites is also visible in figures showing that the median GS grade for whites is 8.7 in contrast with a minority mean of 5.[67]

With blacks overrepresented in the two lower sets of grades (GS 1–4 and 5–8), emphasis should be placed on bringing more blacks into the upper half of the General Schedule jobs. Although Figure 1 shows that substantial progress has been made in the higher positions, the rate of improvement is slowing down. The rate at which blacks have gained GS 9–11 jobs has actually been lower since the 1965 executive order than it was during the preceding triennium.[68] Although blacks were added to the GS 12–18 ranks at a slightly higher rate after 1965, the first half of 1973 witnessed a reverse, which if continued for any length of time would bring the post-1965 rate for this group below the 1962–65 rate. This indicates that although improvements are being made, they are now coming more slowly.

Underrepresentation of blacks in the higher positions of federal employment stems from two factors. First, as noted in the discussion of private employment, there is a limited supply of blacks available for the better paying jobs. Second, the CSC has not done all that it could to expedite equal employment opportunities. It refused to acknowledge that goals and timetables might be useful tools until 1971,[69] thereby ignoring a useful—if not essential—benchmark for evaluating agency progress. For years the CSC accepted plans lacking statistical information essential for evaluation, and plans which had failed to bring progress in the past.[70] Moreover, while 1972 legislation called upon federal agencies to devise training programs to prepare minority employees for better jobs, the CSC has not required data on upward mobility programs by race, nor does it evaluate the programs. Finally, the CSC practices institutional racism. The Federal Service Entrance Examination, which screens applicants for more than 200 job categories, has not been validated as discrimination free. EEOC Chairman Brown charges that "the federal civil service entrance exam would be declared unlawful if it were used by private industry."[71]

The preceding evaluation reveals the CSC's performance to be flawed by the same voluntary approach as were the OFCC and the EEOC. Although executive orders seemed to empower CSC to require agency adoption of equal employment programs, the CSC demurred. Until 1972 it acted as a consultant rather than as an enforcer. "Despite [its] mandate, CSC's role under E.O. 11246 was characterized more by passivity rather than 'leadership'; more by neutrality than by 'guidance'."[72]

Not until 1972 did the commission begin to crack down. Since the commission has assumed a more active role, it has found large numbers of agencies to have defective affirmative action plans.[73] These efforts, if pursued, could eliminate many of the weaknesses in past CSC behavior.

Expanding Employment Opportunities

Equal employment programs have enabled many minority workers to obtain jobs on a par with their training. Blacks having adequate training or education can now, theoretically, enter apprenticeship and management trainee programs and rise as high as talents and ambition will carry them. But what of those who lack the requisite training? Removing racist barriers does little to broaden the horizon of men whose assets are limited to strong backs. The person who lacks marketable skills and is therefore a janitor, maid, or garbage collector will probably continue in that job long after his or her employer conscientiously embarks upon an affirmative action program. Nor will the elimination of employment discrimination benefit the minority person who has been unable to find work.

If untrained and uneducated members of the labor force are to maximize their contribution to the economy and to improve their own conditions, they must have the opportunity to realize their potential. In a period of economic growth, private employers may assume primary responsibility for training the unskilled. Private training programs are financially advantageous when their cost is exceeded by the cost of luring experienced workers away from other jobs. When, however, the demand for experienced workers is low, it is cheaper to hire them than to train the unskilled. At that point, if training programs are operated, they will be funded by the government. Since the unemployment rate has exceeded 4 percent for all but 4 of the last 20 years, federal training programs were needed during most if not all of the period. Unemployment rates for blacks—especially for young blacks—reveal that even during periods of high labor demand, large numbers of blacks lack jobs. Therefore if large numbers of minority members are to receive training, it will have to come from federal programs. While training programs offer hope for a better life to all untrained workers, the benefits may go disproportionately to blacks who are more likely to be poorly educated, to be unemployed, and to earn inadequate wages.

Since the early 1960s, numerous federal programs have been devised to upgrade the skills of the untrained. The programs differ in clientele. Some, like the Job Corps, have been aimed at the young whereas others, like Operation Mainstream, have been planned for older people who were out of work. Most projects are operated and paid for by the federal government, although in some the federal government acts in partnership with public or private employers. Although there are a number of manpower programs, they are of two general types. One type aims at imparting specific job skills through a structured training program. The other simply seeks to give work experience to people unaccustomed to the routine of a job. Of course participants in the latter type of program may acquire some job skills, but such a program is not organized to prepare enrollees for specific jobs. The most important of the federal job training programs will now be described and evaluated.

Structured Training Programs

Manpower Development and Training. The Manpower Development and Training Act of 1962 (MDTA) committed the federal government to retraining experienced workers who lost their jobs because of technological advances. In 1964 the Economic Opportunity Act reoriented the program to emphasize training the disadvantaged. Three years later welfare recipients became an important clientele for the MDTA. In FY 1973, 62 percent of the MDTA participants were economically disadvantaged.[74]

The bulk of MDTA resources have been directed into two types of training programs. Between September 1962, when MDTA training began, and June 1973, almost 1,390,000 people received institutional (classroom) training. Another 800,000 underwent on-the-job training (OJT). Black participation in MDTA institutional programs grew from 21.4 percent in FY 1963 to 45.4 percent in FY 1968, before sliding to 30.1 percent in FY 1973. During its first decade, 35.9 percent of all MDTA institutional enrollees were black, a figure three times as large as the black proportion of the total population but only slightly above the black proportion (31 percent in 1973) below the low-income level. Blacks have constituted a smaller proportion of OJT participants, ranging from 13.1 percent in FY 1963 to 35.4 percent in FY 1969 and then receding to 21.9 percent in FY 1973.

Black participation in MDTA programs peaked in the wake of the urban riots and slumped during the benign neglect of the Nixon presidency. The decline in black enrollments also coincides with the post-Vietnam economic slowdown. As white unemployment lines lengthened, blacks were being displaced from training programs.

Although evaluations of MDTA programs typically do not present data separately by race, if results are comparable across racial lines, then black graduates have benefited. Analyzing a sample of 1969 MDTA enrollees a year after training, Mangum found that mean income gains were $1,876 for institutional trainees and $1,614 for OJT.[75] Of those who were employed prior to MDTA training, institutional program participants experienced a mean increase in annual income of $841, whereas OJT completers experienced a mean increase of $921. Length of training correlated with income gains, with those who completed MDTA programs showing gains three times greater than the dropouts (although even the dropouts showed some improvement). A disappointing finding of Mangum's study was that mean post-training earnings hovered near or below the poverty level. Graduates of institutional programs earned $3,400, whereas those who had undergone OJT averaged $400 more.

In Mangum's sample, unemployment rates for the institutionalized trainees dropped from 34 to 10 percent, whereas the rates for OJT graduates dropped from 10 to 4 percent. Overall, during the first decade of MDTA, unemployment rates plummeted from 80.3 prior to training to 24.2 percent afterwards among institutionally trained and the rates dropped to 12.1 percent for those in OJT.[76] Nonwhites have, however, had lower rates of employment after training than have comparable whites.[77]

One very successful OJT program has been the Training and Technology (TAT) program operated by Oak Ridge Associated Universities to train workers for Atomic Energy Commission contractors.[78] A 1972 study of 472 TAT graduates found that 90.5 percent were employed at an average annual salary of $7,051; up from an average starting income of $5,990. (In 1971–72, 32.9 percent of the graduates were black.) The annual earnings of the 1971–72 class increased from a pretraining mean of $1,142 to $5,941. The higher earnings and greater increases for TAT than for MDTA in general may be attributable to TAT providing exclusively on-the-job training. Also wages are generally relatively high in the industry for which TAT prepares workers. Third, the TAT study was done two years after Mangum's.

An OJT effort aimed largely at minorities is the Opportunities Industrialization Centers of America (OIC).[79] Begun in Philadelphia in 1964, OICs are now in more than 100 cities and have trained 150,000 people. Job placements have been rather low with only 30 to 45 percent of the graduates finding work. Low job placements may be partially due to the unwillingness of some white employers to hire minorities. The 14,000 alumni of the program in Philadelphia average $5,500 a year, more than the mean found by Mangum, thus indicating OIC's success.

Job Opportunities in the Business Sector. Sponsored by the Department of Labor and the National Alliance of Business, Job Opportunities in the Business Sector (JOBS) provides on-the-job training in the private sector. Operating in 163 cities, 823,000 people were placed with 20,000 companies between June 1968 and December 1971.[80] JOBS will reimburse businessmen for added costs incurred in training disadvantaged workers enrolled in the federally financed portion of the program. However, more than half of the JOBS trainees have been in programs fully financed by the private employer. (These are participants in the JOBS-Optional Program which accepts as many as 50 percent advantaged. The federally supported aspect of JOBS is limited exclusively to the disadvantaged.) As in the MDTA programs, the proportion of blacks in JOBS has declined in recent years; dropping from 77.5 percent in FY 1969 to 40.5 percent in FY 1973.[81]

Since JOBS provides on-the-job training, each person placed by the Department of Labor automatically has a job. In the absence of production cutbacks by cooperating employers, those who complete the training have jobs with a future. Since participants are assured of jobs, it is disappointing that only half of the enrollees complete the training program.[82]

Job Corps. At its inception, the Job Corps was modeled after the Civilian Conservation Corps, with large numbers of rural camps where enrollees worked on conservation projects. More recent emphasis has been on urban training centers, and many rural camps have been closed. Training provided in urban centers is more likely to prepare the participants for our increasingly urban society. In addition to job training, corpsmen are offered educational programs intended to upgrade their verbal and quantitative skills, to provide counseling, and to improve their health care. By FY 1973, more than 400,000 people had entered the Job Corps. In that year 59.2 percent of the corpsmen were black.

The Job Corps has been widely criticized and was threatened with dismemberment during the War on Poverty's great retreat in the late 1960s. Critics have pointed to antisocial behavior at some training centers, high costs, and high dropout rates. One cannot but wonder to what extent criticisms are prompted by the fact that three-quarters of the corpsmen are from minority groups. Even if one acknowledges some merit in the charges, criticism must be tempered by a recognition of the nature of the raw material which is recruited. In FY 1973, 28 percent of the corpsmen had had less than 9 years of education and fewer than 10 percent were high school graduates.[83] In FY 1972 they were the poorest participants in the training programs, with 39.8 percent coming from families having annual incomes of less than $1,000. A third of them had been arrested and 64 percent had been asked to leave school. These data indicate that the Job Corps is trying to reclaim young people who have severe handicaps. That they would be expensive to train and at times unruly is hardly surprising. Despite the obstacles, 78 percent of the youth completing the Job Corps in FY 1973 found jobs, joined the armed services, or re-entered school.[84] Out of those who found jobs, the whites generally earned more than the blacks.[85]

Work Experience Programs

Neighborhood Youth Corps. The Neighborhood Youth Corps (NYC) has the largest enrollment of the manpower programs. This program provides public service jobs for poor youth 16 to 21 years old who are out of school, and after-school and summer jobs for students. In FY 1973, 48.4 percent of the students and 44.2 of the nonstudents were black. NYC helps students earn enough money to stay in school if currently enrolled and to return if they have dropped out. Remedial education and counseling are offered both sets of participants.

The program has remained popular with Congress and has continued to grow, even though answers to questions raised in cost-benefit analyses are mixed. While NYC is supposed to be providing work experiences which will prepare enrollees for meaningful participation in the labor market, many enrollees are given make-work jobs.[86] This, coupled with low wages (enrollees earn the minimum wage), results in many program dropouts. However, Borus et al. report that nonstudent males experience significant gains in earnings after completing NYC.[87] Among students, NYC participation is associated with a greater likelihood of graduation among black females and a greater likelihood of attending college among black male high-school graduates.[88] Still needed are thorough appraisals of the success of NYC in luring dropouts back to school.

Work Incentive. The Work Incentive Program (WIN) is designed to place welfare recipients (especially women)[89] in gainful employment, freeing them from dependence on welfare. Because it promised to reduce welfare rolls while simultaneously improving its participants' standards of living, WIN was given special emphasis during the Nixon presidency. Since many program enrollees are mothers, WIN subsidizes day care centers at which children can stay while their mothers are being trained and then later when they are working. While in the program, participants can avail themselves of various social services, including remedial education and health care.

Recipients of Aid to Families with Dependent Children (AFDC) are required to register for WIN participation. Exceptions are extended to mothers of children under 6, youth under 16, students, the ill, and the elderly. AFDC mothers who get jobs can retain a portion of their welfare benefits, with the amount of welfare declining as wages increase. This is a notable deviation from earlier procedures which terminated all benefits once earnings reached a specified level (well below what would be necessary for a minimally decent standard of living).

Funds are available to employers who subsidize WIN on-the-job training. Additionally, tax credits equal to a fifth of the wages paid WIN workers are extended to employers who keep WIN completers in non-subsidized jobs for a year. A tax break is also available to employers providing day care facilities.

By the end of FY 1973, 644,600 trainees had entered WIN programs, 41 percent of whom were black.[90] While both private and public employers can participate, private on-the-job training is increasingly preferred by program administrators. During the first quarter of FY 1973, there were almost 7 privately employed trainees for each public one.

WIN has not met its proponents' hopes that it would enable one million people to become self-supporting. During the first two years, 41 percent of the enrollees dropped out and only 7 percent earned enough to no longer receive welfare.[91] Even after several changes were implemented, the proportion of the program participants who worked their way off welfare rolls was still under 10 percent in FY 1973.[92] The program's performance was particularly poor as it related to blacks who made up 45 percent of the participants but only 26 percent of those who worked their way off welfare.

The program has suffered from a number of defects. It has not attracted as many trainees as had been expected, partially because only half of the needed day care facilities have been developed, thus preventing interested mothers from enrolling. A second problem has been that the jobs for which WIN trainees are prepared often pay very little. For example, WIN trainees in the District of Columbia are frequently prepared for federal GS 2 positions. As Steiner shows, the earnings of a GS 2 are so low that despite the program's name, there is little financial incentive for a mother to forgo food stamps, Aid to Families with Dependent Children, and free lunches for her school-age children in order to take a job.[93] Indeed, mothers with three or more children may have *a lower standard of living* once the costs of transportation, office clothing, and baby sitting are deducted. As the Department of Labor recognized, WIN "succeeded in moving only modest numbers of [welfare recipients] into stable employment."[94]

A third problem has been that the program probably does little to increase the supply of jobs available for WIN completers.[95] Since these people leave the programs with few skills, WIN may simply be enticing people into the labor market who are prepared to compete for a shrinking supply of jobs.

Fourth, placement of WIN enrollees is contingent upon employer bias. Indeed a 1972 study found that the type of training received was a less important correlate of job placement than were local attitudes toward WIN participants.[96] Middle-class biases against welfare recipients and minorities reduce the opportunities available to WIN trainees.

Concentrated Employment Program. The Concentrated Employment Program (CEP) represents a merger of Department of Labor and OEO efforts to serve the employment needs of ghettos and impoverished rural areas. CEPs are usually operated by community action agencies, local administrative units created to handle War on Poverty programs.[97] Areas with CEPs provide a coordinated smorgasbord of manpower programs in which the state Employment Service offers counseling, testing, and job placement through NYC, Public Service Careers, and other training programs.

By the end of FY 1973, CEP had enrolled 537,300 poor people. Of the FY 1973 enrollees, 94 percent were unemployed and 38.3 percent had been without jobs for more than half a year and 99 percent were classified as impoverished. CEP enrolled more blacks in FY 1973 (58 percent) than did any other manpower program except the Job Corps. In the course of its six years, more than 60 percent of CEP trainees were black.

During FY 1973 CEP was moderately successful when compared with other programs. The proportion of enrollees who obtained jobs, 65 percent, was slightly above that for all the Department of Labor manpower programs.[98] CEP completers, however, were poorly compensated. Of six manpower programs for which average hourly earnings are available for FY 1973, CEP graduates were among the poorest paid, averaging $2.33 an hour. CEP was, however, the only program in which blacks earned more than whites ($2.33 to $2.28). Nonetheless black graduates averaged $93.20 for a 40-hour week, a scant $14 a week above the 1971 average low-income for a nonfarm family of four.[99]

Public Employment Program. Rising unemployment of the early 1970s led to the creation of the Public Employment Program (PEP), which was given $2.3 billion to fund public employment for two years. It had a triggering mechanism, dispersing funds to state and local agencies when national unemployment stood at 4.5 percent for three consecutive months, with additional funds available in areas experiencing three months of 6 percent unemployment.

PEP places less emphasis on training than do most manpower programs. Its objective is to secure immediate employment for the jobless, especially Vietnam veterans and those who have completed manpower training. This is not exclusively a short-range, stopgap program like the Works Progress Administration of the Depression. Participating state and local agencies must agree to keep at least half of their PEP participants employed for a year *after* the program's funds expire.

PEP workers averaged $2.89 an hour during FY 1972, a figure which leads the Department of Labor to conclude that, on the average, they began with slightly better than entry level jobs.[100] PEP men averaged $.09 an hour less than in their last jobs, but women enjoyed a $.70 an hour increase over previous wages. The relatively good wages earned by PEP enrollees—compared with those of participants in other programs—are partially a product of "creaming," (that is, not ministering to the worst-off strata).

Although all PEP participants during FY 1972 were either unemployed (91.2 percent) or underemployed, a smaller proportion (37.6 percent) qualified as disadvantaged than in other programs. Because

PEP emphasized immediate employment instead of training, and made no funds available for purchasing equipment, public agencies tended not to hire low-skill personnel.

PEP would be of little benefit if upon completion of a stint in the program people were unable to find jobs. If this were the case, the program would simply delay the hardships which accompany unemployment. Happily, of a national sample of PEP completers, 73 percent had jobs or were in training programs within a month after leaving PEP.

Given the wages paid enrollees and the success of placement after completion, one would hope that blacks would be heavily represented in PEP. However, only 26.1 percent of PEP members were black in FY 1973. This was 50 percent below the average for all manpower programs that year.

The Emergency Employment Act of 1971 funded PEP through 1973. The high levels of unemployment in 1973 coupled with gloomy predictions for 1974, produced strong congressional support for extending PEP. Before accepting President Nixon's manpower revenue-sharing legislation, Congress extracted presidential approval of a continuation of PEP through FY 1977. During this extension, PEP funds will be available for public service employment in areas where unemployment exceeds 6.5 percent (2 percentage points above the threshold in the 1971 legislation). The 1973 Act is less well-financed than the earlier law. While $2.3 billion was authorized in 1971, the first two years under the 1973 law have only $600 million earmarked for public service jobs. Obviously, although it has been continued for four more years, it will be a more restricted program.

Comprehensive Employment and Training Act of 1973. Legislation extending PEP also moved manpower programs in the direction of Nixon's new federalism. The Department of Labor, while retaining general supervisory responsibilities, will no longer operate manpower programs through the almost 11,000 contractors. Henceforth, programs are to be run by some 500 prime sponsors, that is, state and local government units with populations of at least 100,000. This does not exclude the involvement of community organizations, which can still operate programs such as Opportunities Industrialization Centers. Community agencies will, however, be dependent on the state or city as a conduit for funds.

In the wake of the 1973 legislation, a number of manpower programs which focused on specific sectors of the unemployed will be swept away. Prime sponsors will be allowed to spend funds on what they perceive to be the greatest needs in their locales. Prime sponsors will have the option of sponsoring on-the-job training or classroom programs, or of putting the unemployed to work on public service projects.

Revenue-sharing, with few strings attached, provides leeway to create programs maximally responsive to local problems. It will be interesting to see whether the designers' expectations are realized. That is, will the programs run by prime sponsors result in higher rates of job placement and in better compensation (adjusted for changes in the cost of living) than did the categorical programs which have been supplanted? Or will money be used to hire the unemployed to perform menial functions with no efforts made at improving job skills.

Manpower Program Impact

Data presented thus far show that manpower training has helped participants, particularly those who have completed the programs. Available research indicates that graduates' earnings increase after participating in the programs. Also it appears that employment rates rise for completers. Nonetheless there appear to be several shortcomings in the operation of manpower programs. Latest data reveal that more than a third of the people who leave manpower training programs do not find work. Moreover wages earned by program completers are often meager. Criticism can be directed at four aspects of these programs.

Objectives. In most manpower programs, the primary objective has been quantity rather than quality. Efforts to maximize the number of new enrollees result in people not spending long in manpower programs. By 1973 the average time spent in an institutional MDTA program was down to 3.4 months, far short of the 24 month maximum authorized.[101] Since many of the enrollees are woefully unprepared for work, a quick exposure to training, education, health care, and counseling is often inadequate. A partial remedy would be to either increase funding or spend the same amount of funds on fewer people who would receive longer, more intensive preparation.

Generally it has been found that length of training is associated with income gains.[102] Certainly if the preparation of skilled workers becomes the objective, more extensive training will be necessary. Technological advances make short programs geared to preparing low-skill workers less and less desirable. As Vivian Henderson has said, "In a significant way, we trained blacks to move from unskilled unemployment to various shades of skilled unemployment and underemployment."[103] This points up another deficiency in part of the manpower effort. Too often there has been little relationship between the jobs for which enrollees are prepared and the needs of employers.

Technique. The first of the manpower programs was oriented toward skill preparation. More recently the emphasis has been on work experience. In FY 1973, there were 1,117,700 new enrollees in work experience programs compared with 362,000 new enrollees in structured training programs.[104] Funding also reflects the priority given to work experience programs, which receive more than 75 percent of the FY 1973 manpower budget.

Current evidence suggests that training program graduates are more likely to find employment and earn higher wages than are those who have been through work experience programs. People who have received OJT seem to do particularly well. Follow-up surveys find up to 90 percent of OJT graduates have jobs. In FY 1973, MDTA–OJT completers averaged higher wages per hour than other groups. Moreover there is evidence that in the absence of skill training, the provision of basic education in manpower programs does little to enhance income or job-holding ability.[105]

Davis offers a particularly damning evaluation of the work experience emphasis.

> [W]e may say that the long-run effects of present training and manpower policies will contribute to a perpetuation of black community poverty by giving the illusion of effective training programs. This is true because the bulk of the trainees are in the "work experience" type of programs, which are (1) specifically designed to get Negroes off relief rolls into poorly paid jobs (for example, the Work Incentive Program) or (2) to get Negroes into low-paying jobs before they get on welfare (for example, the Neighborhood Youth Corps).[106]

Clientele.   Manpower programs are not aimed at those most in need, ignoring people who have multiple problems. Some careful students of manpower training conclude that "MDTA–OJT has never been able to prove conclusively that its trainees were any different in characteristics and needs from those the employer would have hired in the absence of any subsidy."[107] Other programs have engaged in varying amounts of "creaming." One suspects that the frequency of not completing programs is positively associated with the number and degree of problems which the enrollee had prior to entering the program. Consequently manpower programs may fail to attract or to retain many people who desperately need them.

Size.   By the end of FY 1973 manpower programs had enrolled more than 9.6 million people.[108] This is an impressive number, more than 10 percent of the labor force. However from another perspective, one could judge the enrollments insufficient. Whether the millions of jobless men and women have undergone job training or not, it is obvious that manpower programs have not lived up to their advance billing. Millions of people remain on the periphery of the economy, unable to maximize their economic potential and enjoy a fuller life. Consequently one can argue that manpower training should be expanded until all those who can benefit from it are able to find work. In this vein, an evaluation of the Work Incentive Program, which by FY 1973 had become the largest program serving adults, concluded that "it remains a small program in relation to the size of the problem it addresses."[109] Estimates are that current manpower programs reduce the overall unemployment rate by less than 0.5 percent.[110] This is inadequate in light of present needs.

Demand For Labor

Despite training programs, black unemployment remains approximately twice as high as white unemployment. The surges and declines of the white economy appear as late afternoon shadows, enlarged and distorted, when the impact on blacks is traced. In January 1975, the familiar pattern of much higher black unemployment persisted with 13.4 percent of the black and 8.5 percent of the white labor force out of work.

Figure 2 shows that between 1960 and 1974, the total unemployment rate has fluctuated between 3.5 and 6.7 percent. While rates of under 4 percent may conform with notions of full employment, total labor force figures reveal that nothing even approaching full employment has ever been achieved among blacks. When, thanks to the Vietnam War, the white rate bottomed out at 3.1 percent in 1969, it stood at 6.4 percent for blacks. In 1974 when 5.0 percent of the white labor force was jobless, 9.9 percent of the black labor force was out of work.

Discouraging as these figures are, they tell only part of the story. A complete picture of black employment requires consideration of two additional factors. First, high unemployment discourages some people from even seeking work, so they are no longer counted as part of the labor force. Keyserling suggests that because of what he labels the "concealed unemployment" of labor force dropouts, real unemployment rates may be double the official figures.[111] Blacks are disproportionately represented among discouraged workers, constituting a fourth of those leaving the labor market but only a ninth of the labor force.[112] Second, some of those who have jobs can find only part-time work. This sub-employment rate was found to reach 6.9 percent in a 1966 study of slum areas and is probably higher today.[113]

Figure 2 presents another bit of dismal information, the unemployment rates of nonwhite teenagers. Even the economic stimulus of the Vietnam War brought the unemployment rate for these youth no lower than 24 percent. The cooling economy of peace (or more accurately, United States disengagement) caused the rate to soar to 33.5 percent in 1972, the highest in decades. The 1973 rate, 30.3 percent, was more than 2.25 times that of whites.

To evaluate the problem of unemployment, we must determine the minimum level to which unemployment can be reduced. There is always

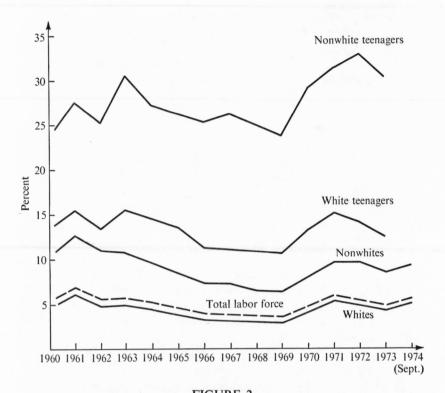

FIGURE 2
Unemployment Rates by Race for Entire Labor Force and for Teenagers,
1960–1974. SOURCE: Department of Labor, *Manpower Report of the President*
(Washington, D.C.: Government Printing Office, 1973), pp. 133–135.

some frictional unemployment, that is, people changing from one job
to another. Economists, beginning with Phillips, have noted a trade off
between employment and inflation. When the supply of labor is insufficient to meet demands, competition for workers will lead to higher
wages which translate into higher consumer prices. The point at which
labor becomes so scarce that competition for it produces inflation is
subject to debate. Study of the British labor market led Phillips to conclude that relative price stability was possible with unemployment as
low as 2.5 percent.[114] Thus full employment does not mean that the
unemployment rate will stand at zero but only that joblessness beyond
the level of frictional unemployment will be eliminated.

Since World War II, full employment has been endorsed as part of
our national policy. The Employment Act of 1946 stated as an objective,

> All Americans able to work and seeking to work have the right to useful,
> remunerative, regular and full-time employment, and it is the policy of the
> United States to assure the existence at all times of sufficient employment
> opportunities to enable all Americans to freely exercise this right.

While we ostensibly retain this goal, the definition of maximum employment has been redefined. Little is heard of achieving unemployment rates of 2.5 or 3 percent. Government planners now cite 4.0 to as high as 5.5 percent unemployment as acceptable. Experience indicates that if national unemployment is at this level, there will be at least eight percent unemployment among blacks.

Gösta Rehn, internationally known manpower specialist, points out that 4.5 percent unemployment would be unthinkable in Europe.[115] Some American economists are also critical of the willingness to tolerate higher unemployment. In the words of former Labor Secretary Wirtz, "This country is getting dangerously close to the view that unemployment is a price of peace, or technological advancement, and of economic stabilization."[116] To opt for high unemployment is to assess a disproportionately large share of the presumed cost for controlling inflation on society's unfortunates. It is middle-class complacency at its worst which leads to acceptance of four million unemployed (4.5 percent of the 1973 civilian labor force unemployed).

The notion that at least 4 percent unemployment is necessary to achieve stable prices can be challenged. Since unemployment rates are not constant across racial, occupational, or social lines, an overall rate of 4 percent masks wide variations. For example, in early 1974, the percent unemployed ranged from 1.8 for managers and administrators to 24.8 among construction laborers and from 1.8 percent in the communications and utilities industries to 14.1 percent in the construction industry.[117] Clearly there were large numbers of people laid off by the construction industry who could take jobs before unemployment in that industry dropped to 4 percent. Our wage-pull inflation is not fueled by a general scarcity of labor but by bidding for the services of workers in specific occupations in which supply is insufficient, such as managers and administrators. Thus even in 1968 when total unemployment had receded to 3.6 percent, there was unacceptably high unemployment among operatives (4.5 percent), service workers (4.4 percent) and laborers (7.2 percent). Therefore 4 percent unemployment, or even lower rates, should not be accepted as necessary unless there is evidence that the incidence of unemployment is fairly constant across occupations and industries.

It should be feasible to retrain and find work for people in high unemployment occupations without producing rampant inflation. Where high demand occupations have relatively low-skill prerequisites, the unemployed could be placed immediately and learn on the job. Occupations in which high demand exists but for which there are extensive prerequisites might be filled through an upgrading strategy. Workers one step below those for whom demand is great could be prepared for advancement, with the same process being repeated at each lower level to provide candidates to fill vacated jobs. Ultimately the process would create vacancies in entry level positions for which the untrained could be prepared. Repeating this cycle would allow ambitious workers who had obtained entry level jobs in a previous cycle to become candidates for advancement rather than being locked into the least rewarding jobs. A second attribute which should be included in programs to provide workers for occupations in which there is demand would be to facilitate relocation. This would enable the jobless to move from job-scarce areas, for example, from Appalachia or urban ghettos to locales where the demand for labor is brisk.

The recondite workings of the current economy have dealt with the poor more cruelly than does the undulating of the Phillips curve. Higher unemployment has not been offset by stable prices as the Phillips' model predicts, but instead has been paralleled by rising prices (the Consumer Price Index has risen from 106.7 to 156.0 between January 1969 and January 1975). Many lower-class blacks who have been particularly hard hit by rising prices have had their hardships intensified by the drying up of the labor market.

The surplus of labor, particularly among people with minimal skills or education, can adulterate the effect of training programs. Without an economy which can absorb those who have recently undergone training programs, graduates may simply displace equally needy but less well-trained job incumbents. Instead of introducing general improvements to the lower strata of society, manpower training may stimulate struggles for a place on the bottom rung of the economic ladder. Another consequence of a sluggish economy is that some recent trainees will find no work. In FY 1972, only 45 percent of manpower program terminations were followed by employment.[118]

The failings of current manpower policies to resolve the problems of those in the lower ranks of the labor force has become compounded as the 1974–75 recession deepens. A weakened economy generates few new jobs, causing employers to hire fewer graduates of training programs. Private concerns may also become less willing to sponsor on-the-job training if faced with laying off regular employees, due to declining demand for the goods they produce. In addition to slack demand for new trainees, some past beneficiaries of manpower training will lose their jobs. To the extent that the graduates of training programs are relatively low in seniority, they are more likely to be laid off as companies retrench. In industries which have recently expanded black employment opportunities, black workers may be disproportionately among those thrown out of work.

It seems unlikely that the economy as it now functions can provide employment for all graduates of job-training programs, much less achieve full employment. Therefore we will now consider proposals for creating additional jobs.

Public Employment

An economic downturn, especially a full-scale depression, would lend support to pleas that the federal government become the employer of last resort. Proponents note that during the Great Depression, Works Progress Administration projects fulfilled this function, hiring people to perform a variety of public services ranging from raking leaves to painting murals in post offices. Advocates of the reinstitution of federal employment programs note the need for aides to help professionals in education, health care, recreation, law enforcement, and so on. An Office of Economic Opportunity study discovered the potential for hiring almost 4.3 million subprofessionals to provide public services.[119]

A major difference between the programs of the 1930s and the projects of the 1970s is that the WPA generally provided jobs for people who had been employed before the economic collapse and who had skills which would enable them to reenter the private labor market once demand made that possible. The intended beneficiaries of a 1970s public works program should include many who have previously been on either the fringes of private employment or unemployed. Moreover, it is possible that for some people public works employment, instead of being an emergency measure, would become permanent.

The possibility that some people might be permanently employed on public works projects is not inherently bad. It would be a problem only if the jobs offered no opportunity for advancement. As manpower specialists generally recognize, an essential aspect of the training–job opportunity sequence is that the job not be a dead end.[120] Consequently, while there is a need to provide various professionals in public employment with assistants, it may not suffice to meet the needs of the aides if their positions are on one-rung advancement ladders. Unfortunately most of the types of jobs which are suggested for employing the jobless do not, in our contemporary job structure, constitute apprenticeships for positions having greater authority and commensurate rewards. Teachers' aides do not generally become teachers, nor do nurses' aides become nurses.

Although some aides to professionals will find their positions sufficiently rewarding, others will want promotions. A survey of workers in 1972–73 found that blacks wanted promotions more often than did whites.[121] Blacks, however, perceived their chances of promotion as less favorable than did whites. Therefore to bolster morale, a public employment program should provide means by which the person hired as an aide can at least earn salary increases. It should be possible to establish programs through which the ambitious could prepare for promotions to more demanding jobs. For example, the agency could subsidize a training program or credit work experience toward advanced certification.

Although public employment offers the best chance for absorbing large numbers of unemployed workers, there are proposals for expanding black job opportunities on a smaller scale. Two of these involve channeling the money spent by blacks to black-owned businesses.

Black Capitalism

The proposal of black capitalism enjoyed some popularity during the early days of the Nixon Administration. It involved lending money to blacks who wanted to open or expand businesses in the ghetto. These businesses, it was hoped, would facilitate retention by blacks of some of the money (estimated at 80 percent or more of black expenditures) which currently flows from black consumers to white businesses.[122] The proposal also included the idea that expenditures to supply, maintain, or build public facilities in the ghetto go through black middlemen or directly to black suppliers and contractors. As a step in this direction, federal agencies annually purchase more than $50 million worth of goods and services from minority firms under noncompetitive contracts.[123] Since these businesses probably could not compete with larger white firms, these contracts build in a subsidy. Money remaining in the ghetto would, hopefully, create additional jobs and funds for community development. In time some black concerns might compete outside the ghetto for white dollars.

It will not be easy to develop programs which will succeed, since the needs of black capitalism are great.

> Black capitalism, if it is to succeed, requires the finding and training of black entrepreneurs and managers, a radically liberalizing set of criteria for lending, bonding, and providing insurance of all kinds, and large-scale technical assistance and the identification and cultivation of profitable market opportunities. It will further require sheltered markets and subsidies reaching the heights of $20–$30 billion per year, a sustained white corporate involvement and partnership, and a reversal of the flow of capital and other resources from the central city to the suburbs.[124]

The federal response, while sometimes grand in rhetoric, has been limited in funds. Beginning in 1964 the Small Business Administration offered loans of up to $25,000 to people who would open businesses in depressed areas or who would hire minorities. Efforts were accelerated during the last days of the Johnson Administration. Under Project OWN, loans reached an annual rate of $100 million, and by guaranteeing 90 percent of the loans, the Small Business Administration induced banks to make available more funds for minority entrepreneurs. Another source of federal funds has been the purchase of shares in Minority Enterprise Small Business Investment Companies which make low-interest loans to minority businessmen.

Programs of this magnitude are unlikely to have anything more than marginal impact. Even greater efforts would not meet the job needs of blacks.

> If it achieved even the most optimistic expectations, the new jobs created would account for only slightly more than half of the growth in the Negro labor force. So, in 1980, black capitalists would be able to employ no more than 12 percent (and in actuality probably a much smaller proportion) of the jobs Negroes would need.[125]

Achievements of even this size appear increasingly remote. Many businesses which in the wake of the riots made ghetto investments have been disengaging from their commitments. The economic slowdown of the 1970s has led them to retreat from such unprofitable ventures. Economic uncertainty also mitigates against the successful establishment of new black-owned enterprises.

Community Development Corporations

A number of blacks reject the capitalist model for ghetto development. Julian Bond has said of it, "Black capitalism seems to be an insurance policy offered by big business: 5 percent down so 95 percent won't be burned down."[126] Some fear that even if black capitalism succeeded in developing new black capitalists, the new class might exploit poorer blacks as white merchants and employers often have.

A substitute, developed by the Congress of Racial Equality, is the creation of community development corporations (CDCs).[127] CDCs would differ from black capitalism in several ways. Where capitalist ventures are evaluated on the profits earned, Tabb suggests that CDCs should be judged on the number of workers trained, the number of jobs created, or the number of homes built or rehabilitated.[128] Funding of CDCs could come from contributions of the federal government and industry, from the sale of shares to local residents, and from the sale of goods and services by CDC businesses. The 1968 Community Self-Determination Bill proposed the establishment of community development banks and a financing system like the Farm Credit System to fund CDC enterprises.

The business ventures would vary. "The corporation would own a family of businesses, which might range from a shoe shine stand to a major factory. . . ."[129] Ultimately proponents of this idea would like to see CDCs attract a large share of the billions of dollars spent annually by blacks.[130] Some portion of whatever profits earned by CDC businesses could be plowed back into the community in day care facilities, recreation programs, and other improvements of services.

Although there would be problems in establishing CDCs, the idea has merit. If federally provided seed money underwrote viable minority

businesses and thereby expanded the minority job market, the investment would be sound indeed. CDCs could reduce the reliance upon a
strong economy and public service jobs as techniques of black employment. Although an experiment with CDCs seems preferable to the
status quo, recent administrations have been chary of the program.[131]

A Proposal to Improve Black Employment

In this part four prerequisites to improving the situation of black
labor and methods of providing these prerequisites will be discussed.
The prerequisites are the removal of racial barriers, increased employability, adequate employee rewards, and sufficient demand.

Racial Barriers

Strides have been made toward achieving equal employment opportunity. Conscientious application of the available tools should largely
eliminate racist obstacles. Progress could be accelerated by requiring
all employers—private and public—subject to the 1972 Equal Employment Opportunity Act to submit goals and timetables for minority
employment. Time-frames would of course vary, with more time allowed
for employing black professionals than for having a black sales and
clerical staff equal to the proportion of blacks in the area's labor force.

Although setting specific objectives is often essential to fully desegregate a labor force, success will require an effective enforcement
mechanism. Employers will have to be convinced that enforcement
officers consider the goals to be serious obligations and not simply good
intentions. Because of the laxity characteristic of much of the fair employment enforcement effort, it will be necessary to substantially increase
federal oversight efforts. Once federal commitment has been demonstrated, it may be possible to sustain momentum through spot checks of
reports filed by employers and through processing minority complaints.
To get the program underway, however, something more aggressive
than complaint processing will be needed.

In conjunction with mandatory goals and timetables, a thorough
validation of employment prerequisites is necessary. Reliance on educational requirements and aptitude scores, while simplifying the chores
of personnel managers, disproportionately exclude minorities. Therefore employers should be required to discard educational and other
prerequisites which disadvantage minorities *until* such requirements have
been shown to be essential to the functioning of the organization.
Eliminating all prerequisites and placing the burden on the employer
to justify their reimposition should have more effect than does challenging specific requirements on a case-by-case basis.

Even if job prerequisites are bias free, employers must try to recruit black workers. Because of past discrimination, many blacks doubt whether they will be employed even after a firm adopts an equal employment program.[132] Consequently enlarging the number of black workers may necessitate active recruiting in black schools and neighborhoods. Retention of newly hired blacks may require the development of greater understanding among white supervisors.

Employability

As used here "employability" is broadly defined. It includes skill preparation and undertaking to juxtapose geographically black workers and jobs. Experience from manpower programs points toward investing more resources in structured training programs. Providing on-the-job training seems to hold the greatest promise for subsequent job security. In designing training programs, careful attention should be paid to present and future demands of the labor market so as to insure, in so far as is possible, that jobs will be available for program completers. Once manpower programs develop a reputation for placing graduates, they may have fewer dropouts.

Achievement of employability will probably require longer and more intensive training. Technological change is constantly reducing the demand for low-skill workers who can be quickly turned out by manpower programs. Costs will also rise if manpower training serves those who are least prepared to compete in the labor market. As recruitment reaches further down, increasing numbers of participants will require counseling, behavioral preparation, basic education, and medical treatment, in addition to job training. Full-scale commitment to preparing all who seek jobs for today's and tomorrow's labor market will require meeting these needs.

A broad-gauge manpower effort should not limit itself to those currently unemployed. A preventive approach dictates paying greater attention to high school vocational training. Courses and experiences which would prepare students for jobs might reduce high school dropout rates and constitute a better use of school tax dollars. Another set of people who should be the concern of manpower program planners are the employed whose skills will soon become obsolete. A far-sighted program would identify these occupations and make available to these workers opportunities to prepare themselves for jobs for which there is a demand.

An adjunct to training is that completers be able to take available jobs. Urban sprawl, with blacks living in core cities while many commercial and industrial enterprises locate in suburbia, divorces blacks from jobs. One corrective would be a substantial improvement in public transportation so that minorities could go from the ghettos to the jobs. Rising gasoline prices mitigate against ghetto residents who have cars driving great distances to work.

Other methods for bringing blacks and jobs together involve the location of moderately priced housing, plants, or both. The Department of Housing and Urban Development has taken tentative steps toward expanding black housing opportunities in suburbia. Its open communities concept encouraged the development of suburban tracts with inexpensive housing. A less direct approach made the receipt of funds for several HUD programs, for example, urban renewal, contingent upon a city having a program for expanding inexpensive housing and eliminating discrimination. The first program never really got off the ground. The second fell victim to Nixon's New Federalism, which denied funding to categorical community development programs beginning in January 1973. These programs were recently replaced with no-strings-attached block grants.[133] Without either incentives for broadening housing options or federal efforts to create suburban housing for minorities and the low- to moderate-income groups, suburban communities are unlikely to act on their own.

If blacks are not given an opportunity to live in suburbia near the jobs, an alternate strategy would be to locate factories in or near the ghetto. It was once hoped that urban renewal land would be used for this purpose; however, businesses have been reluctant to build on these sites. Consequently, further incentives to induce businesses into the core city will have to be offered. Inducements might include federal tax breaks or dispensations from local property taxes for a specified term.

Intrametropolitan mobility will not solve the needs of the jobless living in depressed areas. For them, federal loans could be provided to facilitate relocation to regions in which labor demands are stronger.

A very different aspect of job access involves poor mothers who wish to work.[134] For some of them, jobholding is not feasible in the absence of reliable, inexpensive day care facilities. A need exists both for all-day care of pre-schoolers and late afternoon supervision of students.

Employee Rewards

Manpower programs cannot be fully effective if they simply prepare people for low-paying, dead-end jobs. A person may be willing to work at a hard, low-status, and even boring, task if he sees it as a stepping-stone to greater rewards. The ambitious will experience growing frustration if they see little likelihood of improving their position. Although the jobless manifest strong commitment to the work ethic, they quickly lose interest if they perceive a job to be "made work."[135]

In so far as possible, manpower programs should concentrate on preparing people for jobs which offer opportunities for advancement. Manpower programs could augment employer or union programs to facilitate the development of skills leading to better pay for those who are currently employed. For example, workers might be able to progress, in time, from being aides to becoming paraprofessionals, and ultimately to becoming professionals. Where promotions to positions of greater responsibility are not likely, workers should at least be eligible for merit salary increases. Moreover, personnel managers and supervisors could redefine some jobs so that workers have some discretion in performing their work. This would also contribute to a greater sense of dignity and pride.

Sufficiency of Demand for Labor

If proper planning goes into designing manpower programs, part of this need will be met, that is, people will not be trained for nonexistent jobs. Nonetheless, even the best planning cannot avoid dislocations caused by recession. To meet such exigencies, the federal government should be able to hire, or underwrite state and local hiring of, the jobless. While performing these tasks, workers could, when appropriate, be preparing themselves for other jobs or upgrading their skills for more demanding tasks. Hopefully people in these jobs could be equipped either to return to private employment or to take decent paying positions within the public sector.

Community development corporations and other proposals for creating more black jobs should be tested. Instead of spreading appropriations thinly across a number of communities, it would be better to launch well-funded experimental programs in several urban areas. Whites who are displaced should be compensated for losses and offered relocation assistance or retraining.

Of more basic concern, however, is the maintenance of a strong economy. In the absence of this, public service projects will be glutted with applicants and community development corporations will be starved for consumer dollars. Manpower programs could be designed (perhaps along lines proposed earlier) so as to permit unemployment to be reduced to lower levels without fueling wage-pull inflation. This would provide jobs for thousands of additional blacks.

Unemployables

Thus far I have dealt with efforts to improve the position of those in the labor market. Even complete realization of the goals of fair employment and manpower programs would leave blacks disproportionately

among the nation's poorest citizens. Adequate training opportunities
and a plentitude of discrimination-free jobs would not benefit American
families who have no one in the labor force. The aged, the lame, and
husbandless mothers and their children would continue to eke out an
existence on the dregs of the world's most productive economy.

In 1971, 39 percent of the elderly blacks (those over 65) were impoverished, as were 41 percent of the children under 14. More than half
(53 percent in 1973) of the black female-headed families are poor.[136]
Blacks constitute 11 percent of the nation's population but account for
31 percent of all families below the low-income level and 38 percent of
the families receiving public assistance.

The nation's poor, especially those who cannot work, are eligible for
one or more welfare programs. Categorical assistance programs provide
money for the aged, families with dependent children, the permanently
disabled, and the blind. Those who have previously worked may be able
to draw Social Security and Medicare benefits. Some poor people participate in programs which reduce their expenses for food and housing.

Although there are a number of programs, they are all subject to the
same criticism. In the words of Mitchell Ginsberg, "The Welfare system
is designed to save money instead of people and tragically ends up doing
neither."[137] Problems with the current system are so great that making
minor adjustments is not acceptable. Primary difficulties relate to the
inadequacy of the benefits reaching the needy:

1. The benefits per person vary extensively from state to state and within
   states. In 1969 the eleemosynary impulse registered $10 per month
   per AFDC recipient in Mississippi. The largess of New Jersey, $65
   per month, was the most generous.[138] A second variation involves not
   the amount but the existence of benefits. Food stamps which are
   sold at a discount to the poor and thereby increase their purchasing
   power are unavailable in some counties. While food stamps enable
   their users to buy more, some poor people cannot afford them.[139]
2. Even within the same jurisdiction, families of comparable sizes and
   with comparable incomes may receive different amounts of benefits.
   For example, many people who qualify for public housing must wait
   months or years before a unit becomes available.
3. The ethos of welfare distribution mitigates against service. Welfare
   programs are riddled with suspicions that benefits may be going to
   those who could be self-supporting, save for their indolence. Because
   of the negative connotations and the verbal abuse and prying which
   recipients may have to endure, some of the eligible do not participate.
4. Benefits are structured so as to discourage outside earnings. Once
   recipients have even meager incomes, they may lose eligibility for
   welfare benefits. Consequently, as with the previously discussed WIN

graduates who could get GS 2 jobs, there is often little economic incentive to take jobs.

Any reforms of the present patchwork of welfare programs should be addressed to the above problems. The idea of a negative income tax geared to the cost of living seems to offer a better way. A negative income tax would provide a minimal income to everyone who makes less than a specified amount. The amount provided would be uniform throughout the country, subject to family size. Recipients of funds could be determined by the Internal Revenue Service from tax returns. This would eliminate the inconvenience and harassment which often accompany means tests. Simplifying the criteria for qualification, and supplanting contemporary programs with a single new one in which income and number of dependents would be the only criteria, would reduce administrative costs. Furthermore the benefits of the program should reach a much larger number of those who qualify.

Proponents typically set a relatively low figure to be received by anyone having no outside income. The Nixon Family Assistance Plan suggested $1,800 for a family of four, while President Ford has mentioned a more realistic figure of $3,600. Earnings would decrease benefits by a proportionate amount until a break-even point was reached. Thus, those who took part-time or low-paying work would retain some benefits —say 50 percent. An illustration of how a negative income tax works may be useful. Suppose that a family of four were to receive $3,600 as the basic amount from the federal government. For each two dollars earned by the family, its federal payment would be reduced by one dollar. Thus, if the family earned $1,000, its total income would be $4,100. Annual earnings of $2,000 would result in a total income of $4,600. Annual earnings of less than $7,200 would be augmented by federal funds. If the break-even income were this high, the negative income tax would help many of the 2 million American families who are poverty stricken even though the head of the family works full-time. A negative income tax would correct the problem described by Mangum: "For increasing numbers [of Americans], the choice between work and welfare is a real one, not because the latters' benefits are excessive, but because the former's are abysmal."[140]

Despite advantages of uniformity and lower administrative costs, as well as the built-in support of the Protestant work ethic, the negative income tax is an idea whose time has not yet come, although it may be approaching. Presently it appears as the most logical proposal for the future. Experimentation on the AFDC program—the most costly and least popular welfare program—has taken various forms, none of which has led to improvements.[141] Nontheless it is naive to believe that the old hodgepodge, unsatisfactory as it is, will be easily replaced.

Outlook for the Future

Recent events give an indication of what the immediate future holds. The most striking recent change was the implementation of manpower revenue sharing. Because of its newness and the flexibility allowed state and local governments, one can only guess about its consequences. The Comprehensive Employment and Training Act (CETA) calls for local development of program combinations best designed to meet the needs of each area's "economically disadvantaged, unemployed, and under-employed." Although the Secretary of Labor is authorized to approve plans and can terminate funding, this oversight may be loosely exercised. The latitude allowed is such that although the Assistant Secretary for Manpower doubts whether a prime contractor would spend all his funds on a single program, for example, subsidized public service jobs, this would be possible.[142] There is little assurance that greater emphasis will be given on-the-job training or that training programs will be geared to meeting the needs of the labor market.

Some black leaders view the shift in policy authority from federal to state and local officials with misgivings. Vernon Jordan has warned,

> The effect of revenue sharing on white people is likely to be harmful; for black people it promises to be devastating. The federal government has historically been the protector of minority citizens. While it has often been the frailest of reeds, historically it has been more responsive than state or local governments.[143]

The CETA seems designed to weaken not only federal control but also the influence of local poverty groups who have run some programs in the past.

Even if state and local officials act in the best of faith, the future is ominous. Funding for public employment has been slashed, and it is estimated that appropriations for manpower programs will grow at a pace slower than the rate of inflation.[144] This augurs ill for the development of innovative programs or establishment of lengthy training projects.

The outlook for more aggressive civil rights enforcement is somewhat better. Minority group employment in the federal government continues to grow at all levels, even as the size of the federal work force declines.[145] The EEOC is making much greater use of its authority to initiate suits. Improved liaison with state fair employment practices commissions should reduce the EEOC's work load, although this has not yet happened. If states become competent in resolving complaints of discrimination, the results may contribute to greater efficiency in complaint processing and simultaneously allow more time for affirmative action. Although comprehensive data are not yet available, all three of the agencies that have fair employment responsibilities seem to be increasingly requiring employers under their supervision to take affirmative action.

Rigorous administrative enforcement offers the best possibility of further progress, since the likelihood that additional equal employment standards will be legislatively imposed seems remote. As the job market becomes weaker, whites increasingly charge that they suffer from reverse discrimination. Whites' complaints that they lose promotions and jobs to less qualified blacks makes more stringent equal employment legislation unpalatable to most white congressmen. If the furor becomes too great, we may even see a decline in current levels of enforcement, comparable to what occurred in school desegregation after 1969. Already black employment quotas which were supposed to be rigidly enforced have been replaced with goals and timetables which are treated merely as objectives. The semantics may seem obscure but the effect is to reduce pressures on employers.

The area in which new legislation seems most likely is welfare reform. As the size of the budget appropriated for welfare has grown, there has been an accompanying crescendo of calls for corrective action. One possible reform would be for the federal government to assume responsibility for financing Aid to Familes with Dependent Children. This would provide uniformity in the amounts received by recipients in various states. A precedent for a federal takeover of AFDC came in 1973 when Congress replaced the federal–state matching programs, which aided the elderly, blind, and disabled, with full federal funding. Federal takeover of AFDC, while easing the burden on the states, would increase federal expenses.

Another possible reform is the adoption of some version of a negative income tax. The desirability of such a change would depend upon the level of benefits and the availability of aid under other programs. If a negative income tax was simply added to existing programs providing subsidized housing, food, and health care, smaller benefits would suffice. If, however, a negative income tax took the place of other aid programs, then more generous support would be needed. The path leading to enactment of a negative income tax is a narrow trail between conservative opposition to overly generous benefits and liberal opposition to penurious funding.

Harrell R. Rodgers, Jr.
UNIVERSITY OF HOUSTON

4

On Integrating the Public Schools: An Empirical and Legal Assessment

S ince 1954, school desegregation has been the focus of perhaps more litigation, legislation, administrative action, rhetoric, and controversy than all other areas of civil rights combined. Yet, by all signs, the struggle to desegregate schools has only begun. The struggle will continue because progress in school desegregation has been limited and because difficult questions and problems raised by school segregation in metropolitan areas and in Northern school districts are only beginning to be dealt with.

This chapter has a simple thesis: that school desegregation can be achieved in all American communities and that successful school desegregation will ultimately have positive consequences for American society. In an effort to establish the validity of this thesis, this chapter will (1) review the progress of school desegregation to identify the areas in which this conflict must expand in the future if full school desegregation is to be achieved; (2) identify the factors that have limited progress to suggest the obstacles that must be overcome if progress is to continue; (3) assess the current standards of the Supreme Court on school desegregation and speculate on the implications of these standards for achieving further desegregation in both Southern and Northern school districts; (4) evaluate the benefits of interracial school systems and the merits of some recent attacks on school desegregation; and (5) suggest some methods of facilitating school desegregation.

Progress

The starting point for school desegregation was the 1954 decision of the Supreme Court in *Brown* v. *Board of Education*.[1] In *Brown*, the Court ruled that dual school systems were inherently unequal and therefore unconstitutional. It ordered Southern school boards to dismantle the dual system "with all deliberate speed." Resistance was ubiquitous. Governors denounced the decision, state legislators subverted it, school boards ignored it, United States district courts frequently refused to enforce it, and President Eisenhower pleaded innocence in the whole matter.[2] Understandably, therefore, progress was slow, almost unusual. Ten years after *Brown*, 7 of the 11 Southern states had not placed even 1 percent of their black students into integrated schools.[3] As late as 15 years after the decision, only one of every six black students in the South attended a desegregated school.[4]

The first signs of real progress in school desegregation were not evident until the 1966–67 school year; in that year 12.5 percent of all black students in the 11 Southern states attended schools with whites.[5] A breakthrough in the stalemate over school desegregation was made possible by the 1964 Civil Rights Act. Title VI of this act provided that federal funds could be terminated in school districts that refused to desegregate, and the attorney general was given authority to file suit against recalcitrant districts. The Office for Civil Rights (OCR) in the Department of Health, Education and Welfare (HEW) was given responsibility for enforcing Title VI. The OCR formulated guidelines for desegregation and began to put pressure on those districts that failed to comply. As the guidelines were made sharper and the pressure on districts became more intense, progress began in earnest. In the 1967–68 school year, 18.4 percent of all black students in the 11 Southern states attended majority-white schools—triple the number of the 1965–66 school year.[6] During the next two years school desegregation doubled in the Southern states (see Table 1). In the 1969–70 school year 39.4 percent of Southern blacks attended majority-white schools. During the next two years progress slowed considerably, with only a 5 percent increase over the 1969–70 school year—44.4 percent. Northern and Western states lagged behind the South; in the 1971–72 school year, only 29.1 percent of black students in these areas attended majority-white schools.

Table 1 allows us to assess the progress of school desegregation. It is clear that some very substantial gains have been made since 1963, especially in the South. In 1968, 78.8 percent of Southern black students attended schools that were 80 to 100 percent black. By 1972 this figure had dropped to 31.6 percent. Moreover in 1972 only 9.2 percent of Southern blacks attended 100 percent minority schools, compared with

TABLE 1

FALL 1972 PROJECTIONS OF PUBLIC SCHOOL BLACK ENROLLMENT COMPARED WITH FINAL FALL 1968 AND 1970 DATA

| Geographic Area | Total Pupils | Black Pupils | | Black Pupils Attending Schools Which Are: | | | | | |
| | | | | 0-49.9% Minority | | 80-100% Minority | | 100% Minority | |
		Number	Pct	Number	Pct	Number	Pct	Number	Pct
Continental U.S.									
1968	43,353,568	6,282,173	14.5	1,467,291	23.4	4,274,461	68.0	2,493,398	39.7
1970	44,877,547	6,707,411	14.9	2,223,506	33.1	3,311,372	49.4	941,111	14.0
1972	44,485,568	6,641,343	14.9	2,446,239	36.8	2,953,991	44.5	721,757	10.9
North & West[a]									
1968	28,579,766	2,703,056	9.5	746,030	27.6	1,550,440	57.4	332,408	12.3
1970	29,451,976	2,899,858	9.8	793,979	27.5	1,665,926	57.6	343,629	11.9
1972	28,970,304	2,831,080	9.8	822,480	29.1	1,581,871	55.9	284,273	10.0
South[b]									
1968	11,043,485	2,942,960	26.6	540,692	18.4	2,317,850	78.8	2,000,486	68.0
1970	11,570,351	3,150,192	27.2	1,230,868	39.1	1,241,050	39.4	443,073	14.1
1972	11,601,027	3,165,229	27.3	1,405,435	44.4	1,001,211	31.6	289,638	9.2
Border & D.C.[c]									
1968	3,730,317	636,157	17.1	180,569	28.4	406,171	63.8	160,504	25.2
1970	3,855,221	667,362	17.3	198,659	29.8	404,396	60.6	154,409	23.1
1972	3,914,255	645,034	16.5	218,323	33.8	370,909	57.5	147,844	22.9

[a]Alas., Ariz., Cal., Col., Conn., Ida., Ill., Ind., Iowa, Kan., Maine, Mass., Mich., Minn., Mont., Neb., Nev., N.H., N.J., N.M., N.Y., N.D., Ohio, Ore., Pa., R.I., S.D., Utah, Vt., Wash., Wis., Wy.
[b]Ala., Ark., Fla., Ga., La., Miss., N.C., S.C., Tenn., Texas, Va.
[c]Del., D.C., Ky., Md., Mo., Okla., W. Va.

68 percent in 1968. These are important and dramatic changes, but progress may be more substantial than HEW's figures (based on the number of black students in majority-white schools) indicate. Since many school districts in the South have black majorities, it would be impossible for schools in these districts to become predominantly white once they are integrated. In fact, the more desegregation occurs in these districts, the fewer black students there will be in majority-white schools. If these largely black districts were considered, progress might be increased by another 8 to 10 percent. Also if the data were divided on an urban–rural basis, we would see much greater compliance in rural areas where the logistics of desegregation are less severe.

Although much remains to be done, considerable progress in school desegregation has been achieved in the South. Nationwide, however, progress has been minimal. In both rural and urban areas of the North and the West, school segregation is pervasive. A 1972 study revealed the extensiveness of segregation nationwide:

> . . . 519 million out of 9.3 million minority-group students, or more than 60 percent, still attend predominantly minority-group schools. At the same time 72 percent of the nation's nonminority-group students attend schools which are at least 90 percent nonminority. Four million minority-group students attend schools which are 80 percent or more minority, and 2 million are in classes which are 99–100 percent minority.[7]

Thus, substantial problems remain in the area of school desegregation, the most serious of which involve the North and the West, and metropolitan areas in all regions of the United States.

Lessons of the Past

A host of factors are responsible for the slow rate of progress in school desegregation.[8] To begin with, from the start Southern officials had no intention of obeying *Brown* unless they were forced to do so. The decision played into the hands of Southern officials because it was ambiguous to the point of not placing school districts under any real obligation. In arguing the *Brown* case on behalf of the NAACP, Marshall asked the Court to establish specific deadlines for the start of school desegregation.[9] Hindsight reveals that the Supreme Court made a serious mistake in ignoring Marshall's plea.

In *Brown* the Supreme Court directed the district courts to ensure that communities in their jurisdiction make a "good faith start" toward school desegregation. However, Southern judges were little inclined to take on this obligation. Most federal judges in the South were native Southerners and knew only too well that they would be ostracized in their own communities if they enforced the law; and some of the judges disagreed with the decision.[10] Generally, therefore, the Supreme Court was abandoned by the lower courts.

The Supreme Court became completely isolated when the Congress and President Eisenhower refused to endorse or help implement the decision. As a result, school boards were under almost no real legal or political pressure to desegregate. Southern blacks were themselves reluctant to pressure local officials for compliance. In many communities if blacks pressured local officials they risked physical violence or economic coercion. Also if private pressure failed, most Southern blacks could not afford to hire an attorney to press their case.

The passage of the 1964 Civil Rights Act signaled a number of important changes. First, the act constituted strong backing by Congress of civil rights goals. Acts had been passed in 1957 and 1960, but they were weak and largely symbolic, and they focused primarily on voting rights. Although the 1964 act failed to provide strong enforcement mechanisms for some civil rights, it put Congress firmly behind the principle of school desegregation. The act also allowed a much more systematic attack on school desegregation, since a case law strategy could be abandoned by civil rights forces for more uniform standards to be applied by HEW. With this new law, and a President who supported the goal of school desegregation, real progress seemed imminent.

The first guidelines generated by HEW (1965–66 school year) reflected a gradual approach by requiring that all school districts make a "good faith start" toward desegregation. This was interpreted by HEW to mean that districts were required to integrate "the first and any other lower grade, the first and last high school grades, and the lowest of junior high where schools were so organized."[11] Despite the fact that the guidelines were timidly enforced and contained obvious loopholes, some progress resulted. HEW allowed school districts to use any of three methods of compliance: (1) Execution of an Assurance of Compliance form, stipulating that race, color, and national origin were not factors in student assignment, reassignment, or transfer; that faculty and staff were not segregated; that the facilities, activities, and services of the school system were not segregated; and that no other vestige of segregation remained. (2) Submission of a final desegregation order by a federal court, together with a statement from the school district of its willingness to comply and a progress report. (3) Submission of a desegregation plan approved by the United States Commissioner of Education. This plan would have to specify that the school system had designed a workable desegregation program.

Many school districts submitted voluntary plans and then reneged at the last moment. Other districts voluntarily submitted to court orders that required considerably less desegregation than HEW's standards.[12]

If a district was judged dilatory by HEW, the procedure for cutting off federal funds was long and torturous; it included an appeals procedure that allowed a district to continue to receive federal funds for 6 to 12 months after being judged noncompliant by HEW field officers. Nevertheless, federal funds to several hundred districts were cut off between 1967 and 1969.

Perhaps the greatest weakness of the HEW guidelines was that "freedom of choice" was considered an acceptable approach to school desegregation. Under freedom of choice, any black who dared was "free" to attend a white school. The United States Commission on Civil Rights documented many violent acts by whites reminding blacks that they better not dare.[13] In 1968 the Supreme Court ruled that desegregation plans that relied on freedom of choice could not be used if any other method would more quickly achieve desegregation.[14] Inasmuch as freedom of choice has never been known to produce significant desegregation, the decision in effect overruled its use. Still, many school districts managed to avoid large scale desegregation for another year while it was being "proven" that freedom of choice did not work in their community.

Just as the momentum of compliance with HEW guidelines was building up, Richard Nixon was elected President.[15] During his 1968 campaign Nixon made it "perfectly clear" that his support for civil rights was weak, and that he favored neighborhood schools and opposed busing to achieve desegregation. During the campaign Senator Strom Thurmond and other prominent segregationists stumped the South spreading the word that Nixon, if elected, would take the heat off school desegregation.

Nonetheless, retreat did not immediately follow the election. Nixon's Secretary of HEW, Robert Finch, and the Director of the Office for Civil Rights, Leon Panetta (a Finch appointee), were liberal Republicans who felt obligated to enforce the law. Although Southerners felt betrayed by Nixon's campaign pledges to take the pressure off school desegregation, Finch and Panetta pushed desegregation efforts for some 14 months. During this period, however, Southern politicians put considerable pressure on the White House for relief. This pressure was constantly transmitted from the White House to the OCR, resulting in a number of defeats for Panetta.[16] The White House persisted in making statements about deeemphasizing school desegregation, while Panetta continued to show by actions and words that he had no intention of doing so. The result was considerable confusion about administration intentions, and many school districts abandoned desegregation plans in the anticipation that a federal retreat was imminent.

Ultimately Nixon fired Panetta, Finch later resigned, and the retreat on civil rights began.[17] After the departure of Panetta, the administration would probably have brought progress to a halt had the Supreme Court not overruled some compromise maneuvers by HEW (discussed later in the Alexander decision), thus holding HEW to the obligations of the law. Still, under the newest Secretary of HEW (Casper Weinberg), the administration began a "spirit of cooperation rather than coercion" in enforcing civil rights laws. The result was a mere 5 percent increase in desegregation between 1970 and 1972 in the 11 Southern states, a 4 percent increase in the 6 Southern Border states and the District of Columbia, and a mere 1.6 percent increase in the 32 Northern and Western states. Obviously in school desegregation, cooperation is a poor substitute for coercion.

What the past tells us about accomplishing school desegregation is fairly obvious: (1) School officials, especially but not exclusively in the South, will normally obey civil rights laws only under coercion. (2) Legal standards for school desegregation must be unambiguous and forceful. (3) Greater progress is achieved if the three branches of the federal government are reasonably unified and uncompromising in their approach to desegregation. (4) The burden for achieving school desegregation must rest with school officials, not with black citizens and their children. (5) The Administration must be prodded and carefully supervised by the federal courts if significant progress is to be made.

Current Supreme Court Standards: Implications for Completing Desegregation in the South

As noted, Brown was the catalyst for little change in school desegregation for some ten years. By 1964 the Supreme Court was beginning to show displeasure with the slow progress of desegregation. In Griffin v. County Board[18] the Supreme Court noted the long history of dilatory and unlawful behavior of Southern officials in avoiding their obligation under Brown and concluded that the standard of "all deliberate speed" never contemplated an infinite number of delaying tactics to defeat desegregation.[19]

Progress continued to lag, however, and in 1968 the Supreme Court began to specify the obligations of Southern school districts. In Green v. New Kent County School Board the Supreme Court ruled against the use of nonproductive "freedom of choice" plans; school boards were obligated to "come forward with a plan that promises realistically to work . . . now . . . until it is clear that state imposed segregation has been completely removed."[20] School boards were ordered to take whatever steps were necessary "to convert to a unitary school system in which racial discrimination would be eliminated root and branch."[21]

The *Green* decision was extremely important because it set a much more explicit standard and made it clear that school boards were responsible for undoing the consequences of their past actions. Equally important was *Alexander* v. *Holmes County Board of Education* (1969), which removed any doubt about the time-frame within which school boards were required to make significant progress. The suit challenged an attempt by HEW to grant 33 dilatory school districts in Mississippi a one-year delay in implementing desegregation plans. Noting the 15 years that had already passed since *Brown* and the long-standing recalcitrance of the districts, the Court disapproved the delay and ordered school districts "to terminate dual school systems at once."[22] The *Green* and *Alexander* decisions combined to produce considerable desegregation in many communities throughout the South. The considerable controversy stimulated by many district court orders based on these decisions led to one of the most important of recent Supreme Court cases on school desegregation.

The Swann Decision

In *Swann* v. *Charlotte-Mecklenburg Board of Education et al.* (1971),[23] the Supreme Court dealt forcefully with a number of problems left unresolved in earlier decisions. Basically, the case raised questions about the extent of a school board's obligation to achieve desegregation and the extent of a district court's authority to produce desegregation if the school board defaulted its obligation. The Court's answers were direct. First, school boards were obligated to achieve *immediate* desegregation; plans for gradual progress were no longer adequate. Second, if the local board defaulted its obligation to achieve desegregation, the district courts had broad discretion to develop desegregation plans. In *Swann* the school board had devised a plan that substantially desegregated the junior and senior high schools but left the elementary schools segregated. A district judge had ordered the school board either to devise a plan that would desegregate all the schools or to accept a comprehensive desegregation plan formulated by a court-appointed expert. The court's plan included extensive busing, rezoning, pairing, [24] clustering,[25] closing of schools, and specific ratios for the assignment of students, faculty, and staff.

Racial Ratios

The Supreme Court upheld the district court's imposition of the expert's plan and the specific techniques in it. In a 1959 case the Court had upheld the use of fixed ratios for faculty assignment, and they merely restated their position on this point.[26] For the first time, however, the

Court held that ratios could also be used in student assignment. Although it said that it would not uphold inflexible mathematical formulas, the Court held that ratios were acceptable as "a starting point in the process of shaping a remedy."[27] Whereas some people have argued that the Fourteenth Amendment requires "color-blindness," the Court took the position that blacks could only be protected by color *consciousness*.[28] "Awareness of the racial composition of the whole school system is likely to be a useful starting point in shaping a remedy to correct past constitutional violations."[29]

Attendance Zones

In *Swann* the Court also defined the district court's authority to alter the attendance zones of school districts. Since it was the obligation of school districts to *achieve* desegregation, assignment policies that were merely "racially neutral" or based on a "neighborhood schools" plan would not be adequate if they did not promote desegregation. To accomplish desegregation, the district courts were given authority to alter attendance zones by pairing, clustering, closing, or grouping schools. Further, the Supreme Court stated that new zones did not need to be compact or contiguous. The impact of zone restructuring was duly noted by the Court.

> The remedy for such segregation may be administratively awkward, inconvenient, and even bizarre in some situations and may impose burdens on some, but all awkwardness and inconvenience cannot be avoided in the interim period when remedial adjustments are being made to eliminate the dual school systems.[30]

One-Race Schools

The Court was somewhat ambiguous about whether one-race schools could be left in a unitary school system. It noted that under some circumstances one-race schools might remain until housing patterns changed or new schools were constructed; existence of a few one-race schools would not itself indicate that a school system had continued to practice discrimination. However, the Court held that in a system with a history of discrimination, "The Court should scrutinize such schools, and the burden upon the school authorities will be to satisfy the Court that their racial composition is not the result of present or past discriminatory action on their part."[31] Since the *Swann* decision seems to consider school segregation in a district that once operated a dual system to be state-imposed,[32] it would seem extremely difficult, if not impossible, for such districts to prove that one-race schools were *not* the result of past or present discrimination.

Busing

In perhaps its most important statement in *Swann*, the Court placed its imprimatur on the use of busing to achieve desegregation. This decision was based on three points. First, the Court noted that because busing is so common there was no legitimate reason for excluding it as a method of achieving desegregation. Backing for this conclusion was provided by an HEW survey in 1970 which found that "42 percent of all American public school students are transported to their schools by buses; an additional 25 percent ride public transportation."[33] This survey also revealed that only 3 percent of all busing was for the purpose of achieving desegregation and that only 1 percent of the annual increase in student transportation was attributable to school desegregation.[34]

Second, the Court noted that the busing ordered by the lower court was comparable to busing practices *before* the desegregation plan: "This system compares favorably with the transportation plan previously operated in Charlotte under which each day 23,600 students on all grade levels were transported an average of 15 miles one way for an average trip requiring over an hour."[35] The one-hour bus ride to school required in Charlotte seems to be common to many communities.

Third, the Court pointed out that busing might be the *only* way to achieve desegregation. "Desegregation plans," the Court said, "cannot be limited to the walk-in school."[36]

The Court noted that busing could not be unlimited and that at some point it might even become harmful. It felt, however, that it could not articulate any specific guidelines for busing. It stated only that "An objection to transportation of students may have validity when the time or distance of travel is so great as to either risk the health of the children or significantly impinge on the educational process."[37] The Court also said that "the limits on time of travel will vary with many factors, but probably with none more than the age of the students."[38] Since 60 and 90 minute bus rides by school children seem to be rather common, the Court's statements imply that there can be little limitation on the use of busing to achieve desegregation.

In sum, the *Swann* decision comes close to being the last nail in the coffin of dual school systems. The presumption of guilt for segregation is weighted toward school boards, the mandate is for immediate change, and the courts have been given authority to employ broad remedial powers to dismantle dual schools.

The Dereliction of HEW

After *Swann* the major obstacle left in the path of the complete dismantling of dual systems was the lack of vigorous enforcement efforts by HEW and the OCR. In early 1973 a district court decision took a step toward remedying this problem. In *Adams* v. *Richardson*,[39] declaratory and injunctive relief against HEW and the OCR for default of their administrative responsibilities under the Civil Rights Act was sought. The case against HEW and the OCR was substantial. For example, the record showed that

1. Between January, 1969, and February, 1970, 10 states were judged guilty by HEW of operating segregated systems of higher education in violation of Title VI. Each state was given 120 days to effect a suitable remedy. By early 1973 none of the states had responded adequately, but no action had been taken by HEW and all still received Title VI funds.
2. Seventy-four districts judged noncompliant in 1970–71 were still not in compliance in early 1973, but all continued to receive federal funds.
3. Eighty-seven districts had been allowed an additional year to desegregate after the Supreme Court ruled in *Alexander* v. *Holmes* that districts were to desegregate "at once."[40]
4. After *Swann* established "a presumption against schools that are substantially disproportionate in their racial composition,"[41] HEW continued to take no action against districts with substantial minority schools.
5. Six hundred and forty districts that were subject to court-ordered desegregation plans were presumed in compliance by HEW without the benefit of any monitoring.
6. Between 1964 and 1970 HEW initiated approximately 600 administrative proceedings against noncomplying school districts, with about 100 proceedings a year in 1968 and 1969. With the appointment of Panetta's successor no proceedings were initiated for some 12 months. Since February, 1971, only a token number of proceedings have been initiated and no funds have been terminated since the Summer of 1970.

The district court made three points: First, HEW and the OCR were obligated to achieve compliance with Title VI. Second, HEW and the OCR could not exercise unlimited discretion in seeking voluntary compliance. Third, when a substantial period had passed without compliance, HEW and the OCR had to see that Title VI was enforced. Judge Pratt's words were explicit:

> As the undisputed record demonstrates, defendants' efforts toward voluntary compliance have been unsuccessful in the case of many state and local educational agencies which continue to receive substantial federal funds in violation of the statute. Defendants now have no discretion to negate the purpose and intent of the statute by a policy described in another context as one of "benign neglect" but, on the contrary, have the duty, on a case-by-case basis, to employ the means . . . to achieve compliance.[42]

HEW and the OCR made three trips to the courts of appeals in efforts to reverse the decision but failing announced that the decision would be obeyed. In April, 1973, letters were sent to the 10 states in which higher education systems had been judged segregated and to some 200 school districts telling them to achieve compliance. In addition, the OCR announced that it was doing the paperwork necessary to enforce the decision. By early 1975, however, the OCR was still shuffling papers and making excuses.

Current Supreme Court Standards: Implications
for Achieving School Desegregation in the North

The implication of the *Green, Alexander, Swann* and *Adams* decisions for states that formerly operated dual school systems is quite clear— they must completely dismantle the dual school system and all vestiges thereof. Until lately the implications of the Supreme Court's more recent decisions for school segregation in Northern communities have been rather unclear. Traditionally the courts have made a distinction between segregation based on legal or official acts (de jure) and segregation that is supposedly fortuitous (de facto). Until recently most Northern districts have escaped the obligation to correct segregation on the grounds that the Supreme Court's mandates have been directed toward de jure segregation and that Northern segregation is de facto.

The logic of this approach to school segregation is not very persuasive. There would seem to be no justification for forcing Southern districts to eliminate segregation while Northern districts remain segregated. If school segregation is unconstitutional and harmful in one part of the country, surely it is equally invidious wherever it exists. As noted earlier, school segregation is now more extensive in the North than in the South, and it is particularly acute in Northern metropolitan areas. Recent figures indicate that "over 80 percent of all black metropolitan residents live in central cities, while more than 60 percent of white metropolitan residents live in suburbs. Of minority-group students, 62.4 percent outside the South attend center-city school districts in which a majority of students are from minority groups."[43] Segregation in the North is pervasive, then, but the question is whether Northern districts are now obligated to desegregate.

During the 1960s three of the United States courts of appeals held Northern segregation to be constitutional,[44] whereas one circuit court and a number of district courts reached the opposite conclusion.[45] These cases arose, however, at a time when freedom of choice was the only obligation being placed on most Southern districts.[46] Since *Green* established an affirmative obligation on districts to remedy segregation, many more school districts outside the South have been required by the courts to correct segregated school conditions.

There are basically two broad theories under which Northern districts have been held responsible by federal and state courts for school segregation.[47] Most frequently the courts have held that while school segregation in the North may not be based on a formal legal mandate, it is still the product of intentionally discriminatory actions. For example, in a recent case the ninth court of appeals said, "In context of . . . racial segregation the term 'de jure' does *not* imply criminal or evil intent but means no more or less than that school authorities have exercised powers given them by law in a manner which creates, continues, or increases racial imbalance. . . ."[48] When actionable segregation is based on this broad a theory of de jure segregation, the courts can investigate such factors as whether segregated schools have resulted from discriminatory actions on the part of state and local officials in the areas of housing laws and codes, bank lending policies, school attendance and construction policies, school site selections, and so forth. This theory of actionable segregation could probably be sustained in most Northern communities with substantial numbers of black students, because the communities often use discriminatory techniques to create and maintain segregation and because it could probably be shown that the actions of most school boards have worked to minimize integration at one time or another.

In recent years this theory has been used to hold school segregation actionable in Detroit,[49] San Francisco,[50] Los Angeles, [51] Denver,[52] Pasadena (California),[53] Oxnard (California),[54] Pontiac (Michigan),[55] Las Vegas,[56] and Indianapolis.[57] In the Detroit case the court found that school segregation was de jure rather than de facto because of

> Federal housing Administration and Veterans Administration loan policies that encourage 'racially and economically harmonious neighborhoods'; judicial enforcement of racially restrictive covenants prior to their prohibition by the Supreme Court in 1948; and such school board acts as altered attendance zones, transfer programs that allowed whites to escape from identifiably black neighborhood schools, and busing programs that operated to move only black students out of geographically closer overcrowded white schools into predominantly black schools with available space.[58]

In a number of the other communities the courts relied on a less extensive catalog of discriminatory actions, but ruled that school segregation was de jure because the school boards had used their powers over attendance zones, school site construction, and faculty assignment to perpetrate racial imbalance that had been caused primarily by residential patterns.[59] For example, in the Indianapolis case the seventh court of appeals held that the school board had practiced discrimination because

> It has built additions at Negro schools and then zoned Negro students into them from predominantly white schools; it has built additions at white schools for white children attending Negro schools; it has generally failed to reduce overcrowding at schools of one race by assigning students to use newly built capacity at schools of the opposite race. The Board has also constructed simultaneous additions at contiguous predominantly white and Negro schools, and has installed portable classrooms at schools of one race with no adjustment of boundaries between it and neighboring schools of the opposite race.[60]

In addition, the court found that there had been "approximately 350 boundary changes in the system since 1954. More than 90% of these promoted segregation."[61] In the Pasadena case the court held that if it could be shown that racial discrimination caused segregated housing patterns, "school officials have the burden to show that there are no educationally sound and administratively feasible alternatives available to overcome the existence of segregated schools."[62]

The second broad theory involves some showing that minority children are being denied equal educational opportunities. In one form this theory is unconcerned with past discriminatory actions and centers attention exclusively on segregated educational patterns. The mere existence of segregated patterns would be plenary evidence of a constitutional violation. This theory is consistent with the Supreme Court's conclusion in *Brown* that "Separate educational facilities are inherently unequal."[63]

In the case of *People* v. *San Diego Unified School District*, the theory that an unbalanced school system constitutes a denial of equal protection was adopted. The state court of appeals held that when segregation existed within the schools, the burden was on the state to prove that all children in the system were receiving a genuinely equal education or that achieving desegregation was impossible.[64] This same reasoning was applied in a case involving Springfield, Massachusetts.[65] Expressing a somewhat more moderate theory, the courts of appeals in the District of Columbia and in San Francisco held that segregated schools denied black children an equal education.[66] In the District of Columbia case the court held that black children had also been denied equal protection of the law because minority schools manifested inferior physical facilities and had received fewer economic inputs.[67]

A careful reading of *Swann* provides some support for both theories, but much more for the discrimination than the equal education theory. It may be inherent in the *Swann* opinion that segregated schools are unconstitutional[68] but repeatedly the Court bases the right of relief on the existence of discriminatory state actions. For example, at one point in *Swann* the Court says, "Policy and practices with regard to faculty, staff, transportation, extracurricular activities, and facilities are the most important indicia of a segregated system, and the first remedial responsibility of school authorities is to eliminate invidious racial distinctions in those respects."[69] The reference to facilities indicates that any type of inequality between black and white schools would be considered a constitutional violation. However, the Court seems to be saying that separate facilities that are basically equal would not necessarily be unconstitutional. To be ruled unconstitutional a showing of discrimination in creating or maintaining the separate facilities would be required.

Another section of the opinion supports this reasoning. In perhaps its most revealing words, the Court said,

> Absent a constitutional violation there would be no basis for judicially ordering assignment of students on a racial basis. All things being equal, with no history of discrimination, it might well be desirable to assign pupils to schools nearest their homes. But all things are not equal in a system that has been deliberately constructed and maintained to enforce racial segregation.[70]

Thus, a showing of a constitutional violation in the form of discriminatory actions of some type seems critical to relief.

Additionally, when the Court discusses the conditions that constitute a constitutional violation, they are phrased in terms of discriminatory acts and not the mere existence of segregated attendance patterns. For example, the Court said,

> Independent of student assignment, where it is possible to identify a 'white school' or a 'Negro school' simply by reference to the racial composition of teachers and staff, the quality of school building and equipment, or the organization of sports activities, a prima facie case of violation of substantial constitutional rights under the Equal Protection Clause is shown.[71]

The Court's phrasing is very important because it seems to discuss actions that are independent of laws mandating segregated schools.[72] The acts described seem to define separate constitutional violations that many districts (North and South) are no doubt guilty of. In defining the type of activities that are unconstitutional, the Court also said, "In ascertaining the existence of legally imposed school segregation, the existence of a pattern of school construction and abandonment is . . . a factor of great weight."[73] Again it would appear that if it can be shown that school site and construction policies have been manipulated to perpetuate school segregation, a constitutional violation has occurred regardless of where the district is located.

This reasoning was substantiated in June, 1973, when the Supreme Court head *Keyes et al.* v. *School District No. 1, Denver, Colorado*,[74] the first full hearing of a segregation case from a non-Southern city. The

Court ruled that if the district judge found that intentional racial discrimination by school authorities had caused substantial school segregation in any part of Denver, then the whole district could be considered a dual system subject to full constitutional relief. "Common sense," the Court said, "dictates the conclusion that racially inspired school board actions have an impact beyond the particular schools that are the subjects of those actions."[75] In addition, the Court said that the distinction between de jure and de facto segregation hinged on whether there had ever been any intent to segregate the races in a community, not on whether segregation had been mandated by law. Thus, a community has a "history of segregation" if "a pattern of intentional segregation has been established in the past."[76] Also, if the effects of past discrimination persist, the remoteness of past discriminatory actions is not important. "If the actions of school authorities were to any degree motivated by segregative intent and the segregation resulting from those actions continues to exist, the fact of remoteness in time certainly does not make these actions any less 'intentional.' "[77]

Equally important, the Supreme Court said that if the district judge did find that the city was operating a dual system, the burden would be on the school board to prove that they had not caused or contributed to the existing segregation. The Court said that the burden would be on the board to show that its policies with respect to construction, site and location of schools, student transfers, and other factors such as the "so-called 'neighborhood schools' concept" were not adopted to maintain segregation in the core city or "were not factors in causing the existing condition of segregation in these schools."[78]

The implications of *Swann* and *Keyes* for Northern school segregation seem obvious. The message is that Northern school segregation is unconstitutional if it can be shown that the segregation is de jure rather than de facto. More important, however, the Court has defined de jure segregation broadly and has put the burden of proof on school boards. For Northern boards to prove that their policies have not contributed to, or caused, segregation should be extremely difficult since the specific school board activities that the Supreme Court has identified as evidence of discrimination are activities that are practiced widely both North and South. This is not an ideal approach to school desegregation, but it is viable to the extent that segregated conditions can be attacked, North and South.

Consolidation: A Major Question

The most important issue presently unanswered by the Supreme Court is exactly how much authority the courts have to devise desegregation plans that cross political boundaries. In many areas of the United States, especially large central cities, it is impossible to eliminate "racially identifiable" schools because the white population of the inner city is too small. It takes little imagination to prove that the frequent concentration of black Americans in central cities and whites in the suburbs is not an accident of history. Racial isolation in housing is the result of dozens of types of official and private discrimination.[79] The critical question, therefore, is the conditions under which inner city and suburban students can be assigned across city or county boundaries to overcome this historic segregation.

This issue was first raised in the recent case of *Bradley* v. *School Board*.[80] The district judge was faced with the problem of dismantling a dual school system in the city of Richmond, Virginia. Richmond has only a 30 percent white student population. The Judge felt that the school system was charged with the affirmative duty under *Green, Alexander*, and *Swann* to achieve a unitary school system. The only way to accomplish this goal, however, would have been to combine the schools of Richmond with those of two surrounding counties which were predominantly white. Weighing the merits the Judge ordered the Richmond schools combined with those of the two counties for the purpose of achieving a desegregated system.

The decision was based on three points. First, Judge Merhige concluded that the duty to provide all children with an equal education was an obligation of the state not the local government. Consequently local divisions were irrelevant to this obligation. Second, the court found that all three districts were guilty of having operated dual school systems, of which the district lines were a vestige. Judge Merhige held that maintenance of the district lines had the effect of perpetuating segregation, and that they had been deliberately maintained for that purpose. Third, the boundaries between Richmond and the two counties had been ignored for purposes of achieving and maintaining segregation. Under the dual school system, Judge Merhige found that massive busing over long distances and over the county lines had been employed to segregate the schools. The busing had been so extensive that the Judge concluded that in reality the tri-jurisdictional area was one community.

Support for Judge Merhige's decision would seem to be substantial. If district lines could be crossed for purposes of segregation, surely they can be crossed for purposes of overcoming the resulting imbalance. The Judge's conclusion that education is a state, not a local, obligation also seems sound. Under the Fourteenth Amendment the states are obligated to see that all their citizens are provided equal protection under the law, and the state is held responsible for the actions and consequences of the acts of its agents.

There also seems to be legal precedent for assuming that intrastate boundaries cannot stand as obstacles to legal rights. In the reapportionment cases the Supreme Court held that political boundaries could not be continued if they denied citizens an equal vote. Furthermore the Court said, "Political subdivisions of states—counties, cities or whatever —never were and never have been considered sovereign entities. Rather they have been traditionally regarded as subordinate governmental instrumentalities created by the state to assist in the carrying out of state governmental functions."[81] However, in a recent reapportionment case the Supreme Court made a distinction between local government apportionment and state and federal apportionment.[82] The Court said it would allow small numerical deviations in reapportionment if it was necessary to preserve political subdivisions. What the Court seemed to be saying, however, was that it would sustain a close case only if the state could show a legitimate reason for maintaining the subdivision. In a case such as *Bradley*, where a history of discrimination and prior busing across boundaries is involved, this case would not seem to be prevailing.

Surprisingly, perhaps, the Court of Appeals for the Fourth Circuit reversed *Bradley*, and the decision was upheld when the Supreme Court, Mr. Justice Powell abstaining, divided 4–4. The circuit court held that "Because we are unable to discern a constitutional violation in the establishment and maintenance of these school districts, nor any unconstitutional consequences of such maintenance, we hold that it was not within the district judge's authority to order the consolation of these separate political subdivisions."[83] The Supreme Court's nondecision did not indicate agreement with the circuit court's reasoning but left the lower court decision intact.

There have been a number of other cases which have involved various aspects of this problem. It seems clear that if it can be shown that district lines were purposely drawn or redrawn to achieve segregation, they can be overturned or transgressed. For example, in *Turner* v. *Littleton-Lake Groton School District*, the fourth circuit held that the school districts had been reorganized for the purpose of achieving and maintaining segregation.[84] Also, in the case of the *United States* v. *Scotland Neck City Board of Education*,[85] the Supreme Court refused to allow a new school district to be established in a county where the effect would be to remove most of the white students from the county. Similarly, in *Lee* v. *Macon County*, the fifth circuit refused to uphold the secession of a city from a county school system. Judge Wisdom ruled that "the city cannot secede from the county where the effect—to say nothing of the purpose—of the secession has a substantial adverse effect on desegregation of the county school district."[86]

However, if the boundaries are neutrally drawn and later become barriers to integration they are not necessarily unconstitutional. In

Spencer v. *Kugler*,[87] a New Jersey statute establishing school districts conterminous with political boundaries was challenged on the grounds that the boundaries created severe racial imbalance in some parts of the state. The district court held that the statute was constitutional since it was not based on a racial motive, and the Supreme Court affirmed.[88] This decision does not rule out the possibility that the Supreme Court might allow neutral boundaries to be breached for the purpose of executing a specific desegregation plan.

The Supreme Court was directly faced with the issue of consolidation during the 1973–74 term, but their decision still left the issue clouded.[89] The Court heard arguments in a case involving Detroit, Michigan. The Sixth Circuit Court of Appeals had agreed with a district court ruling that the schools in Detroit were segregated by official action and inaction on the part of local and state officials.[90] The court also agreed that a Detroit-only desegregation plan would not achieve significant desegregation and that only a metropolitan plan including 52 suburban districts in three counties would be effective. The court said, "The discriminatory practices on the part of the Detroit School Board and the State of Michigan revealed by this record are significant, pervasive and casually related to the substantial amount of segregation found in the Detroit School system by the district judge. . . . The Court feels that some plan of desegregation beyond the boundaries of the Detroit School District is both within the equity powers of the district court and essential to a solution to this problem."[91]

In a 5–4 decision, the Supreme Court refused to uphold the lower courts. Chief Justice Berger, speaking for the majority, refused to hold either that local divisions were irrelevant or that school desegregation was a state rather than a local obligation. However, Berger said that "Boundary lines may be bridged where there has been a constitutional violation calling for interdistrict relief." The type of constitutional violation that would warrant an interdistrict remedy seemed to be a showing that all the districts involved in a consolidation plan were guilty of some form of intradistrict or interdistrict school discrimination. Thus, Berger stated that relief would be forthcoming for Detroit if it could be shown that "petitioners drew the district lines in a discriminatory fashion, or arranged for white students residing in the Detroit district to attend schools in Oakland and Macomb counties. . . ." Since Berger felt that the record before the Court did not document any significant violations "by the 53 outlying school districts and no evidence of any interdistrict violation or effect," he remanded the case to the court of appeals for further investigation.

Four judges vigorously dissented from Berger's position, but the most important opinion in the case may have been written by one of the members of the majority. Justice Stewart concurred in the decision of the Court but listed a much broader and more liberal set of conditions that would warrant an interdistrict remedy. "Were it to be shown, for example, that state officials had contributed to the separation of the races by drawing or redrawing school district lines, or by purposeful, racially discriminatory use of state housing or zoning laws, then a decree calling for transfer of pupils across district lines or for restructuring of district lines might well be appropriate." This seems to indicate that officials in the outlying districts would not necessarily have to be found personally guilty of any illegal acts. If the actions of state officials produced discrimination in a district, it would be liable to a consolidation plan.

Until the Court deals with some cases that try to document intradistrict violations, the implications of the Detroit case will not be clear. It would seem that the conditions documented in the Richmond case would certainly warrant an interdistrict plan, and this would probably be the case for most Southern cities. But the implications for many Northern communities must await further litigation.

If the Court will not allow forced consolidation, or if they limit it to only a few instances, it will be difficult or even impossible to desegregate many inner city schools. With consolidation, however, even the schools of such cities as Washington, D.C., and Detroit could be successfully desegregated. Even though metro plans would lead to more desegregation, some reservations about such systems have been expressed. Most frequently it is argued that metro systems would be large to the point of being unwieldy and that children would have to be bused excessive distances in such systems. Such arguments are misleading. Many large cities have metro school systems (for example, Houston, Charlotte, and all cities in Florida) and they have not found such systems to be unmanageably large. In fact, a recent report reveals that metro desegregation plans have proceeded smoothly in Florida districts involving Jacksonville, Orlando, St. Petersburg, Tampa, and Ft. Lauderdale.[92]

The evidence also indicates that metro school districts have some distinct advantages over the typical city or suburban school district. Gordon Foster of the Florida Desegregation Center points out six advantages: (1) A metro plan may require less busing. For example, rather than students having to be bused across a city to achieve desegregation, they may be able to travel only a short distance to a suburban school; (2) experience indicates that in a metro system the physical facilities and resources of all schools are quickly equalized; (3) metro tends to stabilize communities and reduce resegregation because there are no segregated communities for whites to escape to; (4) metro contributes to an equalization of tax burdens and revenues; (5) metro reduces competition between city and suburban schools for the best teachers; and (6) metro can combine the best of efficient centralization of operation with considerable decentralized control.[93] Metro systems, therefore, seem to offer advantages that go beyond the issue of desegregation.

The Educational Park

Even if the Supreme Court does rule that central city and suburban schools can be combined for the purpose of desegregation, it may still be difficult to desegregate some schools without burdensome busing. As noted earlier, consolidation does not necessarily lead to more busing; it may in fact substantially reduce the need for busing. Still, the considerable geographical separation of the races in most cities and in some metropolitan areas may necessitate considerable busing. Defining the point at which busing becomes dysfunctional is, of course, very difficult. An hour trip each way seems excessive, although this time span is rather common in American communities. If a limitation of an hour trip each way was placed on busing, however, it might be difficult to desegregate some communities.

The educational park is a concept that might be combined with consolidation and busing to produce viable desegregation plans.[94] The educational park is a large and comprehensive public school that can be located advantageously for purposes of desegregation. The educational park would be located on 60 to 100 acres, contain 10 to 20 schools ranging from kindergarten to 12th grade, and accommodate 10,000 to 20,000 students.

There are good reasons besides achieving desegregation for serious consideration of the educational park system. First, school consolidation saves money on expensive items that are massively duplicated under the present system—libraries, science labs, swimming pools, gymnasiums, and so on. These savings can go into teacher salaries, innovative teaching methods and aids, individualized instruction, and a broader curriculum.

The construction of an educational park would, of course, be expensive but no more so than are current school policies. Some have argued that the size of the parks would make them very impersonal. Most city schools are already large and impersonal, so the situation would probably not worsen, especially since students would be headquartered in specific units of the park. It is also argued that the idea is extravagant since present schools would be wasted. This is only partially true. Many schools are ready to be razed, some can be sold to private interests, and some can be used for other community purposes (for example, meeting halls, city offices).

In sum, the educational park deserves serious consideration, both as a tool of desegregation and as an educational device. Through the use of educational parks, consolidation, and busing, even the largest metropolitan areas could be desegregated.

The Impact of School Integration

An obvious question about school desegregation is what impact is it having on those involved? Realistically, it is much too early to assess accurately the impact of school desegregation on children, their parents, schools, or society. Current evidence does indicate that desegregation is frequently a traumatic experience for everyone concerned. Children may be shifted to new schools, many of their friends may be displaced by strangers of another race, the school they were proud boosters of may be renamed or even closed, a new teacher may have to be faced; and the year they thought they would be seniors in junior high and in dominance in the areas of athletics, journalism, and romance they may find that because of grade restructuring they are instead lowly freshmen in high school. To top it all off, their parents are often upset. The problems for teachers and school administrators have been equally severe.

It is important to realize how difficult school integration frequently is, because until tensions ease and new arrangements become routine, it will be impossible to assess fully its impact. Under the best of circumstances a half-a-dozen years are perhaps a minimum for real adjustment. Unfortunately there are few communities in which significant desegregation has been in effect for that period of time. Consequently most of the available research is based on desegregation experiences of only one to three years. These studies can provide important insight but they are still tentative. In addition, measuring the impact of desegregation on school children is much more complicated than it might seem. A scientific study necessitates pretest, posttest, and control data. The child must be tested before the integrated experience, after the integrated experience, and then compared with similar peers who have not been integrated. This is an elaborate and expensive research project and such studies are rare. Of those longitudinal studies available many cover only one or two years and some fail to control for important variables such as the socioeconomic status of the children's parents.[95] Most of the available research is based on cross-sectional designs where children are simply studied on a one-shot basis after being integrated. Thus, available research on integration is tentative and must be treated as such until time allows more and better research. Despite all the limitations, this research basically reveals that integration can have a very positive impact. We will review the available literature on three important areas —achievement, racial attitudes, and life opportunities.

Achievement

More studies of the impact of integration on the achievement level of black and white children have been done than on the other topics to be surveyed. The prevailing tendency is to view school integration as a device for improving the academic achievement of black students. The thrust of this view is that if school desegregation does not result in higher academic achievement for blacks, it is a failure and should be abandoned. This reasoning is faulty on several counts. First, the Supreme Court's decisions on school desegregation were based on the finding that black Americans were segregated because they were considered inferior by white society. To allow such discriminatory treatment, the Court said, denied black Americans the equal protection of the law and caused racial estrangement. The obligation to desegregate the public schools, then, was based on a legal principle guaranteed to all Americans by the Constitution, not on a pedagogic speculation.

Second, it would be extremely peculiar if school desegregation had to prove its value as an academic device to justify its continuation. After all, segregated schools existed for decades without any demands that its existence be justified on any grounds other than the pernicious doctrine of white supremacy. Third, to center attention almost exclusively on the academic potential of school desegregation neglects a number of areas in which school desegregation may have its most important consequences for society. Thus, while we will survey the academic imput of desegregation, we shall also try to show its broader implications.

Although academic gains is not the best standard for evaluating desegregation, the evidence indicates that black students in racially mixed schools generally make gains over those left in segregated schools. As one reviewer concluded, "The 'before and after' studies of the desegregation of school systems or individuals suggest that following desegregation, of whatever type or at whatever academic level, subjects generally perform no worse, and in most instances better."[96] In some instances the gains made by black children are not very substantial but in others gains of one to two years are made.[97] It is extremely rare for studies to reveal any decrease in white achievement when schools are integrated.

Interestingly, a few studies report that both black and white achievement levels increase significantly in racially mixed schools.[98] It may seem strange that the achievement of white students would improve when they are placed in a classroom with black students, many of whom may be low achievers. A logical explanation may be that a panic mentality set in motion by integration helps account for these improvements. A

1967 study found that when integration takes place, school officials frequently try to compensate for the arrival of minority students by making special efforts to improve the curriculum and teaching for *all* students.[99] It is also possible that when schools are integrated, both black and white parents become concerned about their childrens' performance (for fear that they may fail or that they will not learn as much) and are more conscientious about seeing that their children complete their homework.

One point is forcefully made by current studies. Simply mixing the races in schools or classrooms will not necessarily produce positive results. It is doubtful whether children learn better simply because they are in a classroom with children of another race. If children are to gain academically from integration, some other factors have to be kept in mind. The available research has identified three major variables that seem important in determining whether children will make academic gains in integrated schools. The first is that students must be provided with a positive environment. If interracial tensions and/or poor support from faculty and staff exist, academic gains seem to be much lower.[100] Second, academic gains are greatest when children are integrated at the beginning of their school experience.[101] Elementary integration allows the students to adapt to one another more easily and may also provide the black children with a better educational environment from the start. By the junior or high school years it may be too late for children to overcome very much of their educational disadvantage.

The third factor involves socioeconomic rather than mere racial integration.[102] Studies show that the most important school factor in determining a child's achievement level is the socioeconomic status of his classroom peers.[103] All children seem to perform best in a middle-income milieu because of the well-known "peer effect." Studies reveal that in a group situation the values, aspiration levels, work habits, and achievement levels of the more socially prestigious members of a group tend to be emulated by the others.[104] As Pinderhughes has said,

> [W]hat the pupils are learning from one another is probably just as important as what they are learning from the teachers. This is what I refer to as the hidden curriculum. It involves such things as how to think about themselves, how to think about other people, and how to get along with them. It involves such things as values, codes, and styles of behavior. . . .[105]

Recently Jencks reanalyzed data from the Coleman report on Northern sixty-grade students and concluded that the value of socioeconomic integration is more substantial than it was originally believed.

> Poor black sixth graders in overwhelmingly middle-class schools were about 20 months ahead of poor black sixth graders in overwhelmingly lower-class

schools. Poor students in schools of intermediate socioeconomic composition fell neatly in between. The differences for poor white sixth graders were similar.[106]

When Jencks controlled for the education of the children's families, he found that "poor white sixth graders in middle-class schools scored 10 months ahead of poor white sixth graders in lower-class schools; and poor black students in middle-class schools continued to score almost 20 months ahead of similar children in disadvantaged schools."[107]

The importance of these findings is that only through desegregation can many black children be placed in a middle-income milieu. Given the economic inequality between black and white Americans, most black children find themselves in a lower-income milieu where the quality of instruction and the achievement level of their classmates is generally low. In lower-income schools with large classes and a typically depressed environment, it is not uncommon for teachers to contribute to low achievement levels by averaging down their expectations.[108] When teachers expect their students to be slow-learners, a self-fulfilling prophecy may be set into operation. Thus, one study of ghetto schools bore the ominous title *Death at an Early Age*.[109] It is not surprising, therefore, that studies indicate that moving students to middle-class schools frequently has an educational impact.

Racial Attitudes

The impact of racial mixing in the public schools on racial tolerance is difficult to evaluate because schools have often been desegregated under very tense and negative conditions and because this variable has rarely been examined in longitudinal studies. One study uncovered literally hundreds of desegregated schools in which the most invidious kinds of racial discrimination persisted.[110] Given the number of racially mixed schools in which discrimination and tensions remain, it is not surprising that some studies have found that desegregation has not led to increased interracial tolerance; and that desegregation has been viewed as disappointing by both black and white students in some cases.[111]

Still the available cross-sectional evidence reveals that interracial contact frequently leads to racial tolerance, especially if positive conditions are present. Field studies in a number of Southern communities revealed that incidents between black and white students declined sharply after the initial inception of desegregation and that racial attitudes improved considerably thereafter. The principal of one school said, "racial attitudes of students are better this year than ever before. Many of our kids have helped educate their parents on racial issues."[112] A black administrator explained, a whole new socialization process is going on that didn't go on before. The black kids have to work out their identity. There are growing pains until they get their identity, then they will loosen up. Of course, white kids are going through the same struggle of how to relate.[113]

In other words, racial mixing will not produce overnight results, but in the long haul the results look promising. No amount of racial mixing will alleviate racial prejudice, however, unless a positive environment is created in the schools. As Pettigrew cautions, "Increasing interaction, whether of groups or individuals, intensifies and magnifies processes already underway. Hence, mere interracial contact can lead either to greater prejudice and rejection or to greater respect and acceptance depending upon the situation in which it occurs."[114] After a careful survey of the literature, Allport specified that ideally the conditions for positive interracial contacts included the pursuit of common goals, cooperative dependence, equal status and affirmative institutional support. [115] Other studies have stressed the importance of these and other positive conditions if interracial contacts are to yield beneficial results.[116]

The positive implications of interracial schools are emphasized in a number of recent studies. Several reports reveal that both black and white students who had attended interracial schools are more inclined than students without this experience to prefer to attend racially mixed schools in the future.[117] Further, students attending racially mixed schools are more inclined to say they trust and feel at ease around members of the opposite race.[118] Additionally, a study of 252 desegregating school districts during the 1970–71 school year found that "About 70 percent of the blacks and about 60 percent of whites agreed that both races were becoming more open-minded as a result of interracial busing."[119] A larger study of 879 schools in desegregating districts during the 1970–71 school year also reported basically positive findings:

> Forty-one percent of students attending desegregated schools for the first time reported changes for the better on "going to school with students of another race," while only 5 percent reported changes for the worst.
> Eighty percent of students interviewed agreed that "students are cooperating more and more as the year goes on."
> While 33 percent of black students and 23 percent of white students said they would rather go to another school if they could, only 6 percent reported they did "not like it here" and 80 percent reported learning more in school than the previous year.
> A substantial majority of teachers and principals reported improvements in interracial relationships among students, and only 2 percent reported worsening relationships.[120]

Thus, it would seem that interracial contact does have the potential to improve race relations if some consideration is given to creating a positive environment for interaction. In the final analysis this could be the most important impact of school integration.

Life Opportunities

Perhaps the one finding that all studies (both longitudinal and cross-sectional) of interracial schools agree upon is that the life opportunities of blacks improve considerably if they attend a racially mixed school. Blacks who attended interracial schools are more likely to graduate from high school, to attend college and to attend a better college, and to obtain a better job and receive a higher income.[121] Crain speculates that black gains in jobs and income probably do not result primarily from the educational gains made in racially mixed schools. Instead, he argues that blacks attending interracial schools learn to deal with and trust whites, which may improve their ability to succeed in their post-school environment. Crain also points out that since many jobs are obtained through informal social contacts, and since blacks who attended desegregated schools are more likely to have white friends, they are more likely to learn of good jobs from these friends.

In summary, one fact seems clear: the record for integrated schools is generally positive, especially given the lack of attention to the creation of a favorable environment for interracial schools. Not only do blacks frequently achieve better in integrated schools, but blacks attending interracial schools tend to be more trusting and tolerant of whites, and white attitudes are also more positive. The life opportunity of blacks is so improved that on this point alone integration would seem justified.

The Attack on School Integration: The Armor Study

Given the finding surveyed, it might seem surprising that school integration has been under attack by some academicians. The reason for these attacks, however, is that some scholars have combined unrealistic standards with flawed methodology in their studies of interracial schools. The chief antagonist of integrated education, David Armor, has argued that school integration has failed on a number of counts and thus should be terminated. Armor restricted his call for a termination of integration only to mandatory busing programs, but since he has not actually studied busing programs, his thrust is actually directed at all school integration. Armor's attack hinges on a number of faulty premises, the first of which is that judges, legislators, and social scientists have maintained that "mere contact" between the races will lead to improved achievement, aspirations, self-esteem, and life opportunities for blacks while improving interracial tolerance.[122] This reasoning fails on two counts. In rendering school desegregation decisions the Supreme Court relied on social science research which showed not that "mere contact" led to improvements, but on research which revealed that segregation had a very negative impact on black self-esteem, achievement, aspirations, and life opportunities. Armor makes no attempt to refute these findings.

Second, as pointed out earlier, social scientists have not argued that "mere contact" between the races will lead to positive change. They have argued that under the type of positive conditions specified by Allport, integration can be beneficial. Armor relies on Allport's research, but distorts and reduces his theory to a "mere contact" specification, and then bases his research and expectations on this intellectual mutation. In reality, therefore, Armor does not test the assumptions of social science about the impact of integration. In defense Armor says, "my critics' argument that the programs I looked at did not fulfill the proper conditions for integration is beside the point."[123] But the argument is not beside the point. No one would have expected the programs to produce the changes Armor anticipated unless the conditions were fulfilled, and they were not. Also Armor did not conclude from his studies that induced busing should be combined with the fulfillment of the proper conditions for positive change. He argued that all induced integration should be terminated, implying that induced integration per se is bad and unworkable. Nothing in his or anyone else's research warranted this conclusion.

Even if the prerequisites of Allport's contact theory had been present in the schools Armor studied, he could not have obtained evidence on the effects of integration because his methodology was inadequate. Given the type of research design employed by Armor, the only way to determine whether integration assists blacks is to compare (on a pretest-posttest basis) those who are bused with similar blacks who are left in segregated schools. If, using the proper controls, the integrated blacks show significant improvements over segregated blacks, the assumptions are verified. Even Armor seems to realize this but lacking the proper data he compared the bused blacks with their white classmates.[124]

Comparing bused blacks with their white classmates will show a number of things but not whether blacks have been aided by integration. Yet, Armor argues that induced integration should be terminated because the gains of black students in integrated schools during the short study period were not large enough to bring them up to the level of their white peers. This, of course, is not a valid standard for evaluating integration. As we have noted, studies of integration usually reveal that integrated blacks made achievement gains over segregated blacks, and often the gains are quite significant. The gains for blacks in integrated schools may not be enough to overcome all the educational differences between the races in only a few years, but the additional gains normally found could be "the difference between functional illiteracy and marketable skills."[125] Surely this is a significant improvement. Pettigrew et al. make this point forcefully:

> We believe it to be unrealistic to expect any type of educational innovation to close most of the racial differential in achievement while gross racial

disparities, especially economic ones, remain in American society. Further-more, we know of no social scientist who ever claimed school desegregation alone could close most of the differential. We are pleased to note the many instances where effective desegregation has apparently benefited the achieve-ment of both black and white children, and where over a period of years it appears to close approximately a fourth of the differential.[126]

Armor further argues for terminating integration by busing even though blacks may improve in integrated schools, because a gap fre-quently remains between their performance and that of their white peers. Armor argues that this gap might cause serious psychological harm to blacks which may outweigh any beneficial effects of integration.[127] The gap between the achievement level of black and white students should be of concern but probably not for the reasons suggested by Armor. Black students would feel vastly inferior to whites only if almost all blacks did poorly and almost all white students excelled. Obviously it would be highly unusual if this were the case. Normally in any class some blacks will do well and some whites will perform poorly. Thus the black students will have positive referents within their group. Armor's study provides a good example of this phenomenon. A sixth of the black junior high students in his study were such high achievers that they could not have shown improvement during the study period because they initially scored "virtually as high as the achievement test scoring allowed."[128]

Perhaps three conclusions can be drawn from this analysis. First, available evidence does not warrant final conclusions about the poten-tial of school integration at this time. Little research has been done, much of the research suffers methodological problems (some manifest severe problems), and although the evidence basically favors integration (especially in the area of life opportunities), the research findings are mixed. Thus, arguments that school integration should be terminated are highly premature and cannot be justified by available research. More importantly, these arguments are usually narrowly oriented toward the academic impact of integration. The focus needs to be broadened and lengthened to a consideration of the potential of integration to re-structure black and white relations in our society. A second implication is that too little attention has been given to seeing that integration occurs in a positive environment. Courts and administrators should make every effort to see that desegregation plans embody as many of the conditions of Allport's contact theory as possible. Simply believing that contact alone will produce desirable ends will frequently produce inadequate, or even disappointing, results.

A third implication is that the gap between the achievement of blacks and whites in integrated schools should not be ignored. It is both en-couraging and important that integration frequently improves black performance. The fact that improvements may be made indicates that specially trained teachers, working in a creative integrated environment, can probably close a substantial part of this gap. This should be especially true if integration begins at the earliest grades and if progress simultaneously continues in other areas of civil rights.

The Role of Quality Schools: The Jencks Study

A second attack on school integration has been based on biased interpretations of a study by Christopher Jencks et al. which explores factors explaining the economic differences between adults.[129] Some distorted the thesis of the book to conclude that school desegregation and quality schools are of no benefit. What Jencks et al. really argued was that factors such as quality of education, cognitive skills, genes, home background, and IQ explain only about 25 percent of the variation between adult income levels. They were unable to explain the other 75 percent of the differences, but they speculated that perhaps luck and personality were the important variables. Luck, they suspected, might be important in determining whether a person will be in the right place at the right time or whether a person will have beneficial contacts. Personality would determine how well an individual could deal with colleagues, customers, and superiors. Since the authors felt that much of the difference in individual incomes was explained by factors that could not be influenced by schools, they argued that economic inequality should be dealt with by eliminating all forms of discrimination and by restructuring the American system to achieve a socialist society in which capital resources are more equally distributed.

The study did not attack quality schools or school desegregation. The authors said, in fact, that

> . . . the case for or against desegregation should not be argued in terms of academic achievement. If we want a segregated society, we should have segregated schools. If we want a desegregated society, we should have desegregated schools.[130]

Neither did the authors disparage efforts to equalize school resources. Jencks et al. primarily wanted to make the point that school reform alone could not greatly equalize economic levels. However, the study did express reservations about the ability of school desegregation or remedial programs to greatly alter the achievement levels of students. If school resources were completely equalized, the authors believed that the test scores of deprived students would increase by only 9 to 19 percent. This, of course, would be no small accomplishment, but it would not equalize all groups. The authors also believed that current research warranted the conclusion that desegregating the schools would have a positive impact on black students' achievement levels, but that an educational gap would remain between the races. Moreover it was suggested that achievement gains by blacks would improve only by 20 to 30 percent. However, for all the reasons discussed earlier, available research does not warrant writing integration off as having only minor potential at this time.

Also the reservations expressed about remedial programs by Jencks et al. seem premature since all the study could show was that the teaching techniques and curriculum *presently in use* do little to equalize educational performance. But too little attention has been paid to training teachers to deal with educationally handicapped children and few school systems provide specific facilities or curriculum to deal with serious learning problems. Common sense dictates that a concerted effort to deal with educationally handicapped children, along with faster progress in improving the social and economic conditions of black Americans, would produce significant progress. Even Jencks et al. recognized this problem:

> In concluding this discussion we must again emphasize one major limitation of our findings. We have only examined the effects of resource differences among existing public schools. This tells us that if schools continue to use their resources as they now do, giving them more resources will not change children's test scores. If schools used their resources differently, however, additional resources might conceivably have larger payoffs.[131]

The experience with Head Start programs indicates that even special programs will be of little value if students are given remedial help (frequently by untrained teachers) and then sent back into a depressed school environment.[132] Available evidence seems to indicate that special programs will be successful only in an environment in which high standards and high-quality teaching and curriculum are continually present. An innovative biracial program in St. Louis exemplifies how first-rate remedial programs can produce dramatic results.[133] In a special HEW program, highly qualified teachers work with classes of 15 under-achieving children. Achievement tests show that second and third graders make an average gain of a year and a half in one year, an 80 percent increase in rate of learning. Students in the fourth, fifth, and sixth grades average a 14 month gain in 12 months—a 50 percent increase in learning rate. Similar programs in Hartford and Cheshire, Connecticut, and in Berkeley, California, have achieved similar dramatic results.[134] For a number of reasons, therefore, Jencks et al. may have seriously underestimated the value of special educational programs. Remedial programs definitely can work and racial-socioeconomic integration may have a significantly higher potential than present studies indicate.

Even the argument by Jencks et al. that schools cannot affect factors such as luck and personality is not very persuasive. The advantages of attending a prestigious school in terms of establishing important contacts is too obvious to belabor. Also studies of the life opportunities of blacks in interracial versus segregated schools, indicate that factors such as luck and personality may even be affected by the racial mix of a school. This is true since blacks in racially mixed schools may develop more contacts that lead to jobs and they may better learn to trust and deal with whites.

In conclusion, then, Jencks et al. did not argue that schools are unimportant or that good schools do not provide students with important advantages. As Mosteller and Moynihan observe, only the "simple of mind or heart"[135] could conclude from the Jenck's study that schools do not make a difference. Besides the fact that Jencks et al. emphasized the need for equalization of school resources and the value of good schools, a recent study by Guthrie et al. carefully reviews 18 separate studies which reveal that communities with more money have better schools, that students in high-quality schools learn more, and that the graduates of advantaged schools obtain better jobs and earn higher incomes.[136] It is critically important, therefore, that all students (white and nonwhite) receive the best education possible. Because the financial structure of public schools is based primarily on the property tax and because of the systematic discrimination in our society, it is obvious that the only way most black students will be provided with high-quality schools is by integration. Thus, while Jencks et al.'s goal of a more equitable distribution of financial resources as a means of reducing inequality is admirable, we can hardly imagine its achievement in anything approaching the near future. While the theorists plot, therefore, the goal of integration must proceed.

Implementing Integration

Since the South and many Northern districts are now obligated to dismantle segregated schools, it seems only reasonable that school and local officials should take those actions that will allow desegregation to proceed as smoothly as possible. Enough experience with integration has accumulated to allow some insight into the factors that determine whether school desegregation will proceed in a calm, orderly, and efficient manner. Field studies by the United States Commission on Civil Rights[137] of communities undergoing desegregation and a recent study by a Select Committee of the United States Senate[138] suggest that there are a number of essential elements in successful school integration. Perhaps the most important factor is that school board members and administrators must accept responsibility for carrying out the desegregation process and do so firmly and unswervingly. Once this commitment is made, four broad principles seem important. First, the community should participate in the desegregation process. Along this line, the community should be kept well informed about all desegregation plans.

Plans can be mailed to citizens, and information booths can be set up around the community to answer questions and to stifle the inaccurate rumors that frequently circulate in communities in the throes of desegregation. Community organizations can also be asked to endorse and work for the desegregation plan. Biracial citizen committees can be appointed to consult with, and advise, the school board. In a few communities in which public feeling was uncertain or opposed to desegregation, the school board achieved positive results by hiring a public relations firm to create a more accurate and positive image of the plan.

Second, every effort should be made to create a positive environment in the integrated schools. Administrators and faculty must manifest a positive attitude toward desegregation and treat students of all races with equal respect. Under Title IV of the 1964 Civil Rights Act, funds can be obtained to run summer conferences for administrators and staff to teach them to recognize and deal with racist attitudes and behavior. Schools can contribute to a positive environment by attempting to see that students do not feel that one race of students is being dealt with in a partial manner. For example, disciplinary procedures should be firm, fair, and impartial.

In addition, when schools are merged it is important that students transferring to the new school do not feel disadvantaged. If schools are consolidated, a new school name, mascot, and school colors may be chosen so that one group does not lose out completely. Class officers from merging schools should serve simultaneously. Academic requirements for participation in extracurricular activities should be relaxed during the adjustment period so that students who must adapt to new schools, teachers, and perhaps standards, do not feel discriminated against. Local organizations can promote racial understanding between the students by organizing events which allow them to get to know one another. Community events of this type might be particularly important the summer before schools are to be integrated.

The third factor is to make certain that the desegregation plan is educationally sound. This means that steps should be taken to improve the quality of education for all students when desegregation occurs and that the findings of the studies reviewed earlier should be acted upon. Integration should take place in the earliest grades possible, and socioeconomic as well as racial integration should be achieved. Tracking and ability grouping should be minimized because they tend to generate classroom segregation when the black students are from deprived schools.

Fourth, while the desegregation plan must be legally sound it should also be administratively logical. A few examples can be provided, although the specifics will vary according to the type of desegregation problems the community faces. There are five criteria, for example, that are frequently followed by school boards in developing a desegregation plan:

1. All schools should have populations as similar as possible to the whole district's ethnic composition.
2. The neighborhood school concept should be maintained to the extent possible consistent with an integrated system.
3. The shortest traveling distances to effect integration should be used.
4. Optimum use should be made of existing facilities.
5. Population trends and future mobility should be considered in building a plan for permanent desegregation.[139]

In addition, two other principles should be employed. First, if at all possible, no plan should be adopted which will not last a number of years. If the plan is legally inadequate and must be overturned by the courts for a more extensive plan, the resulting reorganization will extract a considerable toll on students and teachers who are shuffled about. Second, the desegregation plan should not place a disproportionate share of the burden for desegregation on any particular racial group. If it does, the tensions are usually considerable.

Conclusions

This analysis leads to three conclusions. First, school desegregation can be achieved. The legal grounds for attacking school segregation have been amply established by the Supreme Court. There is probably no community with substantial school segregation that is not obliged to desegregate under the Supreme Court's recent decisions. In the next five years there should be substantial additional progress in school desegregation because Northern segregation will come under full legal scrutiny and because the legal obligations of the South are so specific that few dilatory ploys are left.

Second, achieving desegregation is easier than many people believe. With honest effort there are probably few school systems in America that cannot be substantially desegregated. The technology to achieve full desegregation is available—pairing, grouping, clustering, rezoning, site selection, busing, and so on. As Foster says, "there is nothing mysterious about the techniques of desegregation. Indeed, all of the tools for desegregation can be and have been used to create or maintain a segregated status for school populations."[140]

Third, school desegregation is worth the effort. Although controversial and frequently hard on those involved, in the long run school desegregation should be beneficial to society. The available empirical evidence only hints at the full potential of school desegregation, but the limited insights gleaned are promising, and this is especially true when interracial education is implemented under positive conditions. In addition, it seems only reasonable that integrated schools are a necessary preparation for interracial living. As a black parent in Rochester said, "Education . . . is preparing yourself to live and work in the world, and in this respect your education is definitely lacking if you are not being prepared to live and work with all types of people."[141] Jencks et al. make a similar point:

> the most important effect of school desegregation may be on adults, not on students. School desegregation can be seen as a part of an effort to make blacks and whites rethink their historic relationship to one another. If blacks and whites attend the same schools, then perhaps they will feel more of a stake in each other's well-being than they have in the past.[142]

A Select Committee of the United States Senate recently made the point even more forcefully.

> It is among our principle conclusions—as a result of more than 2 years of intensive study—that quality integrated education is one of the most promising educational policies that this nation and its school system can pursue if we are to fulfill our commitment to equality of opportunity for our children. Indeed, it is essential, if we are to become a united society which is free of racial prejudice and discrimination.[143]

Neal A. Milner

NORTHWESTERN UNIVERSITY

5

Conventional Police Reform and Racial Hostility

Much of the conflict between blacks and the police has focused on two issues: the lack of police restraint and the lack of police accountability for their actions. The latter refers to unwillingness to respond to the demands of blacks or their supporters. It also refers to police departments' unwillingness to allow outsiders to supervise or even monitor their activities. The police have been hostile to opposing viewpoints, and they have viewed attempts to influence policing by civilians, especially those advocating greater community involvement in disciplining police, as unmitigated threats. This hostility and defensiveness is quite apparent in some of the techniques that police organizations have used:

> Police may use public-relations techniques to "sell" the public on the police way of doing things. Associated with this technique is the assumption that the community is not qualified to make long-range policy regarding police behavior. There is a tendency to allow public-relations techniques to supersede community relations programs, which depend on the recognition of the legitimacy of the community's view. Even when police organizations are willing to grant some access, they can and often do control the choice of who is represented on the group that participates in police policy making. The department decides who are the "responsible" members of the community and become accessible only to those members. Needless to say militant Blacks are seldom considered "responsible." . . . The technique of considering some important demands while ignoring others helps the police organizations to minimize apparent conflict by granting symbolic satisfaction to those to whom they gave access while ignoring those whose tangible conditions are in most need of change.[1]

Police restraint has become a more explosive issue because police actions, which blacks felt were unnecessarily arbitrary or vicious, were the immediately precipitating factors in most of the riots of the 60's. Police officers have often been callous, arbitrary, sullen, and even brutal in their dealings with blacks.

Concentrating on riots or the lack of restraints, however, under-estimates the complexity of black views of restraint and accountability, and thus subtly minimizes their plight. Opinion polls that were taken in the late 1960s showed that black people found themselves in a frustrating and paradoxical position vis-à-vis the police. According to these surveys, blacks were more afraid of crimes than were whites, with black women being the most frightened group in America. On the other hand, they were less willing to trust the police and were more likely to believe that the police were bigoted and brutal. More blacks than whites claimed to have directly experienced police brutality or to have known others who had.[2] It is not really simplying matters too much to say that those who felt they most needed the police trusted them the least.

The following essay looks rather closely at the public policies used to deal with the problems of tolerance, restraint, and accountability. It concentrates on police reform policies that fulfill three criteria. First, they must be premised on the view that the lack of police accountability and restraint is a problem. Second, they must at least implicitly recognize the ambivalence that black communities feel in desiring both more order and more restraints. Finally, they must be premised on the assump-tion that some important improvements in police–black relations can be made even in the absence of basic political or social changes. These criteria obviously eliminate approaches to change that some may con-sider crucial, but the ones I choose are the most common. They have clearly dominated police reform during the 60's and 70's. Many, in fact, have become part of the conventional wisdom. The essay will first describe these attempts at reform and evaluate their assumptions. I shall show that these policies might very well *increase* police isolation, hos-tility, and brutality. I shall then offer an alternative that tries to take into consideration the problems of conventional reform. To do all of this, we must consider each of the following questions:

1. What are the definitions of the problem according to each of two dominant approaches to police reform?
2. What are the assumptions made in each of these approaches?
3. Are these assumptions supported by close analysis?
4. On the basis of this analysis, what are the strategic points in the social and political structure that produce the problem?
5. From what alternative moral point of view might the problems be assessed?[3]

A brief comment about the fifth question. To answer it, I must be explicit about my own values. Though my opinions will be apparent in much of what follows, I think that some preliminary statement is necessary here. Like advocates of conventional reform, I believe that restraint and accountability are important goals, and that to some extent, some important thrusts toward accomplishing these goals can be made independently of more basic political and social changes. I am, however, probably less optimistic than conventional reformers. Thus, the alternatives I present in question 5 aim at achieving these general goals: however, restraint and accountability will take on quite different meanings in the alternative proposal. My definition of restraint stresses self-restraints, whereas my strategies for increasing accountability have in mind a much more encompassing degree of citizen participation.

The task ahead would be much easier if there were a large number of studies that evaluated the impact of police reform. Their absence is not surprising. Evaluation takes up resources that in the eyes of the leadership of an organization, could be put to better use. Police reforms, like policies emanating from other agencies, are frequently symbolic gestures that are intended to alleviate anxieties and thus reduce pressure by showing commitment to "doing something." Evaluation increases the possibility that such reforms would be measured against goals that were more instrumental and concrete than the goal of symbolic anxiety alleviation is. Certainly this helps explain the apparently calculated reluctance of higher echelon police officials to conduct more than a cursory evaluation. A typical strategy is to declare a policy change a success and then to forget about implementing it on a more general scale,[4] thus avoiding resistance from those in the organization who do not like the change. The process of evaluation itself is threatening to those who have risen to power through traditional organizations. It is further threatening because it is a process involving decisions about who sets the standards of comparison or the measurement of success and failure. An evaluation by outsiders who retain a degree of independence from the organization whose policies are being evaluated presumes that those within the organization are not the best judges of that policy's effectiveness.[5]

Because there are few such studies, I also rely on three other sources: investigations of police behavior, general discussions of professionalism, and studies of other organizations that have characteristics similar to those advocated by police reformers.

An Introduction to Police Reform:
Professionalization and Rule Making

To understand the primary directions of police reform, one must have some understanding of professionalization and rule making, because some form of professionalization has been the clarion call of police reformers for at least the past 40 years. This choice of reform has typically been defended on the grounds that it makes police more likely to obey rules. By the 1960s, in response to the civil rights movement as well as the decisions of the United States Supreme Court, professionalization became part of the conventional wisdom of police reform.[6]

Police professionalization has traditionally emphasized improved management techniques, more advanced levels of technology, and higher standards of efficiency—all of these dovetail. Better management means more centralized, and presumably more complete, supervision of the patrolman's street activities. The advocacy of high levels of technology frequently (though not always—weaponry and advanced crime investigatory tools are also advocated) refers to improved communication facilities that help in the process of management. For example, in the eyes of professionalizers, one of the greatest technological advances is communication systems that keep systematic and complete tabs on police activities from the time a citizen makes a request to the time that the officer responds. High standards are integral to this view because better educated and higher paid officers are supposedly more amenable to the control afforded by more pervasive management. Thus they are more willing to be supervised and are less corrupt.

This view of professionalization measures efficiency according to two criteria: how many crimes are solved and how "consistently" a police officer functions. The latter criterion is most important in the present discussion. Consistency, in this case, means how frequently the police officer acts in accordance with formal rules. Rules are general regulations that are supposed to govern behavior in specified situations. Rules are supposed to have a special degree of authoritativeness and officiality. They are formal and explicit attempts to limit or to control the discretion of those within the organization and become the standards against which behavior is evaluated.[7]

The professional officer, according to this view of professionalization, is one who follows the chain of command. He is restrained by his willingness to apply the rules to whatever situation arises. This makes him unbiased and thus increases departmental efficiency. Higher standards of education, combined with better pay, attract the people who are most likely to behave in this way once they become police officers. In short, these police reforms have been very bureaucratic in their emphasis.

Taken alone, this view of professionalization is rather different from professionalization as it is ascribed to other, more traditional professions like medicine and law. Generally a traditional profession is characterized by the existence of an organized and rather esoteric body of knowledge. Members of that profession agree over what properly constitutes this body of knowledge. Partially because the knowledge is viewed as so esoteric, traditional professionalization includes the use of colleagues as the most important judges of a professional's performance. The traditional profession looks to peers rather than the rule book for guidance. Colleagueship is the primary means of control. These colleagues judge on the basis of a code of ethics that is promulgated by the profession itself. Information is communicated through professional associations and professional journals, both of which reinforce the sense of colleagueship.

One reason why police professionalization traditionally has had a different emphasis is because in practice policing is quite different from the traditional professions. The body of knowledge that might be called "working police theory" is unorganized and non-esoteric. Furthermore, there has never been much agreement over what an official body of knowledge would entail if it existed. Consequently there has been no accepted code of ethics. As for control, police departments have depended more upon the chain of command (or at least they have tried to do so). Officially, they are a semimilitary organization, a form of organization that explicitly discourages colleague control.

In recent years, however, police reformers have advocated more traditional forms of professionalization. This was done partially in response to the understanding that policing really and necessarily entailed a great deal more rank and file discretion than the bureaucratic view allowed. It also evolved because in the 60's critics began to talk more in terms of the police officer's relationship with his clientele than his relationship with his superiors. The concern with client relationships is much more a part of traditional professionalization. As we shall consider later, this response to those trying to exert influence on police practices may have been more defensive than reformers care to admit. Whatever the reason, police professionalization has come to mean a combination of the traditional and the police-bureaucratic views. There are important contradictions between the two views, and in the discussion of question 3 we shall look closely at them. Despite these contradictions, we shall consider all of the traditional and bureaucratic characteristics as part of police professionalization because the most influential recent advocates of police reform clearly contain elements of both.

Now let us consider the five questions.

1. Definitions of the Problem:
Two Models of Police Reform

To simplify, the diverse, specific measures may be organized into two groups. Most police reform measures fit into one of two models of police reform which I call the police personnel and the police function model.

The police personnel model concentrates on characteristics of the individual police officer. As a recent Brookings Institution study taking this approach put it, "the heart of the police problem is one of personnel."[8] It advocates both traditional and more management-oriented professionalization, but clearly management takes precedence. Police are insufficiently professionalized in that they lack the appropriate amount of formal education prior to their becoming police officers and are undertrained in their actual preparation for the job. Upper echelon police officers have insufficient knowledge of modern management and other techniques of on-the-job socialization and control. All of these problems are reflected in police work, which tends to be inconsistent with clearer standards. By improving management techniques and hiring officers whose education make them more amenable to supervision, such "erratic" and arbitrary police behavior would be greatly reduced. The personnel model assumes that, in part, citizen involvement in policing increases as the number of professional officers increases.

This model is dominant in actual police reform. Prestigious organizations like the Brookings Institution, the Committee for Economic Development, the President's Commission for Law Enforcement and the Administration of Justice emphasize this model.[9] It is also dominant in the professional police journals.

The police function model, the other view, concentrates on what the police *do* rather than on their individual characteristics. According to this view, the basic dilemmas of policing in this society reduce the likelihood that cops will be tolerant, open, or restrained. There are a number of variations of this view, and many disagreements among its proponents. The problem might be described as a basic tension between due process and the police officer's need to keep order, or it may be described as an incompatibility between the central police mission of keeping order and the freedom of citizens to come and go as they please. The problem may be a racist society, a citzenry implicitly demanding police lawlessness, or a set of criminal statutes whose enforcement is virtually guaranteed to increase the hostility of blacks (for example, some gambling laws). In any case, the locus of the problem is an *inherent* hostility between police officer and citizenry.

Advocates of the police function model may also differ greatly among themselves over the degree that citizen participation should be tolerated in police activities. Some are dubious about any sort of decentralization of police authority, while others urge that police organizations be governed on the basis of neighborhood-oriented participatory democracy. Nonetheless for our purposes all of these fall within the functional model because of their beliefs that there is an *inherent tension between policing as it is basically structured and increasing levels of citizen influence on police departments*. The characteristics of the police officer that the personnel model emphasizes are not completely irrelevant to the function model, but they are tangential.

The police function model is most apparent in the work of social scientists who have written about police behavior and reform. Some of these social scientists have been directly involved in making policy recommendations, but their primary role has been to criticize and evaluate from outside the policy process.[10]

2. The Assumptions of the Two Models

The two models differ basically in their assumptions about the effectiveness of policies attempting to hold police officers more accountable for their actions. The personnel model assumes that there is a direct relationship between raising the standards of police officer education or training and developing an interest in complying with formal and explicit rules. The professionalized patrolman is more likely to accept attempts to regulate his behavior whether these attempts originate from within the department (for example, his bosses) or from outside (for example, civilian review boards).

Though there is no assumption that all rules will meet with a high level of compliance, it is generally assumed that there is more likely to be high levels of compliance in a professionalized department. Modern management techniques reinforce such sensitivity by increasing the department's ability to supervise its officers. Centralization of a department's functions, which the model associates with advanced management techniques, increases the likelihood of rule compliance and improves police services by minimizing bias, arbitrariness, and the use of excessive force.[11] *Most significant of all is the fact that this view of reform sees little tension between professionalizing individuals and increasing the degree to which they are supervised by others.* I shall subsequently spend a good deal of time questioning this assumption, but let us first take a look at the common alternative view.

The police function model assumes that no attempt at institutional change will succeed unless it concentrates upon the basic function of the police. The occupational culture of the police, the need to use discretion, the need to maintain a hostile and suspicious posture, and the constraints of the substantive criminal law are considered to be factors that greatly limit the success of those policies attempting to bring about increased police restraint and compliance. Policing is a job that takes place in a setting that is hard to supervise. The police work alone most of the time. They must be suspicious because being suspicious is what good police work is all about, especially since patrol activities are so isolated. In short, the model is premised on the fact that the police are *rewarded* for behavior that the personnel model sees as the problem. These rewards are based on values about proper police work that go to the heart of what the police are expected to do. Whatever a policeman's education, he must work in this sort of milieu. This occupational culture is strong enough to overcome the effects of his education.

The differences between these perspectives can be seen by taking a closer look at what each model would suggest as an appropriate response to the ambivalence that ghetto residents feel toward the police. The personnel model would urge more efficient use of manpower and better supervision as a means of alleviating the complaints of insufficient police services. Because of the close association between professionalization and restraint, complaints about police brutality would be alleviated if the officers were also professionalized. The functional model would see the conflict as endemic, given the social context in which the police must operate. This is most obviously the case in the ghetto. Putting more officers on ghetto streets may satisfy some of the residents, but it also increases the likelihood that the police will question suspects who are innocent, who resent the questioning, and who complain about their treatment. This makes it more likely that issues of police brutality and harassment will arise. Thus, a solution to one aspect of this problem is accompanied and countered by an exacerbation of the other.

The previous discussion can be summarized and more specifically applied to blacks as follows:

MODELS

	Personnel	Function
Locus of problem:	Defective manpower and management	Inherent hostility in police–citizen interaction, especially in ghetto
Dominant working hypotheses:	1. Professionalization of lower echelon personnel and advanced management techniques will overcome individual resistance to increases in police accountability.	1. The police task mitigates the effectiveness of personnel-oriented reforms.
	2. Professionalization increases restraint on the part of police officers.	2. Only changes in the basic police function leads to greater police restraint and accountability.
Specific reforms:	More formal education for officers, more in-service training in race relations; management training programs; police–community relations programs, more black police officers.	Reduction in the use of the criminal sanction; greater emphasis on and rewards for the service rather than the law enforcement aspects of police work; adoption of police–community relations programs only if they focus on the inherent hostility in the ghetto. Community relations-oriented reforms must not be separated from the everyday behavior of all police officers.

Because most reforms have been oriented toward the personnel model, this discussion will focus more on its hypotheses. The functional model informs my criticism of the personnel model.

3. Investigating the Assumptions

Professionalization, Insulation, and Accountability

The theoretical and other general literature on professionalization, studies of the process of professionalization in other organizations and occupations, and the few studies of police professionalization all suggest that the working hypotheses of the personnel model tend to be disconfirmed, or at the very least tend to be only partially correct. First of all, the research on professionalization clearly shows that professionalization is a means of political control. It is not a reform that intrinsically or automatically works toward the public interest. Professionalization is a process by which an occupation protects itself from the demands of others. It does so by helping the occupation gain "statutory legitimacy and related publicly-sanctioned privileges as well as . . . public acceptance."[12]

Professionalization can be seen as a response by an occupation to protect its authority from other groups attempting to move in on its turf. These competitors include both clients and competing occupational groups. Thus, one function of professionalization is to deflect political demands.[13] Occupations frequently respond to clientele by agreeing to their demands, but occupations also seek to change the nature of clientele response or to deny the legitimacy of that response. Professionalization increases the legitimacy of an occupational claim to deny the validity of its clients' demands or criticisms. It stresses the recognized special competence of the professional to define his clients' needs, especially since in an ideal professional–client relationship the client is supposed to assume unquestioningly the competence of the professional.[14]

In recent years, partially as a consequence of the civil rights and black liberation movements, many professions have found that clients have been increasingly unwilling to defer to the professional's definition of their situation.[15] Some client groups have challenged the teacher's ability to decide what their children can learn, the social worker's and the doctor's ability to tell them what their problems are, and the city planner's competence to advise them on what constitutes the best sort of urban environment. There is now less consensus over the professional's ability to define human needs and less willingness to accept claims to a monopoly on esoteric knowledge.

Also, there has been ferment within the professions themselves, as small but significant numbers of each of the previously mentioned professional groups question the basic premises of their own profession.

Accepting many of these perspectives (for example, advocate planning, community control of schools) requires a serious reconceptualization of the professional's role, since previously so much of the ideal professional–client relationship isolated the client–professional interaction from the environment. These new views encourage occupational competition because they increase the number of relevant perspectives. Problems are less likely to be seen as "purely" medical or "purely" legal or "purely" anything else. These changes are typically seen by professionals as a threat to their *raison d'être*. Such developments create tensions, foster disunity within professions, and lead to the development of a defensive posture on the part of the majority of the professionals.

The police are no exceptions to this. Indeed, despite their differences from the traditional professionals, they may be more vulnerable to the threats that increase the pressure for professionalization.

There are two reasons for this vulnerability. First, the police occupation's professional status has been far too tenuous to stave off its critics. Second, a good portion of the police departments' clientele is not likely to be very submissive to their professional authority in the first place. Unlike the case with other professions, police clientele frequently do not seek help voluntarily. Thus, the tension and hostility toward clients that develops among professions in less tense settings perhaps would be even more likely to develop in law enforcement organizations.[16] Surely these defensive postures could readily develop in relatively professionalized police organizations where policemen are becoming more confident in their abilities at the same time that clients are becoming more hostile and less deferential toward police authority. There is little doubt that many police think that their authority is threatened by their clientele and by other groups competing with them for influence, for example, liberal reform groups, academics, presidential commissions, lawyers, and judges.[17]

The police thus have been experiencing the very forms of competition that lead to defensive professionalization. This leads us to the view that upper echelon police officials readily accept reforms stressing professionalization in part because it protects their status and protects the organization from their clientele and from the views of other non-police groups. Also, while the stress on the need for increased technology, from weaponry to communications, may be primarily a direct response to crime and disorder, it may also have the effect of establishing a definition of a social problem that helps to maintain police status against attacks on its occupational credibility. All of this suggests that the relationship between increasing professionalization and responsiveness to clients may be inverse.

One of the few studies of the impact of police professionalization shows evidence that this disdain for both clients and other groups interested in law enforcement accompanies professionalization. In a survey of officers in a number of small to medium-sized police departments, Walsh found that professionalized officers generally had a more positive attitude toward minority groups. This difference between more and less professionalized individuals, however, is greatly mitigated by some of Walsh's other findings. Seventy percent of those officers whom he classified as "professional strivers" felt that their most unpleasant experience was having their authority challenged. Only 36 percent of the low strivers felt that way. Low professional strivers were much more likely to claim that they would use violence against people who looked or talked tough to them than were the high strivers (45 percent to 7 percent). The importance of this latter difference, however, may be limited because low professional strivers are probably more likely to find such behavior threatening to their authority and to the authority of the entire legal system.[18] What about situations where the most professionalized officer's authority is threatened? Highly professional officers in Walsh's study were indeed more likely to claim that they would use violence against "animals," those people whom police officers encountered but who, in the minds of these officers, had no business with them. Walsh stresses the importance of this conclusion by comparing the latter response to the disdain that physicians have for those who seek their help when in fact they are not sick in a way that a doctor defines as illness.

In this context, it is worth considering some recent efforts at increasing police accountability and citizen participation. They are civilian review boards and neighborhood team policing. Both reforms are usually identified with professionalization. Civilian review boards and other similar attempts at partially removing departmental discipline from internal control have, of course, engendered much conflict, whereas neighborhood team policing has been adopted with less controversy and less police resistance.

Of all the conventional attempts to increase police accountability, none has been resisted as vociferously by the police as civilian review boards. Though their formats vary, these boards generally contain at least some civilians. They hear citizen complaints against police officers and have some authority to follow up on these complaints. To their advocates, such organizations are an integral part of the police–community relations program. Their goal has been to broaden the spectrum of influence by allowing greater community control over law enforcement.

This goal has not been achieved.[19] In some cities, police deparments mobilized against these review boards and became a potent political force in defeating them. Those boards that were ultimately established usually had limited resources for redressing grievances or even for investigating them. Discipline remained firmly under department control, and boards frequently had to depend on police officers themselves to conduct investigations of the complaints.

Other police–community relations programs have also experienced serious difficulties. Community service programs that remained in the hands of police officials were considered by ghetto leaders to be too public-relations oriented and not sufficiently concerned with accountability. On the other hand, those programs that were more interested in increasing the community's role in making police policy tended to be denigrated by most of the officers who were not directly involved. For example, officers who become advocates of black community sentiments, especially if they involved criticizing the police, were typically viewed as bleeding hearts or even turncoats by other officers. Those officers who were directly a part of the community-oriented programs tended to become isolated from the rest of the departments' activities.[20]

In short, there is no evidence that professionalization has been able to break this pattern of opposition or limited implementation regarding review boards or other police–community relations programs. There is, of course, no direct evidence to the contrary, but the broader perspective on professionalization suggests reasons why it may *limit* the adoption of such changes. Outside control and impingement on the decision making process is a threat to the professionals' belief that they alone can best define a situation and decide whether their peers' behavior in a given situation is proper. Outside control deprofessionalizes the occupation, and deprofessionalization is a threat.

The comparative lack of resistance to neighborhood team policing can be understood along these same lines. Neighborhood team policing is an interesting approach because, as I shall later discuss in more detail, it attempts to break out of the rule-oriented limits of the personnel model. It puts control of policy policy making for a particular neighborhood in the hands of a group of police officers who work only in that neighborhood and who have almost the sole responsibility for any policing matter that arises there. Others are called in only if special investigatory work has to be done or if there is an immediate and pressing need for more manpower in the team-policed neighborhood. The basic operating assumption is that because these officers are supposed to work outside the established departmental bureaucracy and because they work more closely with neighborhood leadership, they become more sensitive to the needs of the neighborhood.

Thus in a general sense the neighborhood team policing approach resembles civilian review boards in its concern with police responsiveness.[21] But there are some crucial differences that explain the totally different police response to these programs. They are not oriented toward the investigation or punishment of police misbehavior, and they merge the community relations function with the more general policing functions. (Neighborhood team policing is indeed far more sensitive to the functional model in this very important respect.) But the most important reason for police acceptance is that these programs are *definitely oriented toward maintaining the general pattern of low community participation in police policy making.* As the Urban Institute study that preliminarily evaluates and then advocates neighborhood team policing stated, "While neighborhood team policing is not a program designed to give community control of police, citizen opinions should be carefully considered before plans are completed."[22]

Even this degree of consideration and consultation is narrowly conceived. The Urban Institute report explicitly excludes the Dayton, Ohio, program from its analysis because that program gives to the civilians in the neighborhood too much control over the selection and allocation of police personnel.[23] This exclusion is particularly significant since the Urban Institute's study is the most complete, influential, and favorable review of the subject. Its work will certainly act as a model for future programs. The report stresses the intelligence-gathering advantages that result from consulting with people in the neighborhood. A closer look at Urban Institute summaries of the individual programs shows that in fact this de-emphasis on participation is even greater than that which the report recommended. For example, the St. Petersburg, Florida, program—in many ways the most advanced of the programs—handles citizen complaints in the following manner: "Complaints from citizens concerning conditions, police services, etc., are recorded and the complainant subsequently is contacted again and told that the complaint [has been] received."[24]

That is all the St. Petersburg report says about complaints or police disciplinary procedures; indeed, the issue is ignored generally in the Urban Institute report. Even those portions of the report that direct themselves to community service do so partially because they want to limit some forms of community participation. For instance, the report urges the police to act as advocates for neighborhood complaints against the city, so that the police might become a "legitimate part of the power structure" at the expense of militant groups.

The neighborhood team policing programs have not always been unilaterally accepted by police departments. Resistance has come from middle level supervisory police officials who correctly see the concept as a threat to the usual pattern of hierarchical dominance because that is one of its purposes.[25] Rank and file officers seem to be more favorably disposed, and generally resistance is relatively low because the programs have much appeal for the professionalized officer. The existing patterns of police control over citizens are not threatened, while the realm of police work is expanded for many officers because uniformed police get to do much of the highly prestigious criminal investigation work that is traditionally reserved for detectives. Also, as we shall see below, peer-oriented decision making frees professional strivers from the contraints of bureaucratic rules.

Professionalization, Management, Rules, and Discretion

The personnel model does not consider the weaknesses inherent in a system of control that relies on rules. These weaknesses do not hinder all uses of rule making. Nonetheless, the limits are important enough to get more consideration than they usually do. The use of rules at times makes it difficult to treat the client in meaningful, personal terms. Rules often interfere with client–worker interactions because the work-er's responsibility is to something abstract (the rule) rather than to the client. As a result, over a period of time the client is seen as part of the organization's problems rather than as someone who needs immediate help. The client is blamed for the organization's tensions and failures. This result hurts the poor the most because they are the ones with the fewest resources to circumvent the rules and are least able to be treated on the basis of their individual case rather than on the basis of generali-zations.[26]

Another general weakness of control by rules is that such control may do the most harm to those members of the organization who are most restrained in the absence of rules. The sociologist Erving Goffman tells us that the more easily a person learns to cope with his or her immediate surroundings, the more that ability to cope becomes subconscious. Con-sequently, people with this competency become less able to present a for-mal, explicit rationale for their actions.[27] Without stretching an analogy too much, we might consider a self-restrained police officer as one who finds himself in that paradoxical position. One of the reasons for his re-straint is that his skill in sizing up the environment helps prevent him from overreacting, that is, responding in a way that others would find both out of the ordinary and unnecessary. Forcing this officer to justify such behavior according to the standards set by abstract, general rules might discourage this person from achieving restraint, one of the very goals that rule making seeks to achieve. This might be worth the sacrifice if officers who were less skilled along these lines, or lacked restraint for other reasons, were effectively constrained by rules. Putting it another way, if the following prediction about the effect of rule making were accurate, then the personnel model's emphasis would appear more sound:

> The impact of rule making on the patrolman can scarcely be overstated. Operating under a protective umbrella of departmental rules, the individual police officer could no longer be on his own to interpret a given court

> decision, group of decisions or statutes. His discretion would be channeled by carefully researched and articulated rules—rules formulated in categories meaningful to the policeman. . . .[28]

Unfortunately, this view seems overly optimistic. The author gives no supporting evidence. Those who have investigated and described other organizations argue that compliance with rules is uncertain and depends upon a variety of factors such as the visibility of the behavior to be controlled, the costs of noncompliance, and the tactics people have at their disposal to circumvent the rules, to name only a few. Since, as the functional model emphasizes, everyday police work is not highly visible, the task of policing frequently requires that rules be violated, and the police have many effective means at their disposal to circumvent the rules, this approach to reform may be particularly unrealistic.[29] Another characteristic of rule making is that it works counter to the premises of traditional professionalization. This alone should not be considered a weakness; one might very well want to counter traditional professionalization by eliminating the sense of autonomy and independence. What *is* a weakness about the personnel approach is that it fails to see the contradictions in advocating both professionalization's traditional and bureaucratic forms. This model assumes that rules and central supervision will be more acceptable to an officer who aspires to be professional. This assumption fails to consider the studies of other organizations that show the basic tension between professionalization and bureaucratization. The traditional professional's sense of autonomy is accompanied by a related belief in the need to use discretion to deal with a particular situation. This makes the professional feel unduly constrained by organizational rules.[30] This tension is extraordinarily great in police organizations. Unlike most other organizations, individual police discretion *increases* as one moves down the hierarchy.[32] Patrolmen exercise more initiative than their superiors.

Furthermore, officers who are most interested in a professional-oriented, problem solving approach to their clients are the least likely to accept the need for centralized control, as Susan White's study of the values, policing techniques, and orientations toward command and rules among officers in one large city police department shows.[32] White classifies the officers according to four predominant role types. The type that she labels "problem-solvers," the most positively oriented toward the people they deal with, are also the ones who are among the *least* willing to accept anything other than their self-restraint as proper sources of control over their behavior. On the other hand, those who are control oriented have values and attitudes that *decrease* their sensitivity toward their clients. This poses an interesting dilemma for police reform, a dilemma that surely cannot be solved by a reliance on rule making.

The whole notion about the advantages of centralization may be another shibboleth. The dominant assumption is that through centralization, police services can be offered more quickly and effectively. Furthermore, the model assumes that centralization makes it easier to hold officers accountable for their activities.

A recent study of policing in and around Indianapolis, Indiana, should cast this assumption in a critical light. On the measures of crime victimization, willingness to call the police, and evaluation of police manpower allocation, this study showed that citizens served by relatively decentralized departments received better service.[33] Because the investigated neighborhoods and communities were not predominantly black, the applicability of the findings are somewhat limited. Still, it seems quite possible that decentralization would also be more effective in black neighborhoods where crime victimization is high and willingness to call the police is low.

Of all the popular reforms, the previously discussed neighborhood team policing concept comes closest to recognizing and dealing with the tension between professionalization and rules. These programs try to replace the quasi-military, centralized, bureaucratic model of police administration with its emphasis on detailed, unrealistic orders that police officers frequently ignore and disdain. Instead, policies are supposed to be made by all the working officers. The program depends upon fellow team-officers as the most important source of pressure for good police work. Though this policy might very well handle the tension *within* the organization, it might do so *at the expense of the officer's relationship with the team's neighborhood.* Advocates of neighborhood team policing assume that a cohesive peer-oriented organization will be more amenable to strong pressure from the citizens it serves. Certainly it is the history of other professionals, and is consistent with our earlier discussion of the politics of professionalization, that such peer groups act as much to protect their peers from outsiders as they do to assure accountability to their clientele.

Like traditional professionalization, rule making can also insulate an organization from outside influence. The process of rule making might be adopted in order to add legitimacy to the notion that the organization can regulate itself. Indeed some advocates of police rule making quite clearly see it as a way of keeping courts and lay persons (that is, competing groups) from impinging any further on police policy making.

Perhaps this insulation is indeed part of the hidden agenda of conventional police reform. In any case, if rule making acts to blunt accountability, then clearly the process works counter to the stated goals of conventional police reform.

4. The Locus of the Problem

At this stage, I can offer some plausible statements about the limits of police reform.

First, the process of professionalization may exacerbate the problem of controlling the police. This seems plausible whether we refer to control that is exercised within the organization or to the control that those outside the police department exercise over law enforcement policy making. Thus, the personnel model of police reform may increase the problem of police accountability. Moreover, the reform's greatest impact may be in limiting control by the citizenry and by those who compete with the police for control over police policy making.

Second, reforms oriented toward the personnel model do not alleviate the tension between administration and participation. For instance, neighborhood team policing encourages policies that are rather liberating for more professional-oriented officers, but this may occur at the expense of effective participation by outside groups. On the other hand, measures that are more oriented toward group participation may be resisted by both the professional officer and his less progressive colleague.

In short, the locus of these problems of police accountability and control seems to lie outside the attitudes of the ill-educated officer in a badly organized police department (in the personnel model sense). This is, of course, what the functional model predicts. The problem with the functional model, however, is that it diagnoses far better than it cures. One view within this functional model argues that what is needed is acceptance of this reality and the difficulty of changing it. In this case, community participation is at best a secondary goal.[34] Others argue that the standards of professionalization must be redefined by society to stress self-restraint, but advocates of this change give no guidance about the strategies of change that would accomplish this redefinition.[35] Those who talk in terms of institutional racism advocate the development of grass roots, issue-oriented organizations that attempt to expose white racism.[36]

Thus the functional model offers a Hobson's choice to those who are concerned with broadening community participation in police policy making. The choice can be described in the following way: Either one accepts the notion that cooperation between policeman and citizen must virtually take as given the nature of the police organization, or one must rely on basic but vague and long term social change as a catalyst for developing restrained officers who are amenable to something closer to participatory democracy.

Like the personnel model, the functional model ultimately fails because it does not come to grips with the issue of police restraint. It can criticize the simple professionalization-rules-accountability-restraint view, but it cannot offer a useful alternative. Paradoxically this failure results from the fact that the functional model is itself so caught up in the view, albeit as a critic, that it cannot offer alternatives. What is needed is a perspective on police reform that recognizes the need for standards of behavior but that places far less emphasis on the conventional strategies of change that purport to bring about and sanction the adoption of these standards. Certainly we should not unilaterally dismiss the effectiveness of the rule making process. Anything involving rule compliance is not simply an either/or concept. Rules may work better in some contexts than others. There ought to be more detailed analysis of rule making and its impact, a subject that has received a very little attention from social scientists.[37] Still, we should consider other approaches that try to develop restraint and empathy toward the client without the dependence on rule making or professionalization either in the traditional or the bureaucratic sense. This should be done if for no other reason than to prevent professionalization and management from so monopolizing police reform ideology that they become even more a part of the conventional wisdom. Tentative and fragmentary as the previously discussed evidence is, it at least suggests that alternatives need serious consideration. The subsequent discussion offers an alternative viewpoint and some specific reforms that stem from this view. It de-emphasizes rule making and professionalization in the traditional sense.

5. Alternative Point of View

The alternative viewpoint and the reforms emanating from it also stress accountability and restraint, but in a manner that attempts to take into consideration the limits of the conventional responses. Thus, instead of restraint based on rules and hierarchy, the alternative stresses *self*-restraint. It does not depend upon either form of professionalization to bring about the desired changes; instead it relies on strategies that try to convince officers of the personal benefits associated with tolerance and restraint. The strategies also seek to protect those officers who are sympathetic toward such views but who are frustrated in their attempts to advocate or manifest their positions.

The alternative is based on the premise that some important changes can occur within the existing police organization. Of course, such success is limited as long as our legal system has a racial and class bias, and as long as we rely on the police to do so much of society's dirty work. The strategies associated with this viewpoint might very well help police officers understand how much they actually do impose laws on groups of people that benefit very little from this imposition.

Accompanying this assumption about the possibility of change within the organization is the view that the police are by no means universally sullen, hostile, and distrustful of reform.[38] Moreover, even within a single department there exist important differences of opinion over specific issues like what role rules should play in policing and how policemen should treat critics whether they come from within or outside policing. Despite contrary claims to the public, police officers do not trust their colleagues very much. Though unity, cohesiveness, and defensiveness characterized the police in their response to the peace and civil rights demonstrations, and other crises, policemen generally do not show such enthusiastic agreement with their fellow officers. They do not get along with each other all that well. It is more accurate to see police departments as organizations composed of diverse kinds of people, some of whom are rather tolerant, sympathetic, and open in their attitudes towards the demands of the black community. Police officers with these attitudes often find themselves in a formal or informal organizational setting (the "locker room" culture) that discourages such attitudes. The position of such officers is tenuous, but they often manage to survive, though sometimes their survival is based on a sort of splendid isolation from the rest of the department as a co-called reform-oriented police leadership allows them to try new ideas where they will not bother anyone, least of all the rest of the department.[39] The following alternative tries to use this group as a locus for change without generating the isolation and frustration that typically emanate from such change strategies.

One more word of caution. I am not now saying that the alternative should completely replace conventional police reform, though one should not rule this out as a long-term possibility. What I offer is a somewhat different direction, or what social scientists call a heuristic device. Heuristic devices are catalysts; their purpose is to get observers to see a phenomenon or a problem in a new or rather different light.

The alternative includes four provisions. The first two try to change the nature of police control. The last two are primarily change strategies that help make the first two possible. The provisions are as follows:

1. Reduce the hierarchical nature of police supervision.
2. Stress and legitimate self-restraint as a source of control.
3. Emphasize apprenticeships as the most important form of police education.
4. Rely on gentle subversion as the most important general change strategy.

Reducing Hierarchy

If the rule making process itself is at fault, then we must reduce the extent of internal police supervision on the basis of rules. Police departments are very peculiar organizations in that they justify their operations in very hierarchical terms ("quasi-miltary" is the frequently used phrase), but in fact the rank and file officers use a tremendous amount of discretion. The alternative would accept this fact and would try to decentralize police supervision in order both to facilitate and emphasize discretion. The officer would be held less accountable to those higher in rank or anyone distant from the scene of action. Instead, he (or she) would be held more accountable to himself and to the people he serves in the streets.

Increasing everyday accountability to the people he serves does not mean increasing the use of civilian review boards, at least as they have been typically constituted. Like other attempts at regulating policemen, these boards also show all the inherent weaknesses of rule making. More specifically, they offer very little guidance to the police officer's everyday activities, but they isolate the police from the community by increasing the officers alienation from the community. Their success is limited to dealing with the exceptional case, and any further reliance on them as a more pervasive source of police supervision is likely to have results that are disappointing to their advocates. The problem with review boards is not that insufficient resources have been committed to them. Rather, it has to do with the presumptions that some of their advocates have about what they can accomplish.

The alternative we would stress is the sharing rather than the control aspects of police–community relations.

It would work from and toward a perspective that sees community relations as

> . . . the establishment of a process of *interaction* between police and community, where each group attempted to behave in such a way as to ensure that the relationship would be maintained. . . . At the level of interaction this means training policemen *to see clients not as categories, but as part of the common situation* with the policeman. . . . Throughout, the point would be made that effective police work means retaining a sense of openness between the client and the policeman.[40]

Curbing the hierarchical nature of supervisors is only one step. By itself it would create a situation dear to the heart of the most ardent law and order advocate, so there must be other changes as well. The subsequent strategies speak to the issue of replacing hierarchy. These alternatives are less concerned with imposing a new form of organizational structure— indeed such an imposition would defeat the purpose of the change—than they are with making the police more restrained in settings where little or no such structure exists.

Legitimating and Emphasizing Self-restraint

If formal rules are not the answer and if we do not want the police to be completely unbridled in their work, we must focus on ways to get the police to restrain themselves. We know surprisingly little about the processes that encourage or foster self-restraint or about the individuals who are most restrained in ambiguous situations where they must consider alternative viewpoints. (The latter surely describes a situation the police face all the time.) We do know that most people react to each other in a fairly restrained manner most of the time, even in (or perhaps because of) the absence of formal rules. We also know that *some* police officers are especially adept at this skill and seem "ennobled" by ambiguity, that is, their attitude is, "because standards are so uncertain and opinions are so diverse, I might really be imposing my views on others . . . therefore, I must be restrained in order to avoid the imposition."[41] Most of our knowledge on this subject tends to be quite formalistic. When people write making police less arbitrary and more restrained in using discretion, they generally advocate rule making.

Though I am in some sympathy with those who are cynical toward the advocacy of more research, the subject of self-restraint is so important and our knowledge is so limited that one of the first tasks must be an increase of social scientific research on the subject. Such work requires a meeting of minds; it involves a much more thorough attempt to synthesize the work done by lawyers on the subject of discretion with findings of the sociological and psychological studies that have considered the development of self-restraint in settings that legal scholars ignore. This work requires more than constructing a psychological profile of restrained individuals, police officers, or others. More attention should be paid to street behavior, to the *interactions* between policeman and citizen within the context of such interaction, and to the subtle and not so subtle cues the officer and the citizen exchange. Erving Goffman's approach to the study of "normal" everyday life could be particularly helpful.[42]

It takes more than research to make such changes effective, especially if the changes emphasize ideas that the police establishment, as well as its most persistent critics, distrust. Self-restraint and discretion generally have a bad name in these circles. Conventional reformers do not trust these processes, and police officials do not like to talk of these issues because of their fear that admitting the importance of discretion or the limits of rules will make them more open to criticism. So the issue ends up in the netherworld of policy making. Policemen learn from their fellow officers that rules are unrealistic, that they must use discretion far more than the public believes or wants to admit, but that they must, nonetheless, justify their behavior after the fact on the basis of rules. This increases their cynicism and their hostility toward outsiders.

This process of decision making must come out of the closet. Social scientists again have a role to play. Those who write about public administration can help get others to see the realities of discretion by developing social theories that stress the *endemic* nature of the process.[43] This would be a small but important first step in getting the public to see how unimportant or counterproductive rules can be in many settings. Another related problem is that there is little agreement on what restraint means in regard to policing. This is very serious since it is related to society's ambivalence over what it wants the police to do. Social scientists are not going to solve this problem themselves. As the police function model correctly points out, the ambivalence may be inherent. But social scientists could devote much more attention to developing such standards of proper social control and proper police conduct. Since this is a paper on police reform and not on research methodology, it is not necessary to offer more details. It is enough to say that there are such methods that offer promise in developing such standards by synthesizing our knowledge of organizational behavior with more explicitly value-oriented works in philosophy and jurisprudence.[44]

This process of legitimation would also rely partially on usual forms of communication to get these ideas across. Mass media and traditional police classroom education would be such formats, but these alone would have little success. New formats must be developed to make police officers more amenable to the changes.

That brings us to the third and fourth steps.

Apprenticeships

What is needed is an educational process that better prepares police for restraint in using intuition and initiative. Learning to be intuitive may sound anomalous, but in fact what often seems like intuition involves a very complex if unarticulated form of decision making that draws primarily from past experience. Apprenticeships offer an important way of teaching these subtleties. Apprenticeships emphasize on-the-job training. Implicit is the view that something other than formal rules is necessary and that one can pick up pointers that allow the person to deal with the absence of rules without being erratic or arbitrary. It stresses the need to deal with the situation at hand and relies on peer pressure and the trainee's own bad experiences in the field as the most important sanctions.

For comparison, think of the way plumbers learn their trade or carpenters learn their craft.[45]

Is not this how police learn now? Not exactly, for some very subtle but important reasons. First, on-the-job training now is all too frequently used to subvert the more theoretical, abstract classroom training that officers also receive and thus to denigrate the value of outsiders' views. Second, standards get defined in terms of *formal* education, whether in the police academy or on the college campus, and thus the thrust of police education is away from apprenticeships. The dominant form of education emphasizes traditional classroom activity. It frequently overemphasizes the notion of the certainty of rules.[46] In this regard, formal police education is full of paradoxes. It tries to teach police officers to handle ambiguity by stressing certainty and hierarchy. It tries to get a police officer to react to concrete situations by using a format that divorces that officer from reality.

Thus, as presently used, neither the typical apprentice-oriented street training nor the more formal education merges theory and experience very well. Such a merger would require that universities reverse themselves and play a more modest role in police education. Its role would not be so directly concerned with police training. This is not an easy reversal, especially since in recent years academics have been so willing and uncritical about dipping into the federal till for police training program money. Academia's most important function is a less directly service-oriented one that involves the research and reality-defining mentioned in the previous discussion of self-restraint. Apprenticeships could merge rather than reject these theories.

Changing Attitudes toward Change:
Gentle Subversion

None of the previous steps is likely to be effective unless it is advantageous for the police to act in the desired manner. The fourth provision is based on the assumption that for many individuals the alternative is unconventional and threatening.[47] It also assumes that verbal communication alone will not reduce the threatened feeling.

The first goal of this change strategy would be to reduce this sense of threat. Change agents, that is, those advocating the alternatives we have discussed, would have to emerge from within the ranks of the department. These change agents would not have to be a highly ranked police officer. What is more important is that the agents have good working relationships with the formal department leadership. Proponents of change would initially set about to discover those officers who seem frustrated by the police organization. These frustrated officers would probably be roughly of two types; those who simply want to be restrained in their work and those who believe they can be more restrained and sympathetic in the absence of rules. To both groups the change agents would offer themselves not as dogmatic prophets of the success of their plan but rather as willing listeners.

Initially, the change agents would concentrate on the group of officers who feel that the rules and culture of the organization make it more difficult to be restrained and sympathetic. The strategy would involve establishing informal but open forms of communication among these officers. Because it is so essential for the change agents to demonstrate rather than simply advocate that one can operate effectively and still be open to the views of others, he or she would make no attempt to conceal the identity of this group or their activities. This strategy gives the sympathetic group a chance to coalesce, while making other officers aware of them in a setting that limits distrust.

Accompanying this strategy would be changes that would make this setting even more relaxed and ultimately make it easier for others to be identified with the sympathetic group. One of the most obvious needs is protection. One should be under no delusions about the destructive effects the rest of the police organization can have on this sympathetic group. Police departments are very good at drumming out such people, or at least cooling them out by letting them try their own ideas in a setting that is guaranteed to minimize their impact. To protect the officers from these consequences, one must anchor their positions more securely in the organization and reduce the leadership's feeling that the group threatens it.

To protect the officers, change agents would act as mediators between the group and the formal leadership. Mediation is, of course, most obviously associated with other forms of labor–management issues, but it nicely lends itself to the other issues as well.[48] It seeks to resolve conflicts by convincing the parties that basic principles and ideologies are not the primary issues in the dispute and that the parties to the dispute should view their situations and their priorities quite pragmatically. Because, by definition, mediation is never binding, the mediator's need to obtain compromise is very strong. The process could be used to negotiate an opportunity for the more self-restrained group to try something contrary to existing departmental rules. This would institutionalize lines of communication between these parties and the leadership and thus make it more difficult for the upper echelon to forget about the experiment. This format might be used, for example, to work out an arrangement for officers who wanted to allow for community participation in police policy making to a greater extent than even neighborhood team policing.

Ideally, what would be happening as a result of this strategy? First, the sense of threat would be reduced because initially only those who are committed to the alternative would have to commit themselves to it.

Second, through mediation and through open lines of communication, these individuals get a chance to show their stuff to others. Third, those who are hostile and distrustful observe the advantages of having the ability to merge one's perspectives with those of the people they must deal with every day. Indeed the final goal would be this very merging—a combining of leadership and followers, police and community.

As I implied in the introduction to the discussion of this alternative, one should not be pretentious about this approach. Furthermore, to do so would be hypocritical and counterproductive because pretention is too much like the very prophesy that the change strategy must avoid. Still, the alternatives are worth considering because from the standpoint of police reform they are unconventional and because the assumptions of conventional reform appear so tenuous.

Postscript

Our hope is that this book has impressed two major points upon the reader. First, the problems of racial discrimination and inequality that have been examined are a natural consequence of past and current political realities in our society. This is true not only because our political leaders allowed blacks to be suppressed and exploited for hundreds of years; but, as Savitch has pointed out, because our political system is heavily biased in favor of upper socioeconomic status groups.[1] Those who are favored by the system tend to prosper, those who are not may suffer. As long as these biases continue, many of our current social problems will persist.[2]

Second, the problems that have been discussed have an impact on a large segment of the population, be they white, black, rich, or poor. The failure of the average citizen to recognize this truth is perhaps the greatest obstacle to achieving social change. The average citizen is affected in two ways: First, those characteristics of our political and social system that so drastically vanquish minorities victimize the average citizen as well. The disproportionate influence of wealthy elites in our system means that the thrust of political actions are usually toward protecting the status quo rather than responding to the needs of average citizens.[3] For example, the entrenchment of certain privileged groups in our government allows them to promote and defend excessive profits for corporations on commodities and services, to provide direct and indirect subsidies to big business that exceeds 20 billion dollars a year, to keep the minimum wage down, to defeat laws designed to guarantee workers decent and safe working conditions, to vanquish health programs, to emasculate pollution laws, and so on.[4] As long as wealth is so critical to power and influence in our political system, these events will continue and they will disproportionately suppress all the working class, be they black or white.

The self-interest of citizens is involved in a second way. When certain conditions prevail in our society, all suffer. For example, conditions such as racism spawn poverty and unemployment, which in turn propagate crime,[5] urban decay, and city abandonment. Recent reports reveal that the once insulating suburbs are no longer safe from serious crime, taxes continue to increase to support inadequate and degrading welfare programs, and cities continue to decline. The message is clear: We live in a finite world in which the conditions of all people are interrelated. Poverty, discrimination, and misery affect all. Thus when Savitch says that we must "work to identify out-group demands with the American center," he touches on the heart of the matter. Such a strategy would not be a Machiavellian ploy, it would be the embodiment of an absolute truth.

Notes

1. The Politics of Deprivation and Response

1. The most outstanding representative work of this school of thought is Gunnar Myrdal, Vols. I and II, *An American Dilemma* (New York: Harper & Row, Publishers, 1944). See also Louis Lomax, *The Negro Revolt* (New York: Harper & Row, Publishers, 1962); Nathan Glazer and Patrick Moynihan, *Beyond The Melting Pot* (Cambridge, Mass.: The M.I.T. Press, 1970). The most recent empirical and socioeconomic expression of this thought can be found in Ben J. Wattenberg and Richard Scammon, "Black Progress and Liberal Rhetoric," *Commentary*, 55 (April, 1973), 35–44.

2. The leading treatise on this aspect of racial politics is Stokely Carmichael and Charles Hamilton, *Black Power* (New York: Random House, 1967). See also Franz Fanon, *Black Skin, White Masks* (New York: Grove Press, 1967); Claude M. Lightfoot, *Ghetto Rebellion to Black Liberation* (New York: International Publishers, 1968); and William K. Tabb, *The Political Economy of the Black Ghetto* (New York: W. W. Norton & Company, 1970).

3. See Carmichael and Hamilton, *op. cit.*, Chapters 1 and 2.

4. Robert Dahl, *Who Governs* (New Haven, Conn.: Yale University Press, 1961), p. 84.

5. *Ibid.*, p. 311. See also his *A Preface to Democratic Theory* (Chicago: University of Chicago Press, 1956).

6. For an excellent and detailed treatment of the concept of "bias," see E. E. Schattschneider, *The Semi-sovereign People* (New York: Holt, Rinehart and Winston, 1960), pp. 20–43, *passim*, and pp. 71–72); and Peter Bachrach and Morton Baratz, *Power & Poverty* (New York: Oxford University Press, 1970), Chapter 1.

7. Cf. Peter Bachrach and Morton Baratz, "Two Faces of Power," in Charles McCoy and John Playford (eds.), *Apolitical Politics: A Critique of Behavioralism* (New York: Thomas Y. Crowell Company, 1967); and Schattschneider, *op. cit.*, pp. 20–43, 71–73, *passim*.

8. Cf. Ralf Dahrendorf, *Class and Class Conflict in Industrial Society* (Stanford, Cal.: Stanford University Press, 1959), p. 187.

9. Lester Milbraith, *Political Participation: How and Why Do People Get Involved in Politics* (Chicago: Rand McNally & Company, 1965), *passim*, Chapter 5. Robert E. Lane, *Political Life: Why and How Do People Get Involved in Politics* (New York: The Free Press, 1959), see especially Chapter 16. Also, Angus Campbell, Gerald Gurin, and Warren Miller, *The Voter Decides* (Evanston, Ill.: Row, Peterson and Company, 1954), pp. 187–194; and Bernard Berelson, Paul Lazarfeld, and William McPhee, *Voting* (Chicago: University of Chicago Press, 1954), Chapter 4.

10. See, for example, Grant McConnell, *Private Power and American Democracy* (New York: Alfred A. Knopf, 1966); Murray Edleman, *The Symbolic Uses of Politics* (Urbana: University of Illinois, 1967), Chapter 3; and Harmon Ziegler, *Interest Groups in American Society* (Englewood Cliffs, N.J.: Prentice-Hall, 1964), especially Chapter 10.

11. For an account of how this process actually worked to affect Board policy, see David Rogers, *110 Livingston Street: Politics and Bureaucracy in the New York City School System* (New York: Random House, 1968), pp. 216–220.

12. See, for instance, *The New York Times* (April 7, 1974), p. 6E.

13. See, for example, Edgar Litt, *Beyond Pluralism: Ethnic Politics in America* (Glenview, Ill.: Scott, Foresman and Company, 1970), pp. 46–48; and Daniel Moynihan and Nathan Glazier, *Beyond the Melting Pot* (Cambridge, Mass.: The M.I.T. Press, 1970), pp. vii–xc, *passim*.

14. For a general account of the strike, see Maurice Berube and Marilyn Gittell (eds.), *Confrontation at Ocean Hill-Brownsville* (New York: Praeger Publishers, 1969); and Martin Mayer, *The Teacher's Strike* (New York: Harper & Row, Publishers, 1968).

15. There are nearly as many operational definitions for ideology as scholars who have used the term. Samuel Patterson and S. M. Lipset distinguish ideology from "pragmatic" politics and refer to an "ideological style" which is dogmatic or imbued with "affective commitment." See Samuel Patterson, "The Political Cultures of the American States," in Norman Lutbeg (ed.), *Public Opinion and Public Policy: Models of Political Linkage* (Homewood, Ill.: Dorsey Press, 1968), p. 278; and Seymour M. Lipset, *Political Man* (Garden City, N.Y.: Doubleday & Company, 1959), Chapter 13. Others such as Herbert McCloskey and Robert Lane have used the term in a more neutral sense as I have attempted in this essay. See Herbert McCloskey, "Consensus and Ideology in American Politics," *The American Political Science Review*, LVIII (June, 1964), 362–363.

16. For an interesting discussion of this subject, see Edelman, *op. cit.*, and Michael Lipsky, *Protest in City Politics* (Chicago: Rand McNally & Company, 1970).

17. See Peter Bachrach and Morton Baratz, "Decisions and Non-Decisions," *The American Political Science Review*, LVII (September, 1963), 632–642.

18. For an elaboration of the concept of "administrative impartiality," see Max Weber, "Class, Status, Party," in A. M. Henderson and Talcott Parson (eds. and trans.), *From Max Weber: Essays in Sociology* (New

York; Oxford University Press, 1946), pp. 146–244; and Reinhard Bendix, "Bureaucracy and the Problem of Power," in Robert Merton, Alisa Gray, Barbara Hockey, and Hanan C. Selvin (eds.), *Reader in Bureaucracy* (New York: The Free Press, 1952), p. 132.

19. See, for instance, Edelman, *op. cit.*; and Lipsky, *op. cit.*; and also Theodore Lowi, *The End of Liberalism: Ideology, Policy and Crisis of Public Order* (New York: W. W. Norton & Company, 1969).

20. Lipskey, *op. cit.*, Chapter VII.

21. Charles Silberman, *Crisis in Black and White* (New York: Random House, 1964), p. 23.

22. *Ibid.*, p. 23.

23. Robert E. Martin, "The Relative Political Status of the Negro in the United States," in Harry A. Bailey, Jr. (ed.), *Negro Politics in America* (Columbus, Ohio; Charles E. Merrill Books, 1967), p. 18.

24. Robert C. Weaver, "The Negro Ghetto," in August Meier and Elliott Rudwick (eds.), *The Making of Black America*, Vol. II (New York: Atheneum Publishers, 1969), p. 174.

25. Silberman, *op. cit.*, p. 31.

26. Weaver, *op. cit.*, p. 169.

27. *Ibid.*, p. 166.

28. *Ibid.*, p. 168.

29. Silberman, *op. cit.*, p. 33.

30. Joe R. Feagin and Harlan Hahn, *Ghetto Revolts* (New York: The Macmillan Company, 1973), pp. 78–79.

31. For an interesting journalistic account of this event and the black situation in Chicago, see Mike Royko, *Boss* (New York: E. P. Dutton & Co., 1971), pp. 35–36.

32. *The National Roster of Black Elected Officials*, Vol. 3 (Washington, D.C.: Joint Center for Political Studies, May, 1973), p. xvi.

33. *Ibid.*, p. x.

34. *Ibid.*, p. vi.

35. See, for Example, William H. Towe, *Barriers To Black Political Participation In North Carolina* (Atlanta: Voter Education Project, 1972), pp. 10–12.

36. *Ibid.*, p. 18.

37. See Mario Fantini, Marilyn Gittell, and Richard Magat, *Community Control and the Urban School* (New York: Praeger Publishers, 1970), pp. 228–229. Also, for a comprehensive treatment of community control, see Alan Altschuler, *Community Control* (New York: Pegasus, 1970).

38. Carmichael and Hamilton, *op. cit.*, p. 44.

39. *Ibid.*, p. 44.

40. National Advisory Commission on Civil Disorders, *Report of the National Advisory Commission on Civil Disorders* (New York: Bantam Books, 1968), p. 111; see also pp. 128–135. For some excellent treatments on the

subject, see H. L. Nieburg, *Political Violence* (New York: St. Martin's Press, 1969); Jerome Skolnick, *The Politics of Protest* (New York: Simon and Schuster, 1969), p. 44; and Nieburg, *op. cit.*, p. 165.

2. Housing and Racial Segregation

1. Karl E. and Alma F. Taeuber, *Negroes in Cities* (Chicago: Aldine Publishing Company, 1965), pp. 39–40.
2. Frank S. Kristof, *Urban Housing Needs Through the 1980's: An Analysis and Projection*, Research Report No. 10 of the National Commission on Urban Problems (Washington, D.C.: Government Printing Office, 1968), pp. 7–8.
3. *Ibid.*, pp. 6–7; and 1970 census, *Housing Characteristics for States, Cities, and Counties*, Vol. 1, Part 1, U.S. Summary, Table 2.
4. *Ibid.*, p. 57.
5. *Ibid.*, p. 45.
6. Ben J. Wattenberg and Richard M. Scammon, "Black Progress and Liberal Rhetoric," *Commentary*, 55 (April, 1973) 35–44.
7. *Ibid.*, p. 39.
8. Walter Williams, "Cleveland's Crisis Ghetto," *Trans-Action* (September, 1967), pp. 33–42.
9. *Ibid.*, p. 34.
10. *Ibid.*, p. 35.
11. Edward C. Banfield, *The Unheavenly City: The Nature and Future of Our Urban Crisis* (Boston: Little, Brown and Company, 1970).
12. The Center for Community Change, The National Urban League, *The National Survey of Housing Abandonment*, New York, 3rd ed. (March, 1972).
13. See Brian D. Boyer, *Cities Destroyed for Cash: The FHA Scandal at HUD* (Chicago: Follett Publishing Company, 1973).
14. *Time* (December 17, 1973), pp. 18–19.
15. See, for example, Henry J. Aaron, *Shelter and Subsidies: Who Benefits From Federal Housing Policies?* (Washington, D.C.: The Brookings Institution, 1972), especially Chapter 4; Patricia Llany Hodge and Philip M. Hauser, *The Federal Income Tax in Relation to Housing*, Research Report No. 5, The National Commission on Urban Problems (Washington, D.C.: Government Printing Office, 1968), especially pp. 29–33.
16. Higbee stated in 1960 that suburban growth was consuming up to half a million acres a year. See Edward Higbee, *The Squeeze: Cities Without Space* (New York: William Morrow and Company, Apollo Edition), p. 129.
17. Higbee also foresaw that the "era of the commuter suburb's explosive growth will be rather brief . . . comparable to the flash of a meteor against the long darkness of a winter's night," *ibid.*, p. 114.

18. *Second Annual Report on Housing Goals*, Message from the President of the United States, House Document No. 91–292 (Washington, D.C.: Government Printing Office, 1970), p. 4.

19. William A. Caldwell (ed.), *How to Save Urban America* (New York: New American Library, 1973), pp. 20–21.

20. Toledo *Blade* (December 24, 1971).

21. Chicago Daily News Service dispatch in Toledo *Blade* (June 24, 1973).

22. *Euclid* v. *Amber Realty*, 272 U.S. 365 (1926).

23. *National Land and Invest. Co.* v. *Easttown Twp. Bd. of Adjmt.*, 419 Pa. 504, 215 A.2d 597 (1965).

24. *Oakwood at Madison* v. *Tp. of Madison*, 117 N.J. Super. 11 (Sup. Ct. 1971).

25. *The Construction Industry Association of Sonoma County et al.* v. *The City of Petaluma et al.*, C-73 663 LHB.

26. Frederick C. Mezey, "Beyond Exclusionary Zoning—A Practitioner's View of the New Zoning," *The Urban Lawyer*, 5 (Winter, 1973), 57 (emphasis in the original).

27. *Ibid.*, p. 68.

28. William A. Caldwell, *op. cit.*, p. 21.

29. National Committee Against Discrimination in Housing, *Summary of Recent Court Challenges to Exclusionary Land-Use Practices* (Washington, D.C.: September, 1972), mimeographed, pp. 5–6. The Committee is a good source of information on this topic.

30. *James* v. *Valtierra*, 402 U.S. 137 (1971); *rev'g Baltierra* v. *Housing Authority*, 313 F. Supp. 1 (N.D. Cal. 1970).

31. This is discussed in Robert E. Forman, *Black Ghettos, White Ghettos, and Slums* (Englewood Cliffs, N.J.: Prentice-Hall, 1971), especially Chapters 7, 8, and 9.

32. David R. Hunter, *The Slums: Challenge and Response* (New York: The Free Press, 1964), p. 3.

33. See, for example, Edmund K. Faltenmeyer, *Redoing America* (New York: The Macmillan Company, Collier Books, 1969), p. 27; Miles L. Colean, *Renewing Our Cities* (New York: The Twentieth Century Fund, 1953), p. 41.

34. Cf. Lee Rainwater, *Behind Ghetto Walls: Black Families in a Federal Slum* (Chicago: Aldine Publishing Company, 1970).

35. The Center for Community Change, The National Urban League, *op. cit.*, pp. 15–17.

36. *Ibid.*, pp. 64–65. Since this report there appears to have been an increase in abandonment in Detroit. Much of it, though, seems to be associated with shady deals under Section 235 in which deteriorated homes were sold to financially unqualified buyers who found it easier to simply walk away than to carry the financial burdens of repairs and payments too large for their incomes. See the discussion of the abuse of a federal program earlier in this chapter and also Boyer, *op. cit.*

37. *Ibid.*, p. 25, and cf. p. 89.

38. William A. Caldwell, *op. cit.*, pp. 27–29.

39. *Ibid.*, pp. 29–30.

40. The Center for Community Change, The National Urban League, *op. cit.*, p. 88.

41. *Time* (August 13, 1973), p. 6 and (September 3, 1973), p. E2; Toledo *Blade*, (September 20, 1973).

42. Toledo *Blade* (February 7, 1971); also see Lee Rainwater, *op. cit.*

43. Oscar Newman, *Defensible Space* (New York: The Macmillan Company, 1972), p. 188.

44. *Ibid.*

45. *Ibid.*, pp. 39–49, 191.

46. Al Hirshen and Vivian Brown, "Public Housing's Neglected Resource: The Tenants," *City*, 6 (Fall, 1972), 15–21.

47. *Ibid.*, pp. 15–16.

48. *Ibid.*, p. 18.

49. F. Stuart Chapin, "An Experiment on the Social Effects of Good Housing," *American Sociological Review*, V (December 1940), pp. 868–879.

50. Harrison E. Salisbury, *The Shook-up Generation* (New York: Harper & Row, Publishers, 1958), pp. 75–76.

51. *City Chronicle* (September 1969), p. 1.

52. Information about Cedar-Riverside from John Fischer, "A Laboratory for Urban Living Rises in Minneapolis," *Harper's* Magazine (July, 1973), pp. 14–19; *Minneapolis Tribune*, Picture section (December 9, 1973); Mimeographed material by Cedar-Riverside Associates, Inc.; and visits and interviews at the site by the author.

53. Karl E. and Alma F. Taeuber, *op. cit.*

54. Frederick B. Glantz and Nancy J. Delaney, "Changes in Nonwhite Residential Patterns in Large Metropolitan Areas, 1960 and 1970," *New England Economic Review* (March–April 1973), 6, and see footnote on p. 3.

55. See Robert E. Forman, *op. cit.*, Chapters 1 and 3.

56. Chicago Commission on Race Relations, *The Negro in Chicago* (Chicago: University of Chicago Press, 1922; reprint ed. New York: Arno Press, 1968), pp. 108–109.

57. See, for example, Harrell R. Rodgers, Jr., and Charles S. Bullock, III, *Law and Social Change: Civil Rights Laws and Their Consequences* (New York: McGraw-Hill, 1972), Chapter 6; Rose Helper, *Racial Policies and Practices of Real Estate Brokers* (Minneapolis: University of Minnesota Press, 1969).

58. U.S. Civil Rights Commission, *Federal Civil Rights Enforcement Effort* (Washington, D.C.: Government Printing Office, 1971), p. 142.

59. *Paul J. Trafficante et al., Petitioners* v. *Metropolitan Life Insurance Company et al.*

60. *Time* (February 22, 1971), p. 59, and *Neighbors* (January–February 1973), p. 2.

61. W. E. B. DuBois, *The Philadelphia Negro* (1899; reprint ed., New York: Benjamin Blom, 1967), p. 297; Lucille Clifton, *The Black BC's* (New York: E. P. Dutton & Co., 1971), poem "G is for Ghetto."

62. *Vincent Zuch et al.* v. *John H. Hussey et al.*, 366 S. Supp. 553.

63. The writer wishes to acknowledge the assistance of Toledo City Councilwoman Mrs. Pamela Daoust, who, as leader of a local neighborhood organization, assembled information regarding antisolicitation ordinances in the process of taking action to secure such an ordinance for Toledo.

64. *Prospectus*, Partners in Housing, 8702 Crispin St., Philadelphia, Pa. 19136 (March 21, 1973), p. 25.

65. *Ibid.*, pp. 5–6.

66. *Gautreaux* v. *Chicago Housing Authority*, 296 F. Supp. 907, 304 F. Supp. 736 (N.D. Ill. 1969, *et seq.*).

3. Expanding Black Economic Rights

1. Arthur Fletcher, former Assistant Secretary of Labor, quoted in Bill Hughes, "Rights Weapon Is Forged," Atlanta *Journal* (February 26, 1970), p. 1-A.

2. Evidence on this point is presented in Charles S. Bullock, III, and Harrell R. Rodgers, Jr., *Racial Equality in America: In Search of an Unfulfilled Goal*, (Pacific Palisades, Cal.: Goodyear Publishing Company, 1975).

3. For a brief account of the creation and functioning of the FEPC, see Robert H. Brisbane, *The Black Vanguard* (Valley Forge, Pa.: Judson Press, 1970). The FEPC relied on voluntary efforts, never using its powers of debarment or contract termination.

4. Executive Order No. 9980 (1948).

5. The number of agencies was reduced from 26 to 15 in 1969, then increased to 19 in 1973.

6. U.S. Commission on Civil Rights, *Federal Civil Rights Enforcement Effort* (Washington, D.C.: Government Printing Office, 1970), p. 76.

7. U.S. Commission on Civil Rights, *The Federal Civil Right Enforcement Effort—A Reassessment* (Washington, D.C.: Government Printing Office, 1973), p. 76.

8. *Federal Civil Rights Enforcement Effort*, p. 173.

9. *A Reassessment*, p. 66.

10. Figures on the number of cities in which different types of plans have been implemented are taken from U.S. Commission on Civil Rights, *One Year Later* (Washington, D.C.: Government Printing Office, 1971), pp. 20–22.

11. *Ibid.*, p. 20.

12. "NAACP Claims New York Plan Violates Rights," Atlanta *Journal* (October 11, 1973), p. 32-A.

13. *Federal Civil Rights Enforcement Effort*, p. 235.

14. Other research has found that an unpopular law will probably be ignored or evoke only partial compliance in the absence of what is perceived to be severe coercion. For example, banning religious worship in schools, where there have not been threats of punishment, has often been ignored. As a representative study, see Kenneth M. Dolbeare and Phillip E. Hammond, *The School Prayer Decision: From Court Policy to Local Practice* (Chicago: University of Chicago Press, 1971). In contrast, once Southern officials were convinced that federal standards for school desegregation and voter registration were going to be carried out, by federal officers if necessary and with recalcitrant local officials losing control over the process, compliance became widespread. See Charles S. Bullock, III, and Harrell R. Rodgers, Jr., "Coercion to Compliance: Southern School Districts and School Desegregation Guidelines," a paper presented at the 1974 Annual Meeting of the American Political Science Association, Palmer House, Chicago, Illinois (August 29–September 2, 1974); Harrell R. Rodgers, Jr., and Charles S. Bullock, III, *Law and Social Change: Civil Rights Laws and the Consequences* (New York: McGraw-Hill, 1972).

15. *One Year Later*, pp. 23–24, is the source of much of the material in this and the next paragraph.

16. Dennis A. Derryck, *The Construction Industry: A Black Perspective* (Washington, D.C.: Joint Center for Political Studies, 1972), p. 16.

17. *Federal Civil Rights Enforcement Effort*, p. 241.

18. *A Reassessment*, p. 75.

19. Lawrence J. Peter and Raymond Hull, *The Peter Principle* (New York: William Morrow and Company, 1969), pp. 40–41.

20. *One Year Later*, p. 14.

21. *A Reassessment*, p. 77.

22. *Federal Civil Rights Enforcement Effort*, p. 264.

23. These figures include charges which were recalled from states.

24. *Federal Civil Rights Enforcement Effort*, p. 307.

25. *One Year Later*, p. 29.

26. *Ibid.*, p. 27.

27. "Employment Discrimination," *Congressional Quarterly Weekly Reports* 32 (September 28, 1974), 2592.

28. *Federal Civil Rights Enforcement Effort*, p. 308.

29. Donna Lorenz, "Policy Chaos Clogs Machinery," Atlanta *Journal* (July 12, 1972), p. 10-A.

30. Donna Lorenz, "Who Guards Those Who Guard Against Discrimination in Jobs?" Atlanta *Journal-Constitution* (July 9, 1972), p. 1-A.

31. *A Reassessment*, p. 91.

32. *A Reassessment*, p. 86.

33. *Federal Civil Rights Enforcement Effort*, pp. 371–372.

34. "The Job-Bias Juggernaut," *Newsweek* (June 17, 1974), p. 75.

35. Arvil V. Adams, "Evaluating the Success of the EEOC Compliance Process," *Monthly Labor Review*, 96 (May, 1973), 27.

36. EEOC, *Second Annual Report* (Washington, D.C.: Government Printing Office, 1968), p. 3.

37. EEOC, *Third Annual Report* (Washington, D.C.: Government Printing Office, 1969), p. 24.

38. "Ma Bell Agrees to Pay Reparations," *Newsweek* (January 29, 1973), p. 53.

39. "Workers Due Back Pay," Atlanta *Journal* (April 15, 1974), p. 14-A.

40. "Pact to End Steel Discrimination Is Disclosed," Atlanta *Journal-Constitution* (April 14, 1974), p. 20-B.

41. Bullock and Rodgers, *Racial Equality in America*, Chapters 2–4.

42. *Federal Civil Rights Enforcement Effort*, p. 336.

43. *One Year Later*, p. 30.

44. *Federal Civil Rights Enforcement Effort*, p. 337.

45. *Clark* v. *American Marine Corp.*, 437 F.2d 959 (C.A. 5 1971).

46. Sar A. Levitan, Garth L. Mangum, and Ray Marshall, *Human Resources and Labor Markets* (New York: Harper & Row, Publishers, 1972), p. 485.

47. Attorney General of the United States, *1972 Annual Report* (Washington, D.C.: Government Printing Office, 1972), p. 80.

48. *Griggs* v. *Duke Power Co.*, 401 U.S. 424 (1971).

49. *United States* v. *Sheet Metal Workers, Local 36*, 416 F.2d 123 (C.A. 8 1969).

50. *United States* v. *Bethlehem Steel Corp.*, 446 F.2d 652 (C.A. 2 1971).

51. *Local 53, Intl. Assn. of Heat and Frost Insulators and Asbestos Workers* v. *United States*, 407 F.2d 1047 (C.A. 5 1969).

52. *United States* v. *Ironworkers Local 86*, 443 F.2d 544 (C.A. 9 1971).

53. *NAACP* v. *Allen*, 340 F. Supp. 703 (M.D. Ala. 1972).

54. U.S. Bureau of the Census, Current Population Reports, Special Studies, Series P-23, No. 48, *The Social and Economic Status of the Black Population in the United States, 1973* (Washington, D.C.: Government Printing Office, 1974), p. 69.

55. For a much more elegant statement of these points, see Kenneth J. Arrow, "Models of Job Discrimination," in Anthony H. Pascal (ed.), *Racial Discrimination in Economic Life* (Lexington, Mass.: Lexington Books, 1972), pp. 83–102.

56. Sources for the data in these two sentences are, in order, Gene L. Maeroff, "U.S. Faculty Religious, Older, Stable," Atlanta *Journal-Constitution* (September 3, 1973), p. 20-B; Hubert Humphrey, "Expanding Minority Participation in Engineering," *Congressional Record*, 93rd Congress, 1st Session, 119 (May 29, 1937), p.S. 9790; "Racism in Reverse," *Newsweek* (March 11, 1974), p. 62; "Physician Shortage Worsening," Atlanta *Journal* (November 23, 1972), p. 24-A; J. Stanford Smith, "Needed: A Ten-Fold Increase in Minority Engineering Graduates," reprinted in the *Congressional Record*, 93rd Congress, 1st Session, 119 (January 12, 1973), p. S 610.

57. *Federal Civil Rights Enforcement Effort*, p. 358.

58. *Employment and Earnings*, 20 (February, 1974), pp. 90–98.

59. Looking at the percentage point increase of blacks in professional technical, managerial, and craftsmen occupations, in 14 of 20 possible comparisons the gap between black representation in the U.S. labor force and in one of the five industries increased. For example, the difference between the proportion of black professionals in the labor force and in the construction industry was 1 percentage point in 1966. By 1971 the disparity had widened to 1.5 percentage points.

60. *Social and Economic Status of the Black Population in the United States, 1973*, p. 17.

61. David Nachmias and David H. Rosenbloom, "Measuring Bureaucratic Representation and Integration," *Public Administration Review*, (November–December, 1973), pp. 590–597; Samuel Krislov, *The Negro in Federal Employment* (Minneapolis: University of Minnesota Press, 1967), p. 48.

62. Quoted in *Federal Civil Rights Enforcement Effort*, p. 111.

63. *Ibid.*, p. 113.

64. Civil Service Commission, *Study of Minority Group Employment in the Federal Government* (Washington, D.C.: Government Printing Office, 1967).

65. *One Year Later*, pp. 8–9.

66. *Ibid.*, p. 5.

67. *A Reassessment*, p. 41.

68. Charles S. Bullock, III, and Samuel Yeager, "The Federal Government and Equal Employment Opportunites," mimeographed.

69. For a discussion of how CSC finally came to accept the utility of goals and timetables, see David H. Rosenbloom, "The Civil Service Commission's Decision to Authorize the Use of Goals and Timetables in the Federal Equal Employment Opportunity Program," *Western Political Quarterly*, 21 (June, 1973), pp. 236–251.

70. *A Reassessment*, pp. 43–51.

71. Lorenz, "Policy Chaos Clogs Machinery," p. 10-A.

72. *Federal Civil Rights Enforcement Effort*, p. 65.

73. "Revise EEO Plans, U.S. Agencies Told," Atlanta *Journal* (February 14, 1973), p. 2-C.

74. Department of Labor, *Manpower Report of the President* (Washington, D.C.: Government Printing Office, 1974), pp. 363, 367.

75. Garth L. Mangum, "MDTA: A Decade of Achievement," in Seymour L. Wolfbein (ed.), *Manpower Policy Perspectives and Prospects* (Philadelphia: Temple University Press, 1973), p. 53.

76. Department of Labor, *Manpower Report of the President* (Washington, D.C.: Government Printing Office, 1973) pp. 230–231.

77. Levitan et al., *Human Resources and Labor Markets*, p. 329.

78. Material in this paragraph is taken from *Training and Technology 1972 Annual Report and Statistical Summary* (Oak Ridge, Tenn.: Oak Ridge Associated Universities, 1973), pp. 17–18.

79. This relies on Frederick E. Miller, "Contributions of Community Organizations," in Seymour L. Wolfbein (ed.), *Manpower Policy: Perspectives and Prospects* (Philadelphia: Temple University Press, 1973), pp. 99–107; "A Hand Up," *Newsweek* (December 10, 1973), pp. 105–106; and Thomas J. Bray, "Leon Sullivan Pushes Job Training as Key to Blacks' Success," reprinted in *Congressional Record*, 93rd Congress, 2nd Session, 120 (May 22, 1974), pp. E3223–3224.

80. William C. Woodward, "The Role of Private Industry," in Seymour L. Wolfbein (ed.), *Manpower Policy: Perspectives and Prospects* (Philadelphia: Temple University Press, 1973), p. 126.

81. Department of Labor, *Manpower Report of the President*, (Washington, D.C.: Government Printing Office, 1971), p. 311; 1974 *Manpower Report of the President*, p. 367.

82. 1971 *Manpower Report*, p. 44.

83. 1974 *Manpower Report*, p. 367. Of the manpower programs, only Operation Mainstream had a less educated clientele.

84. 1974 *Manpower Report*, p. 53.

85. Levitan et al., *Human Resources and Labor Markets*, p. 336.

86. Joseph A. Kershaw, *Government Against Poverty* (Chicago: Markham Publishing Company, 1970), p. 31.

87. Michael E. Borus, John P. Breenan, and Sidney Rosen, "A Benefit-Cost Analysis of the Neighborhood Youth Corps: The Out-of-School Program in Indiana," *Journal of Human Resources*, 5 (Spring, 1970), 139–159.

88. 1971 *Manpower Report*, p. 47.

89. In FY 1973, 70 percent of WIN enrollees were women. 1974 *Manpower Report*, p. 367.

90. 1974 *Manpower Report*, p. 367.

91. 1971 *Manpower Report*, p. 53.

92. 1974 *Manpower Report*, p. 133.

93. Gilbert Y. Steiner, *The State of Welfare* (Washington, D.C.: The Brookings Institution, 1971), pp. 68–71.

94. 1973 *Manpower Report*, p. 37.

95. Levitan et al., *Human Resources and Labor Markets*, p. 415.

96. Bradley R. Schiller, *The Impact of Urban WIN Programs* (Washington, D.C.: Pacific Training and Technical Assistance Corporation, 1972) cited in 1974 *Manpower Report*, p. 139.

97. Much of this section draws from Kershaw, *Government Against Poverty*, pp. 156–157.

98. 1974 *Manpower Report*, p. 53.

99. The average low-income for a nonfarm family of four in 1971 was $4,137, or $79.56 per week. U.S. Bureau of the Census, Current Population Reports, P-60, No. 86, *Characteristics of the Low Income Population, 1971*, (Washington, D.C.: Government Printing Office, 1972), p. 17.

100. 1973 *Manpower Report*, pp. 42–46, for this and much of the succeeding material.

101. Sar A. Levitan and Garth L. Mangum, "An Old Budget for New Legislation: Impact 1974," reprinted in the *Congressional Record*, 93rd Congress, 2nd Session, 120 (March 18, 1974), p. E 1529.

102. Mangum, "MDTA: A Decade of Achievement," pp. 41–63.

103. Vivian W. Henderson, "Manpower Development and Equal Employment Opportunities," in Seymour L. Wolfbein (ed.), *Manpower Policy: Perspectives and Prospects* (Philadelphia: Temple University Press, 1973), p. 93.

104. 1974 *Manpower Report*, p. 358.

105. Mangum, "MDTA: A Decade of Achievement," p. 57.

106. Frank G. Davis, *The Economics of Black Community Development*, (Chicago: Markham Publishing Company, 1972), p. 105.

107. Levitan et al., *Human Resources and Labor Markets*, p. 357.

108. 1974 *Manpower Report*, p. 358.

109. *Ibid.*, p. 143.

110. Sylvia S. Small, "Work Training Programs and the Unemployment Rate," *Monthly Labor Review*, 95 (September, 1972), 7–13; Malcolm Cohen, "The Direct Effects of Federal Manpower Programs in Reducing Unemployment," *Journal of Human Resources*, 4 (Fall, 1969), 491–507.

111. Leon H. Keyserling, *How Well is the Employment Act of 1946 Achieving Its Goal?* (Washington, D.C.: Department of Labor, 1966), pp. 8–9.

112. Paul O. Flaim, "Discouraged Workers and Changes in Unemployment," *Monthly Labor Review*, 96 (March, 1973), 12–13.

113. Kershaw, *Government Against Poverty*, pp. 88–89.

114. A. W. Phillips, "The Relation Between Unemployment and the Rate of Change of Money Wage Rates in the United Kingdom, 1861–1957," *Economica*, 25 (November, 1958), 283–299.

115. Gösta Rehn, "Manpower Policy as an Instrument of National Economic Policy," in Seymour L. Wolfbein (ed.), *Manpower Policy: Perspectives and Prospects* (Philadelphia: Temple University Press, 1973), p. 174.

116. W. Willard Wirtz, "Learning and Earning to Live," in Seymour L. Wolfbein (ed.), *Manpower Policy: Perspective and Prospects* (Philadelphia: Temple University Press, 1973), p. 17.

117. *Employment and Earnings*, 20 (February, 1974), p. 38.

118. 1973 *Manpower Report*, p. 55.

119. Figures cited in Kershaw, *Government Against Poverty*, p. 91.

120. See, for example, Wesley J. Hjornevik, "Manpower Policy—An Instrument of Social Change: Equal Employment, Welfare, Poverty," in Sey-

mour L. Wolfbein (ed.), *Manpower Policy: Perspectives and Prospects* (Philadelphia: Temple University Press, 1973), p. 114.

121. 1974 *Manpower Report*, pp. 124–126.

122. Howard J. Samuels, "Compensatory Capitalism," in William F. Haddad and G. Douglas Pugh (eds.), *Black Economic Development* (Englewood Cliffs, N.J.: Prentice-Hall, 1969), p. 61. In Newark, N.J., 96.9 percent of black expenditures go to whites. Davis, *The Economics of Black Community Development*, p. 95.

123. Neil M. Singer, "Federal Aid to Minority Businesses: Survey and Critique," *Social Science Quarterly*, 54 (September, 1973), 304.

124. Raymond S. Franklin and Solomon Resnik, *The Political Economy of Racism* (New York: Holt, Rinehart and Winston, 1973), p. 189.

125. Andrew F. Brimmer and Henry S. Terrell, "The Economic Potential of Black Capitalism," quoted in Davis, *The Economics of Black Community Development*, p. 96.

126. Quoted in Earl Ofari, *The Myth of Black Capitalism* (New York: Monthly Review Press, 1970), p. 84.

127. See John McClaughry, "Black Ownership and National Politics," and Roy Innis, "Separatist Economics: A New Social Contract," both in William F. Haddad and G. Douglas Pugh (eds.), *Black Economic Development* (Englewood Cliffs, N.J.: Prentice-Hall, 1969), pp. 38–59.

128. William K. Tabb, "Viewing Minority Economic Development as a Problem in Political Economy," *American Economic Review*, 62 (May, 1972), 36.

129. McClaughry, "Black Ownership and National Politics," p. 41.

130. The sum was an estimated $24 billion in 1965, Samuels, "Compensatory Capitalism," p. 63.

131. For a good discussion see Arthur I. Blaustein and Geoffrey Faux, *The Star-Spangled Hustle* (Garden City, N.Y.: Anchor Books, 1972), pp. 179–186.

132. Michael Jay Jedel and Duane Kujawa, "Barriers to Minority Employment," *Atlanta Economic Review*, 23 (November–December, 1973), 34.

133. "Housing and Urban Development," *Congressional Quarterly Weekly Report*, 32 (February 9, 1974), 274.

134. Recent research finds welfare mothers quite eager to work, although they have little confidence in their abilities. Leonard Goodwin, "Welfare Mothers and the Work Ethic," *Monthly Labor Review*, 95 (August, 1972), 35.

135. Leonard Goodwin, *A Study of the Work Orientation of Welfare Recipients Participating in the WIN Program* (Washington, D.C.: The Brookings Institution, 1971); 1974 *Manpower Report*, pp. 136–137.

136. U.S. Bureau of the Census, *Social and Economic Status of the Black Population . . . 1973*, p. 30.

137. Quoted in *Report of the National Advisory Commission on Civil Disorders* (New York: Bantam Books, 1968), p. 457. Cf. Francis Fox Piven and Richard Cloward, *Regulating the Poor* (New York: Vintage Books, 1971).

138. Steiner, *State of Welfare*, p. 78.

139. *Ibid.*, p. 213 reports a 40 percent drop off when communities changed from distributing surplus food free of charge to using food stamps.

140. Garth L. Mangum, "Manpower Research Report—Part II," reprinted in the *Congressional Record*, 93rd Congress, 2nd Session, 120 (October 8, 1974), p. E 6349.

141. For a good discussion see Steiner, *State of Welfare*, pp. 31–74.

142. *National Journal*, 6 (February 9, 1974), 213.

143. "Keynote Address by Vernon Jordan," reprinted in the *Congressional Record*, 93rd Congress, 1st Session, 119 (August 1, 1973), p. E 5284.

144. Levitan and Mangum, "An Old Budget for New Legislation," pp. E 1527–1529.

145. Mike Causey, "Government Minority Jobs Rise," Atlanta *Journal* (March 6, 1974), p. 8-C.

4. On Integrating the Public Schools: An Empirical and Legal Assessment

1. 347 U.S. 483 (1954).

2. See Jack W. Peltason, *Fifty-Eight Lonely Men: Southern Judges and School Desegregation* (New York: Harcourt, Brace & World, 1961); Benjamin Muse, *Ten Years of Prelude: The Story of Integration Since the Supreme Court's 1954 Decision* (New York: The Viking Press, 1964), and Harrell R. Rodgers, Jr., and Charles S. Bullock, III, *Law and Social Change: Civil Rights Laws and Their Consequences* (New York: McGraw-Hill, 1972), pp. 69–111.

3. See Thomas R. Dye (ed.), *American Public Policy: Documents and Essays* (Columbus, Ohio: Charles E. Merrill Books, 1969), pp. 18–19.

4. *Federal Enforcement of School Desegregation*, Report of the United States Commission on Civil Rights (September 11, 1969), p. 4. The U.S. Commission on Civil Rights, like the Department of Health, Education and Welfare, defines a desegregated school as a majority-white school with racial mixing.

5. *Revolution in Civil Rights*, Washington, D.C.: Congressional Quarterly Service, 1968, p. 93. These figures indicate how many black students were attending schools with whites, now how many were attending majority-white schools.

6. U.S. Department of Health, Education and Welfare, *Staff Report* (January 4, 1970), mimeographed, p. 1.

7. *Toward Equal Educational Opportunity*, The Report of the Select Committee on Equal Education Opportunity, United States Senate (Washington, D.C.: Government Printing Office, 1972), p. 11.

8. This topic is extensively dealt with in the three works cited in note 2.

9. Peltason, *Fifty-Eight Lonely Men . . .* , p. 15.

10. *Ibid., passim.*
11. *Revolution in Civil Rights . . .* , p. 92.
12. This series of events is best covered and documented in *Federal Enforcement of School Desegregation, passim.*
13. *Federal Enforcement of School Desegregation,* pp. 21–22.
14. 391 U.S. 430.
15. On this section see Rodgers and Bullock, *Law and Social Change . . . ,* pp. 88–97.
16. See Leon Panetta and Peter Gall, *Bring Us Together: The Nixon Team And The Civil Rights Retreat* (New York: J. B. Lippincott Company, 1971), *passim.*
17. *Ibid.,* pp. 350–367.
18. 377 U.S. 218.
19. *Watson* v. *City of Memphis,* 373 U.S. 526 (1964).
20. 391 U.S. 430.
21. 391 U.S. 438.
22. 396 U.S. 19 (1969).
23. 402 U.S. 1 (1971).
24. Pairing involves combining the facilities of two schools. For example, if a community has separate elementary schools for black and white students, one school can be converted to handle all students attending grades K–3 and the other can handle all students in grades 4–6. Because desegregation techniques have been discussed so frequently in other works they will not be surveyed here. For an excellent discussion see Gordon Foster, "Desegregating Urban Schools: A Review of Techniques," *Harvard Educational Review,* 43 (February, 1973), 5–36.
25. Clustering is basically the same concept as pairing except that more than two schools are involved.
26. *United States* v. *Montgomery Board of Education,* 395 U.S. 225 (1969).
27. 402 U.S. 25.
28. On this point see Paul R. Diamond, "School Segregation in the North: There is But One Constitution," *Harvard Civil Rights—Civil Liberties Law Review,* 7 (January, 1972), 8–9.
29. 402 U.S. 25.
30. 402 U.S. 28.
31. 402 U.S. 26.
32. See Owen M. Fiss, "The Charlotte-Mecklenburg Case—Its Significance for Northern School Desegregation," *The University of Chicago Law Review,* 38 (Summer, 1971), 700.
33. *Toward Equal Educational Opportunity,* p. 188.
34. *Ibid.*
35. 402 U.S. 30.
36. *Ibid.*

37. 402 U.S. 31, 32.

38. 402 U.S. 31.

39. 351 F. Supp. (1972). A recent report revealed that HEW's performance did not improve after this decision. See Roger Mills, *Justice Delayed and Denied: HEW and Northern Desegregation* (Washington, D.C.: *Center For National Policy Review*, 1974).

40. 396 U.S. 19 (1969).

41. 402 U.S. 26 (1971).

42. 351 F. Supp. 642 (1973).

43. *Toward Equal Educational Opportunity*, p. 32.

44. *Deal* v. *Cincinnati Board of Education*, 369 F.2d 65 (6th Cir. 1966), certiorari denied, 387 U.S. 847 (1967); *Bell* v. *School City*, 324 F.2d 209 (7th Cir. 1963), certiorari denied, 377 U.S. 924 (1964); *Downs* v. *Board of Education*, 336 F.2d 988 (10th Cir. 1964), certiorari denied, 380 U.S. 914 (1965).

45. *Taylor* v. *Board of Education*, 294 F.2d 36 (2d Cir.), certiorari denied, 368 U.S. 940 (1961) *Blacker* v. *Board of Education*, 266 F. Supp. 208 (E.D. N.Y. 1964); *Branche* v. *Board of Education*, 204 F. Supp. 150 (E.D. N.Y. 1962); *Clemons* v. *Board of Education*, 288 F.2d 853 (6th Cir.), certiorari denied, 350 U.S. 1006 (1956).

46. See Diamond, "School Segregation in the North . . . ," 12.

47. The various theories are best discussed in Diamond, "School Segregation in the North . . . "; Frank I. Goodman, "De Facto School Segregation: A Constitutional and Empirical Analysis," *California Law Review*, 60 (March, 1972), 275–437; Robert I. Richter, "School Desegregation After Swann: A Theory of Government Responsibility," *The University of Chicago Law Review*, 39 (Winter, 1972), 421–447.

48. *Johnson* v. *San Francisco Unified School District*, 339 F. Supp. 1316 (N.D. Cal. 1971).

49. *Bradley* v. *Milliken*, 338 F. Supp. 582 (E.D. Mich. 1971).

50. *Johnson* v. *San Francisco Unified School District*, 339 F. Supp. 1315 (N.D. Cal. 1971).

51. *Crawford* v. *Board of Education*, Civil No. 822854 (Sup. Ct. L.A. Cty. 1970).

52. *Keyes* v. *School District No. 1*, 445 F.2d 990 (10th Cir. 1971).

53. *Spangler* v. *Pasadena Board of Education*, 311 F. Supp. 501 (C.D. Cal.).

54. *Soria* v. *Oxnard School District Board of Trustees*, 328 F.155 (C.D. Cal. 1971).

55. *Davis* v. *School District*, 309 F. Supp. 734 (E.D. Mich. 1970), affirmed, 443 F.2d 573 (6th Cir.), certiorari denied, 92 S. Ct. 23 (1971).

56. *Kelley* v. *Brown*, Civil No. LV-1146 (D. Nev. 1970).

57. *United States* v. *Board of School Commissioners*, 332 F. Supp. 665. (S.D. Ind. 1971).

58. Richter, "School Desegregation After Swann . . . ," 427.

59. These findings were made in Denver; Pontiac, Michigan; Las Vegas; and Indianapolis.

60. 332 F. Supp. 667.

61. 332 F. Supp. 670.

62. 311 F. Supp. 503.

63. *Brown* v. *Board of Education*, 347 U.S. (1954).

64. *Kelly* v. *Gruinn*, 456 F.2d 108 (9th Cir. 1972).

65. *Barksdale* v. *Springfield School Committee*, 237 F. Supp. 543 (D. Mass. 1965).

66. *Hobson* v. *Hansen*, 269 F. Supp. 401 (D.D. C. 1967); *Johnson* v. *San Francisco Unified School District*, 339 F. Supp. 1315 (N.D. Cal. 1971).

67. *Hobson* v. *Hansen*, 269 F. Supp. 419 (D.D. C. 1967).

68. This argument is made by Owen M. Fiss, "The Charlotte-Mecklenburg Case—Its Significance for Northern School Desegregation," *The University of Chicago Law Review*, 38 (Summer, 1971), 697–709.

69. 402 U.S. 18.

70. 402 U.S. 28.

71. 402 U.S. 18.

72. This point is made by Diamond, "School Segregation in the North . . . ," 3.

73. 402 U.S. 21.

74. 413 U.S. 189 (1973).

75. *Ibid.*

76. *Ibid.*

77. *Ibid.*

78. *Ibid.*

79. See Rodgers and Bullock, *Law and Social Change* . . . , pp. 139–161.

80. *Bradley* v. *School Board*, 338 F. Supp. 67 (E.D. Va. 1972).

81. *Reynolds* v. *Sims*, 377 U.S. 533, 575 (1964).

82. *Abate* v. *Mundt*, 403 U.S. 182 (1971).

83. *Bradley* v. *School Board*, Civil No. 72-1058 (4th Cir. 1972).

84. 442 F.2d 584 (4th Cir. 1971).

85. 442 F.2d 575 (4th Cir. 1971).

86. 455 F.2d 978 (5th Cir. 1972).

87. 327 F. Supp. 1235 (D. N.J. 1971).

88. Affirmed Mem., 92 S. Ct. 707 (1972).

89. *Milliken* v. *Bradley*, 94 S. Ct. 3112 (1974).

90. *Bradley* v. *Milliken*, 38 F. Supp. 582 (E.D. Mich. 1971).

91. *Ibid.*

92. Foster, "Desegregating Urban Schools: A Review of Techniques," 6.

93. *Ibid.*, pp. 33–35.

94. For a more thorough examination of the educational park, see Thomas F. Pettigrew, *Racially Separate or Together?* (New York: McGraw-Hill,

1971, pp. 69–81; and N. Jacobson (ed.), *An Exploration of the Educational Park Concept* (New York: New York Board of Education, 1964).

95. See Nancy St. John, "Desegregation and Minority Group Performance," *Review of Educational Research*, 40 (February, 1970), 111–134; Robert P. O'Reilly (ed.), *Racial and Social Class Isolation in the Schools* (New York: Praeger Publishers, 1970); Meyer Weinberg, *Desegregation Research: An Appraisal* (Bloomington, Ind.: Phi Delta Kappa, 1968).

96. St. John, "Desegregation and Minority Group Performance," 127.

97. See the studies surveyed in Thomas F. Pettigrew, Elizabeth L. Useen, Clarence Normand, and Marshall S. Smith, "Busing: A Review of the Evidence," *The Public Interest*, 3 (Winter, 1973), 88–131.

98. See Pettigrew et al., "Busing: A Review of the Evidence," 98.

99. *Racial Isolation in the Public Schools*, A Report of the Commission on Civil Rights (Washington, D.C.: Government Printing Office, 1967), p. 161.

100. This conclusion is shared by St. John, "Desegregation and Minority Group Performance," 128; and Pettigrew et al., "Busing: A Review of the Evidence," 107.

101. *Toward Equal Educational Opportunity*, The Report of the Select Committee on Equal Educational Opportunity, United States Senate (Washington, D.C.: Government Printing Office, 1972), p. 217.

102. *Ibid.*

103. James Coleman et al., *Equality of Educational Opportunity* (Washington, D.C.: Government Printing Office, 1966), p. 42.

104. See, for example, O. J. Harvey and Jeane Rutherford, "Status in the Informal Group: Influence and Influencability at Different Age Levels," *Child Development*, 31 (June, 1960), 377–385; and Kenneth P. Langton, "Peer Group and School and the Political Socialization Process," *American Political Science Review*, 61 (September, 1967), 751–758.

105. Cited in *Racial Isolation in the Public Schools*, p. 82.

106. Christopher S. Jencks, "The Coleman Report and the Conventional Wisdom," in Frederick Mosteller and Daniel P. Moynihan (eds.), *On Equality of Educational Opportunity* (New York: Vintage Books, 1972), p. 104.

107. *Ibid.*, pp. 86 and 87.

108. *Racial Isolation in the Public Schools*, p. 105.

109. Jonathan Kozol, *Death at an Early Age* (Boston: Houghton Mifflin Company, 1967).

110. *The Status of School Desegregation in the South 1970*, A Report by the American Friends Service Committee; Delta Ministry of the National Council of Churches; Lawyers Committee; NAACP Legal Defense and Educational Fund, Inc.; and the Washington Research Project.

111. Charles S. Bullock, III, and Mary Victoria Braxton, "The Coming of School Desegregation: A Before and After Study of Black and White Student Attitudes," *Social Science Quarterly*, 54 (June, 1973); Mary Victoria Braxton and Charles S. Bullock, III, "Teacher Impartiality in

Desegregation," *Integrated Education*, 10 (July–August, 1972), 42–46; and David Armor, "The Evidence on Busing," *The Public Interest*, 28 (Summer, 1972), 102–105.

112. *The Diminishing Barrier: A Report on School Desegregation in Nine Communities*, U.S. Commission on Civil Rights (Washington, D.C.: Government Printing Office, 1972), p. 20.

113. *Ibid.*

114. Pettigrew, *Racially Separate or Together?*, p. 275. A distinction between the term integration and desegregation is frequently made in the research literature. Desegregation is generally defined as simply racial mixing, and integration refers to positive interracial contact. I feel that some distinction needs to be made, but since I often cannot determine which situation exists, I use the terms interchangeably; and, where possible, I make a distinction between racial mixing that occurs under positive or negative conditions.

115. Gordon W. Allport, *The Nature of Prejudice* (Reading, Mass.: Addison-Wesley Publishing Company, 1954), p. 267.

116. See the studies reviewed in Daniel M. Wilner, Rosabelle Price Walkley, and Stuart W. Cook, *Human Relations in Interracial Housing: A Study of the Contact Hypothesis* (Minneapolis: University of Minnesota Press, 1955), pp. 155–161.

117. *Racial Isolation in the Public Schools*, p. 110.

118. *Ibid.*, p. 111.

119. Cited in *Toward Equal Educational Opportunity*, p. 210.

120. Cited in *Ibid.*, p. 229.

121. See, for example, Robert L. Crain, "School Integration and Occupational Achievement of Negroes," *American Journal of Sociology*, 75 (January, 1970), 593–606; Robert L. Crain, "School Integration and the Academic Achievement of Negroes," *Sociology of Education*, 44 (Winter, 1971), 1–26.

122. David J. Armor, "The Evidence on Busing," *The Public Interest*, 28 (Summer, 1972), 90–125.

123. David J. Armor, "The Double Double Standard: A Reply," *The Public Interest*, 30 (Winter, 1973), 124.

124. Armor, "The Evidence on Busing," 97.

125. Pettigrew et al., "Busing: A Review of The Evidence," p. 96.

126. *Ibid.*, p. 99.

127. Armor, "The Double Double Standard: A Reply," p. 121.

128. Pettigrew et al., "Busing: A Review of The Evidence," p. 103.

129. Christopher Jencks, Marshall Smith, Henry Acland, Mary Jo Bane, David Cohen, Herbert Gintis, Barbara Heyns, and Stephan Michelson, *Inequality: A Reassessment of the Effect of Family and Schooling in America* (New York: Basic Books, 1972).

130. *Ibid.*, p. 106.

131. *Ibid.*, p. 97.

132. See, for example, Office of Economic Opportunity, *Project Head Start: Evaluation and Research Summary 1965–67* (Washington, D.C.: Government Printing Office, 1967).

133. Carter Smith, "Lagging Pupils Gain in City's Rooms of 15," *St. Louis Post-Dispatch* (November 24, 1972), p. 11A.

134. Cited in *Toward Equal Educational Opportunity*, pp. 24 and 25.

135. Frederick Mosteller and Daniel P. Moynihan (eds.), *On Equality of Educational Opportunity* (New York: Random House, 1972), p. 21.

136. James Guthrie et al., *Schools and Inequality* (Cambridge, Mass.: The M.I.T. Press, 1971).

137. *The Diminishing Barrier . . . ;* and *Five Communities: Their Search for Equal Education*, U.S. Commission on Civil Rights (Washington, D.C.: Government Printing Office, 1972).

138. *Toward Equal Educational Opportunity*, pp. 233–237. See also Al Smith, Anthony Downs, and M. Leanne Lachman, *Achieving Effective Desegregation* (Boston: D. C. Heath and Company, 1973).

139. *Five Communities: Their Search for Equal Education*, p. 5.

140. Foster, "Desegregating Urban Schools: A Review of Techniques," 26.

141. *Racial Isolation in the Public Schools*, p. 159.

142. Christopher Jencks et al., *Inequality: A Reassessment of the Effect of Family and Schooling in America* (New York: Basic Books, 1972), p. 156.

143. *Toward Equal Educational Opportunity*, p. 3.

5. Conventional Police Reform as a Policy Response to Racial Hostility

1. Neal A. Milner, "The Biases of Police Reform," in Edward S. Greenberg, Neal A. Milner, and David J. Olson (eds.), *Black Politics: The Evitability of Conflict* (New York: Holt, Rinehart and Winston, 1971), p. 162.

2. National Advisory Commission on Civil Disorder, *Supplemental Studies for the National Advisory Commission on Civil Disorders* (Washington, D.C.: Government Printing Office, 1968), pp. 42–43; President's Commission on Law Enforcement and the Administration of Justice, *The Challenge of Crime in a Free Society* (Washington, D.C.: Government Printing Office, 1967), Chapter 2.

3. Lee Rainwater, "Introduction," in Rainwater (ed.), *Deviance and Liberty* (Chicago: Aldine Publishing Company, 1974), pp. 7–11. Rainwater suggests that these questions are good general guides to policy-oriented research.

4. Robert Daley, *Target Blue: An Insider's View of the N.Y.P.D.* (New York: Delacorte Press, 1971). Raymond Parnas, "Police Discretion and Diversion of Incidents of Intra-Family Violence," *Law and Contemporary Problems*, 36 (Autumn, 1971), 539–565.

5. Martin Trow, "Methodological Problems in the Evaluation of Innovation," in Frances Caro (ed.), *Readings in Evaluation Research* (New York: Russell Sage Foundation, 1971), pp. 81–94.

6. This introductory discussion relies heavily on Jack Ladinsky, Irving Piliavin, and George Kelling, "Work Orientations and Attitudes: The Meaning of Professionalism in Policing," MS, August, 1974. Instead of using the term "professionalism" I favor "professionalization" because it better connotes the *process* of becoming professional, my primary interest here. "Professionalism" refers to the ideology that develops in those undergoing this process. H. M. Vollmer and D. G. Mills (eds.), *Professionalization* (Englewood Cliffs, N.J.: Prentice-Hall, 1966), pp. vii–viii.

7. W. Fuch, "Procedure in Administrative Rule-Making," *Harvard Law Review*, 52 (1938), 242. Other relevant discussions of rules are Philip Selznick, *Law, Society and Industrial Justice* (New York: Russell Sage Foundation, 1969), and Philippe Nonet, *Administrative Justice* (New York: Russell Sage Foundation, 1969). See also Kenneth C. Davis, *Discretionary Justice* (Baton Rouge, La.: Louisiana State University, 1969); M. Kadish and S. Kadish, "On Justified Rule Departures by Officials," *California Law Review*, 59 (1971), 905–960.

8. Charles B. Saunders, *Upgrading the American Police* (Washington, D.C.: The Brookings Institution, 1970), p. vii.

9. See, for example, Saunders, *op. cit.*; the Reports of the President's Commission on Law Enforcement and the Administration of Justice; Committee for Economic Development, *Reducing Crime and Assuring Justice* (New York: Committee for Economic Development, 1972).

10. Examples here include much of the work on police behavior done by social scientists who are academicians. Examples of such studies that are quite explicitly oriented toward policy changes are Jerome Skolnick, *Politics of Protest*, staff report presented to the National Commission on Causes and Prevention of Violence (Washington, D.C.: Government Printing Office, 1969). James Q. Wilson, "The Police in the Ghetto," in Robert Steadman (ed.), *The Police and the Community* (Baltimore: The Johns Hopkins University Press, 1972), Chapter 3. Louis L. Knowles and Kenneth Prewitt, *Institutional Racism in America*. (Englewood Cliffs, N.J.: Prentice-Hall, 1969), Chapter 5.

11. Committee for Economic Development, *Reducing Crime*.

12. Heinz Eulau, "Skill Revolution and the Consultative Commonwealth," *American Political Science Review*, 67 (1973), 175.

13. Berenice M. Fischer, "Claims and Credibility: A Discussion of Occupational Identity and the Agent-Client Relationship," *Social Problems*, 16 (1969), 423–433.

14. Eliot Friedson, "The Impurity of Professional Authority," in Howard S. Becker, Blanche Geer, David Reisman, and Robert S. Weiss (eds.), *Institutions and the Person* (Chicago: Aldine Publishing Company, 1968), pp. 25–34.

15. Eulau, *op. cit.*

16. See Fischer, *op. cit.*, and Howard Becker, "The Professional Dance Musician and His Audience," *American Journal of Sociology*, 57 (1951), 136–144.

17. Skolnick, *op. cit.*

18. James Leo Walsh, "Professionalism and the Police: The Cop as Medical Student," *American Behavioral Scientist*, 13 (1969), 705–720.

19. On review boards see Arthur Niederhoffer, *Behind the Shield* (New York: Doubleday & Company, 1967), pp. 171–179; David W. Abbott, Louis H. Gold, and Edward T. Robowsaky, *Police, Politics and Race* (Cambridge, Mass.: Harvard University Press, 1969); James R. Hudson, "Police Review Boards and Police Accountability," *Law and Contemporary Problems*, 36 (1971), 515–538; Ralph Knoohuizen, "The Question of Police Discipline in Chicago" (Evanston, Ill.: Chicago Law Enforcement Study Group, 1974).

20 Wilson, "The Police in the Ghetto."

21. The analysis of neighborhood team policing is based upon Peter B. Block and David Sprague, *Neighborhood Team Policing* (Washington, D.C.: Urban Institute, 1973).

22. *Ibid.*, p. 109.

23. *Ibid.*, pp. 98–99.

24. *Ibid.*, p. 65.

25. For discussion on such resistance see Daley, *op. cit.*, and Block and Sprague, *op. cit.*, pp. 82–83.

26. Gideon Sjoberg, Richard Bryner, and Buford Harris, "Bureaucracy and the Lower Class," *Sociology and Social Research*, 50 (1966), 325–336. See also the works of Orion White: *Psychic Energy and Organizational Change*, Sage professional paper in administrative and policy studies, Vol. I, No. 03-007 (Beverly Hills and London: Sage Publications, 1973); "The Concept of Administrative Praxis," MS, 1972; "The Dialectical Organization: An Alternative to Bureaucracy," *Public Administration Review*, 29 (1969), 32–42. The alternative model is greatly informed by White's work.

27. Erving Goffman, *Relations in Public: Micro Studies of the Public Order* (New York: Harper & Row, Publishers, 1971), p. 259.

28. G. M. Caplan, "The Case for Rule-Making for Law Enforcement Agencies," *Law and Contemporary Problems*, 36 (1971), 502. See also the article by Jerry V. Wilson and G. M. Alprin in the same volume.

29. The works that best illustrate these characteristics of policing are Jerome Skolnick, *Justice without Trial* (New York: John Wiley & Sons, 1966). James Q. Wilson, *Varieties of Police Behavior* (Cambridge, Mass.: Harvard University Press, 1968). I have tried to consider the issue in my article "Supreme Court Effectiveness and the Police Organization," *Law and Contemporary Problems*, 36 (1971), 467–487. Some tentative but potentially important evidence that some rules may be effective for con-

trolling police is Bradley C. Canon, "Is the Exclusionary Rule in Failing Health?" *Kentucky Law Journal*, 62 (1974), 681–721.

30. Richard Hall, "Professionalization and Bureaucratization," *American Sociological Review*, 33 (1968), 92–104.

31. James Q. Wilson, *Varieties of Police Behavior*, pp. 16–83.

32. Susan White, "A Perspective on Police Professionalization," *Law and Society Review*, 7 (1972), 61–85. For a further discussion of White's contribution to the evaluation of police reform, see Neal A. Milner, "Policy Analysis and the Police," MS, 1973.

34. Wilson, "Police in the Ghetto."

35. Jerome Skolnick, *Justice without Trial*, pp. 235–239.

36. Knowles and Prewitt, *op. cit.*

37. Milner, "Policy Analysis and the Police," offers more detailed suggestions along these lines. See also Canon, *op. cit.*

38. This alternative view is derived from Susan White, *op. cit.*, and Jonathan Rubinstein, *City Police* (New York: Farrar, Straus, & Giroux, 1973). The more typical academic view is encapsulated in the following, "Profile of Urban Police": In his review of the literature and "profile of urban police" Harlan Hahn encapsulates these views:

> One of the most striking and unusual aspects of the police vocation is the high degree of solidarity displayed by most officers. United by a shared objective of fighting crime and by a common attitude toward the public, policemen display a degree of cohesion unmatched by most other occupational groups. . . .

> Law enforcement officers usually perceive themselves being in conflict with political and community influences, and protect themselves from the hostile forces by developing a form of solidarity that encompasses all members of the force.

Harlan Hahn, "A Profile of Urban Police," *Law and Contemporary Problems*, 36 (1971), 453–456. I criticize this view in "The Misleading Imagery of the 'Solid Blue Line,'" MS, 1974.

39. The actions of the New York City Police Department in regard to Sergeant David Durk show how this cooling out can be done. See Daley, *op. cit.*, and Peter Maas, *Serpico*.

40. Orion White, "The Concept of Administrative Praxis," p. 16 (my emphasis).

41. Ennoblement as well as other reactions to ambiguity is discussed in William Muir, "The Development of Policemen," a paper presented at Annual Meetings of the American Political Science Association, Los Angeles, Cal., 1970.

42. Goffman, *op. cit.*; Rubinstein, *op. cit.*, has some useful insights along these lines.

43. D. C. Perry and P. Sarnoff, *Politics at the Street Level: Police Administration and the Community*, Sage Professional Papers in Administrative and Policy Studies, Vol. 1, No. 03-008 (Beverly Hills and London: Sage Publications, 1973).

44. Philip Selznick, "Sociology and Natural Law," *Natural Law Forum*, 6 (1961), 84–108. His view is elaborated upon and defended in Jerome Skolnick, "Social Research on Legality: A Reply to Auerback," *Law and Society Review*, 1 (1966), 105–110.
45. James Q. Wilson also suggests that policing might best be viewed as a craft. See *Varieties of Police Behavior*, p. 283.
46. John H. McNamara, "Uncertainties in Police Work," in David Bordua (ed.), *The Police* (New York: John Wiley & Sons, 1967), pp. 163–252.
47. This strategy follows closely the general strategy advocated by Orion White, *Psychic Energy and Organizational Change*.
48. Torstein Eckhoff, "The Mediator, the Judge, and the Administrator in Conflict-Resolution," *Acta Sociologica*, 10 (1966), 158–166.

Postscript

1. For additional information see Michael Parenti, *Democracy for the Few* (New York: St. Martin's Press, 1974); Duane Lockard, *The Perverted Priorities of American Politics* (New York: The Macmillan Company, 1971); Andrew Hacker (ed.), *Corporation Take-Over* (New York: 1965); Mark J. Green, James M. Fallows, and David R. Zwick, *Who Runs Congress?* (New York: Bantam Books, 1972); Grant McConnell, *Private Power and American Democracy* (New York: Alfred A. Knopf, 1966); E. E. Schattschneider, *The Semi-Sovereign People* (New York: Holt, Rinehart and Winston, 1960); Herbert E. Alexander, *Money in Politics* (Washington, D.C.: Public Affairs Press, 1972).
2. The most critical reforms needed are campaign reforms to eliminate politician dependence on large contributions, income disclosure laws for office holders, effective conflict of interest prohibitions for office holders, more effective regulations of lobbying groups, and additional measures to remove unnecessary secrecy from governmental activities.
3. Among political scientists there is little debate about whether our political system is dominated by elites. There is, however, considerable controversy over the desirability of this reality. For a conservative, rationalizing approach see Thomas R. Dye and Harmon L. Zeigler, *The Irony of Democracy* (Belmont, Cal.: Wadsworth Publishing Co., 1970); for a radical, condemning assessment see Parenti, *Democracy for the Few*.
4. For specifics see Parenti, *Democracy for the Few*, pp. 69–90.
5. See Ramsey Clark, *Crime in America* (New York: Simon and Schuster, 1970).
6. *Uniform Crime Report* (1971), U.S. Department of Justice, Washington, D.C.

INDEX

INDEX

DATE DUE